P9-AOW-083

Sharing Faith
Across the Hemisphere

Sharing Faith

Faith

Across the Hemisphere

Mary M. McGlone, CSJ

for the NCCB Committee on the Church in Latin America

ORBIS BOOKS

Maryknoll, New York 10545

The Catholic Foreign Mission Society of America (Maryknoll) recruits and trains people for overseas missionary service. Through Orbis Books, Maryknoll aims to foster the international dialogue that is essential to mission. The books published, however, reflect the opinions of their authors and are not meant to represent the official position of the society.

Copyright © 1997, United States Catholic Conference, Inc., Washington, D.C.

All rights reserved. No part of this publication may be reproduced or transmitted in any form or by any means, electronic or mechanical, including photocopying, recording or any information storage or retrieval system, without prior permission in writing from the publishers.

Published by Orbis Books, P.O. Box 308, Maryknoll, New York 10545-0308.

ORBIS/ISBN 1-57075-132-3

Dedication

This work is devoutly dedicated

to Our Lady of Guadalupe,

Patroness of the Church

throughout the Americas

and star

of the first evangelization.

May this book

serve the new evangelization.

Photo: Charlie Archambault

Table of Contents

Preface

The evangelization of the peoples of America began more than five hundred years ago. Our Church's history in this continent is a rich expression of God's grace unfolding on all of the Americas. It is a human history as well—sister Churches emanating from distinct missionary efforts, growing up side by side, at times making mistakes or seeming to be at odds with one another, and always remaining faithful to the task of building up the kingdom.

Now that we are poised on the threshold of a new millennium and have a deeper awareness of the intricacies of our apostolic mission to evangelize, it seems fitting to prepare a history of the relationship between these sister churches—the Church in North America and the Church in Latin America. With a desire to bring about "deeper unity among all the peoples who make up this great continent of America" (Santo Domingo, no. 17), Pope John Paul II has urged international preparation for the Special Assembly of the Synod of Bishops for America.

In light of this coming event, the Bishops' Committee on the Church in Latin America wishes to offer the Church in our country a resource to help understand our history and to appreciate and celebrate the mutuality that has characterized our relationship as mission-sending and -receiving Churches. It is our hope that *Sharing Faith Across the Hemisphere* will serve as an invaluable resource for pastors, parish staffs, and parish committees, as well as religious educators and teachers in our primary, secondary, and higher education institutions. May it help deepen the awareness of our relationship with the Church in Latin America and highlight the blessings this relationship has brought to the Church in our country. *Sharing Faith Across the Hemisphere,* with its chapter study questions, and our video with the same title, are an appealing and significant guide to discussion about our church history, the nature of Church in mission, and the mutuality of mission.

As the Church universal prepares to celebrate the great jubilee of the year 2000 and begin the third Christian millennium, the call of Christ to unity among all peoples is heard with greater urgency. The Bishops' Committee on the Church in Latin America offers this attractive and timely instrument to inform and help unite all of our peoples in the person of Jesus Christ, which will lead to conversion, communion, and solidarity within the Church in America.

Most Reverend Raymundo J. Peña
Bishop of Brownsville
Chairman, Bishops' Committee
on the Church in Latin America

Introduction

In November 1994, when this work was first discussed by the Bishops' Committee on the Church in Latin America, naiveté, ignorance, enthusiasm, and eagerness to better inform the U.S. faithful all played a part in underestimating the enormity of the project. Over and again in various discussions, we stated the goal of the project as follows: "to tell the story about the relationship of the Church in the United States with the Church in Latin America and the impact of this relationship on the Church in the United States." From the outset, it was clear that the entire story could not be told, and yet something of the story could be told. While much has been written on the contributions of Latin American immigrants to the Church in North America, little has been written about the experience of Church in mission in Latin America. Thus, it was our decision to offer Catholics some insight about the breadth and scope of our relationship by telling a story that has never before been heard.

After considering various research centers, the project was located at Notre Dame University, and Rev. Robert S. Pelton, CSC, was named coordinator. Fr. Pelton is representative for Latin American-North American Church Concerns at the Helen Kellogg Institute for International Studies. Dr. Rodney Ganey of the Laboratory for Social Research at Notre Dame was appointed director of the research itself; in preparing material from the research for publication, the assistance of Dr. Anre Venter was invaluable. A number of people generously gave of their time and talent in the design of the project and in the instruments used. Tom Quigley, of the Office of International Justice and Peace of the United States Catholic Conference and a veteran staff person for the bishops regarding affairs for Latin America, was a frequent and loyal collaborator. In addition, many others met in focus sessions in different parts of the country and contributed in various ways:

Sr. Regina Cole (Religious Education, University of Notre Dame)

Sr. Marlene Condon, MM (Vice President, Maryknoll Sisters, New York)

Jay Dolan, Ph.D. (Professor, University of Notre Dame)

Rev. Steven Judd, MM (Assistant General for Latin America, Maryknoll, N.Y.)

Rev. Gaspar LoBiondo, SJ (Woodstock Center, Washington, D.C.)

Most Rev. Marcos McGrath (Archbishop Emeritus of Panamá)

Rev. Philip Murnion (Pastoral Life Center, New York)

A number of people from dioceses, colleges and universities, religious communities, and various associations generously gave of their time and talent to assist us in gathering information and clarifying questions. In addition to those with whom we met, thousands more took the time to answer our questions and tell us a story from the point of view of their parish, diocese, religious community or institution, high school, college, or university. To these many people, we express a deep gratitude. Your contributions helped shape this book as well as the companion video production of the same title.

To find an author, we searched for a historian and theologian who worked in Latin America and could write in a popular style that could also serve scholarly interests. Such a seemingly impossible combination of talents was found in Sr. Mary McGlone, CSJ, Ph.D., assistant professor of theology at Avila College, Kansas City, Mo. Once Sr. McGlone, a former missioner in Peru, accepted the challenge, she proceeded to participate actively and effectively in the entire project. Most importantly, Sr. Mary McGlone has researched and written an excellent work that makes a significant contribution to the Church at this time. The reader will soon find out firsthand the value of her efforts.

Early in the process it became clear that the objective of the bishops "to tell the story" could best be served by not only the research and the book, but also by a video that used the most graphic and compelling stories from the research. Golden Dome Productions at Notre Dame University was contracted to do the video. Executive producer, Chuck Huffman, and many of the staff at Golden Dome worked tirelessly to achieve a superb final product, beautifully filmed in Latin America and in the United States. Every reader of this book will want to view this engaging and inspiring work. The video has been designed as a companion piece to the book and also contains discussion questions for use in educational and parish settings.

The book and the video do not reflect a graphic statistical report of our findings. Rather, they are true to our original intent, "to tell a story." In order to place the story in perspective, the author has begun with the history of the arrival of the faith in Latin America and in the United States. The first two chapters review this remarkable history and, in a cogent manner, set the scene for the relationship. Chapter three begins the story of collaboration in little-known and fascinating history that helps the reader become aware of the relationship between North and South. The 1960s opened a floodgate of activity between the Churches, and chapter four treats this most challenging time in the history of our Church. Chapters five and six develop the maturing of the relationship as the reader is brought into the suffering of Latin America and the prophetic responses of the sister Church in the North. Chapter seven brings us to the present time and discusses a panoply of involvement and a wondrous explanation of the mutuality of mission.

In the last four chapters, all of the information came directly from stories reported from the research or was influenced greatly by the reports from parishes, religious communities, dioceses, and Catholic colleges and universities. Those looking for specific statistical data about the relationship and its impact will find some of that information in appendix A.

The discussion questions at the end of each chapter are offered especially for parishes, religious communities, and educational institutions. We followed a pattern in developing these questions that looked to the Trinity (creation, salvation, inspiration), the Church, and Our Lady of Guadalupe (different expressions of discipleship) as a model. Sometimes the model is apparent; other times it is less so. Readers are encouraged to use the questions especially in a discussion format.

The data we have gathered and the stories that we have told in the book and video are more than have ever before been collected on these matters and are still incomplete. We are certain there are many parishes, religious communities, and dioceses involved in extraordinary works with Latin America, and we have not yet heard their story. It is our hope that this work will initiate a greater communication between the Secretariat for Latin America and groups within the Church in the United States that have a relationship with Latin America.

It is also our hope that this work will be a beginning. We hope that scholars, missionaries, and others who have more to add will tell the story. This is a wondrous expression of God's grace working throughout the Church in America. It is a time to celebrate all of the great achievements and at the same time to recommit ourselves for the challenges that lie ahead at the beginning of the new millennium. We are inspired by John Paul II's prophetic vision of a Church in America—North, South, Central—which begins the new millennium more united and re-evangelized through the efforts of the bishops meeting in synod as well as other preparations for the celebration of the grand jubilee. It is our collective hope that this offering to the faithful will assist in some tangible ways in raising the consciousness of the faithful throughout the Americas and, under the patronage of Our Lady of Guadalupe, draw us ever closer to the encounter with her Son.

Rev. James J. Ronan
Executive Director
Secretariat for Latin America

CHAPTER ONE

The Origins of Christianity in America

A Letter from Rev. Blas Valero to His Jesuit Superior

Peru, 1560

Reverend Father,

There have been three ways of Christianizing the natives of Peru. The first, by force and with violence, without previous instruction or any other kind of teaching. . . . The preachers were soldiers and the baptizers were idiots; the baptized were brought in collars, chains or tied up. Of those that were baptized like that . . . none received the grace of Baptism . . . they did not want such a thing interiorly. If they appeared to consent exteriorly and allowed themselves to be baptized, it was out of fear that the Spaniards would kill them as they had killed others who had clearly said that they did not want to be Christians. This is true. These natives soon returned to their superstitions. They did not think of themselves as Christians. . . .

Others who wished freely to be Christians, moved by the example or ex-hortations of a religious or priest or a pious Spaniard, received superficial instruction in Spanish or Latin, but not in their own language. This was because of the scarcity of missionaries and the fact that many of those who were here were busy in the Spanish cities, building their monasteries. Thus they couldn't attend the indios. If they attended them, it was through interpreters who knew Spanish poorly, and . . . were not the most capable and educated. Some of the missionaries were responsible for a whole province, which forced them to turn to secular Spaniards who did not always exercise their responsibility as they should. With instructors like that, and without receiving any sacrament other than Baptism, it was impossible that the indios would become attached to Christian practices and abandon their idolatry. That is why there has been little progress in faith among the natives.

The third type were some who not only willingly received Baptism, but who had the good fortune to find someone who taught, instructed and ani-mated them with good example. This [was successful], especially when the catechists dedicated themselves to the task of learning the language. It was not necessary to force these people to abandon their idols. . . . They did it for themselves and cleansed their hearts of old beliefs.[1]

What Father Valero wrote about Peru described a situation that had been developing in the New World for nearly sixty years. In that one letter, Valero not only summarized Spain's three major mission methodologies among the American natives, but he also exposed conflicts that had arisen from the different approaches missionaries had taken toward Native Americans since the time of Columbus's arrival.

Columbus

Neither demon nor saint, Christopher Columbus was a complex man with mixed motivations. He firmly believed that the Holy Spirit inspired his ex-plorations and that they were a part of preparations for the soon-to-come end of the world. King Ferdinand and Queen Isabel's support for his venture began just after they had successfully completed a crusade to oust

Christopher Columbus (etching by Leopold Flameng). Photo from Marquis Auguest de Belloy, *The Life of Columbus*, 1885.

the Moors who had occupied Spanish territory for seven centuries. Their joint reign was characterized not only by the wars of reconquest but also by intense efforts to purify the Church in their realms. To that end they sponsored a radical reform of the Church and also, just after their final victory over the Moors, expelled the Jews from their domains. With Christianity firmly established in the homeland, they were ready to turn their sights to far-off lands where they could both evangelize and expand their fortunes.

Columbus described his first encounter with the Amerindians as a friendly, mute exchange of gifts:

> I, in order that they might feel great amity towards us, because I knew they were a people to be delivered and converted to our holy faith rather by love than by force, gave to some among them some red caps and some glass beads . . . and many other things of little value. . . . Afterwards they came swimming to the ships' boats, where we were, and brought us parrots and cotton thread in balls, and spears and many other things.[2]

Communication was so difficult between the two groups that at first they had to rely totally on signs. As Columbus related his assessment of the people, he also revealed that the two topics of their original communication were weapons and precious metals:

> It seemed to me that they were a people deficient in everything. They all go naked as their mothers bore them, and the women also. . . .
> They do not bear arms or know them, for I showed them swords and they took them by the blade and cut themselves through ignorance. . . .

They should be very good servants and of quick intelligence, since I see that they very soon say all that is said to them, and I believe that they would easily be made Christians, for it appeared to me that they had no creed. Our Lord willing, at the time of my departure, I will bring back six of them to Your Highnesses, that they may learn to talk.

I was attentive and laboured to know if they had gold, and I saw that some of them wore a small piece hanging from a hole which they have in the nose, and from signs I was able to understand that, going to the south or going round the island to the south, there was a king who had large vessels of it and possessed much gold. I endeavoured to make them go there, and afterwards saw that they were not inclined for the journey. I resolved to wait until the afternoon of the following day . . . to seek the gold and precious stones.[3]

As the first Spaniard to interpret the New World and its inhabitants, Columbus introduced the conflicting interests that characterized Spain's involvement in the "Indies." Although he insisted that he set out from Spain with the expressed purpose of spreading the faith, Columbus's first act in the New World was to claim the land for his monarchs.[4] His first significant attempts at verbal communication with the Amerindians had to do with weapons and gold rather than the Gospel. His original assessment of the people set them up to be considered as servants—albeit good ones.

Columbus's words and actions outlined the three major motivations for Spain's mission to the New World: imperialism, greed, and the spread of the Gospel. His perception of the Amerindians as a lesser but basically good people who could probably be instructed in Christianity reflected the middle-of-the-road approach to evangelization that would eventually be adopted for Spain's mission to the New World.

Three Modes of Implanting the Faith in America

The history of the Church in America during the earliest decades of Spanish occupation is sketchy. The first clerics to travel to the Indies accompanied Columbus in 1493. Every fleet that left Spanish harbors thereafter with explorers or settlers was required to give passage to some missionaries as well.

It is hardly surprising that the first clerics to go to the "New World" would have been ill-equipped to deal with the people to whom they were sent. They had grown up in a nation permeated with the militant spirit of religious and political crusades, and their religious formation had taken place under the influence of the great ecclesial and educational reforms sponsored by Queen Isabel.[5] Extremely well versed in their religious tradition and often profoundly dedicated to their religious vocation, they were in no way prepared to meet and evangelize peoples whose language, customs, and social and religious life were completely different from their own.

The "discovery" of America shook the Spanish world. As intellectuals and government officials came to grips with the astonishing reality that America was not the Indies but a land their science had never imagined, new questions began to arise about the inhabitants of that world and their place in humanity and the plan of salvation.[6] While theorists in Spain had the leisure to philosophize, missionaries had to face the concrete demands of meeting and preaching to the inhabitants of the New World.

Three years elapsed before the first native was baptized.[7] Eventually an extended family was converted, and seventeen people were baptized and went to live among the Spaniards. When all of the native Christians were killed by their own people, Friar Ramon Pane, the ecclesiastical superior of the Spanish mission, interpreted the murders as a sign that the natives were naturally prone to reject Christianity.[8] That sort of judgment on the part of a cleric gave credence to what can be called the "conquistador" mission mentality: the belief that force rather than rational persuasion was the only efficacious approach to the Christianization of the native peoples.

"The Baptized Were Brought by Force and with Violence. . . ."

—Blas Valero, SJ

Cross and Sword: Evangelization by Conquest

The conquistador mentality was articulated and defended by scholars who understood Spain's relation to the lands across the ocean through the prism of the just war theory. As they interpreted this theory, the Church, represented by Spain, had the indisputable right to declare war against pagans, submit them to Christian rule, and take their properties, provided that the process was part of an effort made to spread the faith.[9]

This school of thought sought support in the accords that had been worked out between the papacy and the Spanish government. After Columbus made his first report to the Catholic monarchs, they quickly began to make arrangements with Rome to ensure their exclusive claim to evangelize the newfound territory. Through a series of papal pronouncements they procured the overall responsibility for establishing the Church in America. This arrangement, known as "royal patronage," gave the monarchs or their representatives the privileges of collecting tithes and naming ecclesiastical authorities in the territories that they would claim.[10] According to the terms of the papal documents, as long as the peoples of the New World were "uncivilized," the Spanish could maintain that the conquest was based on accepted legal principles.

By the mid-sixteenth century, the major spokesman for this school of thought was Juan Gines de Sepúlveda. Although Sepúlveda had never been to the New World, he had a strong opinion about the native population. He held that they were dull-witted and irrational, essentially natural slaves unfit for self-government.[11] Sepúlveda's main source of information seems to have been a history written by Gonzalo Fernández de Oviedo, a royal official who had served in the Indies.[12] Of all of Oviedo's theories, the most injurious was that the Amerindians were so different from Europeans that they were probably incapable of becoming or remaining Christians. His opinion of them was so strong that he included the following warning in his *History of the Indies*:

> I have observed many times [that] their skulls are four times thicker than those of the Christians. And so when one wages war with them and comes to hand to hand fighting, one must be very careful not to hit them on the head with the sword, because I have seen many swords broken in this fashion. In addition to being thick, their skulls are very strong.[13]

Although the extreme ideas of Sepúlveda and Oviedo were not necessarily the norm, the general lines of their "conquistador" philosophy were frequently carried out in both practice and official policy in the Indies.

Long before Sepúlveda and Oviedo published their tracts, Spain had implemented practices and created institutions in the Indies based on what could be understood as a "divine right of conquest." Under this type

Sharing Faith Across the Hemisphere

of thinking, the effective propagation of the faith was often used as a pretext for legalized brutality.

The most important institution fitting the above description is the *repartimiento* or *encomienda*: the donation of land and native labor to Spaniards.[14] These institutions, which existed from the time of Columbus, gave a Spaniard authority over a group of native people in return for a "very elastic" obligation to see to their physical and spiritual well-being.[15] Although they were advocated as means of organizing the people for the purpose of evangelization, *repartimiento* and *encomienda* often resulted in the virtual slavery of the natives, providing the Spaniards with all the free labor they needed in their quest for wealth.

The combination of war, slave labor, disease, and forced relocation caused massive death among the native peoples. Within a few years, the original population of Santo Domingo was literally wiped out, and up to 90 percent of the inhabitants of some densely populated areas of Latin America disappeared in the first sixty years after Columbus's first voyage.[16]

It is impossible to claim that genuine "evangelization" was carried out by those who operated from the conquistador mentality. As Valero said, those who were baptized were "brought in collars, chains or tied up." The real accomplishment of the people who followed this line of thought was a conquest so thorough that one Dominican described it by saying:

All these indios have been destroyed in soul and body, and in their posterity, the whole earth is parched and burned to the point that they can't even live, much less be Christians.[17]

Such communications from missionaries in the field did not fall on deaf ears. Both royal and ecclesiastical authorities attempted to halt the wanton destruction taking place.

The crown's first reform laws, the Laws of Burgos, were promulgated in 1513, largely due to the reports made by the Dominican missionaries. Throughout the rest of the century, Spain sporadically attempted to accomplish reforms through legislation, the most comprehensive of which were the "New Laws" of 1542. In 1537, Pope Paul III promulgated the bull *Sublimus Deus*, which taught authoritatively that the indigenous people of America were full human beings and therefore could not be deprived of their rights. Unfortunately, America was far enough from Spain that reforms were unenforceable without the collaboration of local authorities—a collaboration that was not only rare, but often minimally successful.[18]

Native "Rebels"

From the native point of view, the invasion by the conquistadors was an absolute cataclysm. They were as surprised as the Spaniards at discovering peoples the likes of whom they had never imagined. The conquest turned their world upside down. It is hard to conceive of the confusion, rage, and despair with which they responded to the Spaniards and the death and destruction that came in their wake. The physical appearance of the bearded, strangely clothed, and armored Spaniards made them unlike anyone the natives had ever encountered. To make matters worse, the Spaniards often first appeared mounted on monster animals (horses) and were accompanied by dogs far larger than any known in the Americas. Either devils or gods, it was hard for the indigenous people to conceive that such creatures shared humanity with them.[19]

For some, the only adequate response to the invaders was war, either physical or ideological. The early history of Latin America is filled with reports of native "rebellions." But given the Spaniards' superior weaponry and distinctive war tactics, the inevitable outcome of physical combat was defeat.[20] A more successful alternative to outright battle was ideological warfare. Those who had undergone a forced baptism often took on the outward appearance of Christianity while secretly preserving their traditional faith.

In Mexico and Peru there are records of natives who attempted to maintain their ancient faiths in spite of forced baptism. They frequently used the new vocabulary of Christianity as a "cover" for their attempt to revitalize the religious traditions of their people.[21] In Peru, the most famous and perhaps most nearly successful of these ideological wars was the movement called *Taqi Ongoy*, or the "dancing sickness."[22]

The Taqi Ongoy movement grew up just as persecution of "idolaters" was reaching its first peak in the Andes. The leaders of this movement called on their people to recuperate their traditional faith through rituals in which the people danced until they were in an ecstatic trance: a state through which the ancient gods could enter them and act through them to overthrow the Spaniards. The movement eventually grew into a religious and military offensive, especially strong in areas where the natives outnum-

Sharing Faith Across the Hemisphere

bered the Spaniards by twelve to one. The Taqi Ongoy devotees succeeded in recovering important areas of their territory and were subdued only as they were about to mount what could have been a triumphant offense against Lima. When they were finally defeated, the leaders were captured and severely and publicly punished to discourage others who might follow.

Both the conquistadors and the rebels used violence and ideology as tools of war against the other. In spite of their bitter enmity, the two groups had much in common. Not only did both use religious beliefs in the service of violence, but their closed interpretations of faith prevented them from engaging in significant dialogue with one another. Their belief systems led them to act with a passion that unquestioningly rejected the other.

"Others Received Superficial Instruction in Spanish. . . ."

—Blas Valero, SJ

Missionaries

A second and far less brutal approach to Christianizing native people can be characterized as the attempt to "convert" them.[23] The missionaries who took this approach gained exclusive responsibility for the mission in a particular geographical area and thereby attained the virtual authority to govern it as well. The primary institutions they used to evangelize the native populations were schools for the children of native leaders and "reductions," which were population centers where previously dispersed native communities were brought to live in a common area for a more effective catechesis.

Life in the reductions could be anything from idyllic to cruel; in some cases the reductions turned out to be little more than ecclesiastical *encomiendas*. In other instances, the religious fought to protect native populations whom they regarded as innocent and uniquely prepared to live the Gospel.[24] Even under the best conditions, the reductions were characterized by a paternalistic attitude toward the natives.

The goal of the schools and reductions was the "conversion" of the natives. That implied that they should be "raised" to civilized ways or kept apart and protected from the evil influence and maltreatment of the Spaniards. In spite of the fact that the purpose of the reductions was to serve the native populations, their effect was a total unraveling of native life. People who had previously lived in dispersed communities, whose social and economic life had been based on clan structures and a highly effective utilization of natural resources, were forced into communities with strangers, away from the areas where they had traditionally sustained their life. When this social and geographical displacement was added to the decimation of their population and the destruction of their traditional places of worship, the result was devastating.

Officially, the institutions of the mission were designed to facilitate the conversion of the native population. In practice, the work of the schools and the regimen of the reductions became a campaign to Hispanicize the natives: to eradicate their unique culture and encourage them to imitate Spanish ways. Such imitation was a task at which the natives could never be entirely successful and a demand that they could not easily avoid.

Novices in a Foreign Culture

The native parallel to the missionary attempt to implant Spanish faith and customs was a cult of imitation. The *mestizos* and natives who adopted this approach accepted the dominance of Spain and tried to conform to the new situation by severing their roots and taking on Spanish language, culture, and faith.[25]

One famous *mestizo* who spent his life in this effort was the Peruvian, Inca Garcilaso de la Vega.[26] Born in 1539, Garcilaso was the son of a conquistador and an Inca princess. Educated in the finest schools, he thought of himself as the product of the best that his two parental nations had to offer. But because his father abandoned the family, Garcilaso had neither an inheritance nor even a legitimate name. He went to Spain as a young man, hoping to integrate himself into his father's culture. In spite of military service and a successful career as a historian, he not only failed in his search for full acceptance but was also deprived of his paternal and maternal inheritances. At the end of his life, Garcilaso became aware that he belonged to no race or nation.[27] Early in his life he had been removed from the indigenous culture, yet he would never be fully accepted in Spain because he was a *mestizo*.

Educated natives often fared no better in their homeland than did Garcilaso in Spain. When religious orders established schools open to the natives, their efforts were not always appreciated by their countrymen. On January 6, 1536, the Franciscans inaugurated a seminary in Tlaltiloco, Mexico, for the sons of noble families. The natives in the school were reputed to have far surpassed the Spaniards in the course of studies. The native students also aided their Franciscan teachers in the translation of sermons, religious instruction, and catechisms into the local languages. Nevertheless, in spite of the excellent seminary training it offered, the school did not produce even one native priest to serve the people.

The lack of indigenous priests was not due to the students' unwillingness or lack of capacity. No native priests were ordained because there was too much powerful opposition to them on the part of some Spaniards. In the words of Jerónimo Lopez, a lawyer who wrote to Spanish officials about the seminary:

> It was an error fraught with dangers to teach sciences to the Indians, and still more to put the Bible . . . into their hands to be read and interpreted as they pleased.[28]

According to Lopez, an elite education had led only to insolence on the part of the natives, an attitude which they apparently demonstrated by their unwillingness to be treated as slaves.

It was not only the laity who protested such schools. The Dominicans in New Spain refused to open schools in the early years of their work. Fray Domingo de Betanzos wrote to King Charles V explaining their objection to schools, and especially seminaries, in the following way:

> The Indians should not preach for a very long time to come because they lack the preacher's necessary authority. . . . Those who have studied are even more vicious than others, and are not different enough from the common run. Besides, the Christian doctrine has not yet sufficiently penetrated their spirit, and it is to be feared that they would spread heresies, as had already happened. Finally, they are not capable of properly understanding the dogmas of the Christian religion and explaining them in a fit and precise fashion.[29]

The friars who set up their schools and took charge of the reductions generally did so in good faith. Their intent was to share the faith and give the natives the opportunity to become "more civilized." What they could not comprehend was that they were inviting the natives to take on an unsuitable and ultimately impossible task. People like Garcilaso and the native seminarians learned that their attempt to take on

Spanish ways would only move them to the margins of both peoples. Because of their origins, they would never be able to meet the standards of "being Spanish," and when they tried, they abandoned their own values and people to the degree that they could no longer fit in their ancestral society.

"The Third Type Had Good Fortune to Meet Someone Who Taught with Good Example"

—Blas Valero, SJ

The Dominicans: Montesinos, Pedro de Córdova, and Las Casas

The injustice of Spain's treatment of the natives and the inadequacies of mission methodologies did not go unchallenged. The first voice to be publicly raised in protest was that of Antonio Montesinos, a Dominican serving on the island of Hispaniola or Santo Domingo. There, in December 1511, Montesinos gave a sermon that astonished his Spanish congregation and had repercussions for decades, if not centuries. Preaching to the authorities on the island, a group that included Governor Diego Columbus, the son of the famous admiral, Montesinos proclaimed this message:

> You are all in mortal sin, you are living in it and you will die in it, because of the cruelty and tyranny that you practice with these people.
>
> Explain yourselves!
>
> According to what law and with what kind of justice do you keep these Indios in such cruel servitude? On what authority do you base yourselves in waging detestable wars against these people who in their lands were gentle and peaceful, where you have consumed an infinite number of them through death and destruction? How can you keep them so oppressed and worn out, without giving them food nor curing the ills which they suffer from the excessive work that you give them to kill them? Better said, you kill them to take out and acquire gold each day.
>
> And what are you doing to see that they learn the doctrine of the faith? That they know their God and Creator? That they be baptized, hear the Mass, keep the feast and Sundays?
>
> Are these not human beings? Do they not have rational souls? Are you not obligated to love them as you love yourselves? Do you not

Bartolomé de las Casas (1474-1566). Photo: Edward E. Ayer Collection, The Newberry Library.

understand this? Can you not feel anything? How can you exist in such a profound and lethargic sleep?

Know this for certain, that in the state in which you are living you can not save yourselves anymore than the Moors or the Turks who both lack and reject faith in Jesus Christ.[30]

Montesinos's radical sermon was not allowed to pass unnoticed. Those who heard it wasted no time before appearing at the Dominican convent to demand a retraction of this new, unorthodox doctrine. The Dominican superior, Pedro de Córdova, responded that the text of the sermon had been signed by the whole Dominican community. There would be no retraction. Montesinos's sermon marked the beginning of a long tradition of religious protest against the conquest and inappropriate methods used to implant Christianity in the New World.

Perhaps the greatest effect of the Dominicans' preaching was the fact that it converted Bartolomé de las Casas. Las Casas, a priest who began his New World career as merchant and adventurer, had received an *encomienda* for the helping in the "pacification" of the island now called Cuba. His transformation took place in 1514 as he prepared to celebrate Pentecost Mass for the settlers of a town called Espíritu Santo. The precise text which caused him to reassess his life and Spain's mission came from Sirach:

> Tainted his gifts who offers in sacrifice ill-gotten goods. . . . He slays his neighbor who deprives him of his living. (Sir 34:18-22)

These words, combined with the questions the Dominican preaching had already raised, led him to preach to the settlers in the Dominican style, to dispose of his *encomienda*, and to begin a campaign on behalf of the native Americans that would last the rest of his life.[31]

Alternating in his residence between Spain and the New World, Las Casas became the bishop of Chiapas and the sixteenth century's most outspoken critic of Spanish policy in America. Unable to master the native languages, his contribution as a missionary and resident bishop was minimal compared with his labor in awakening Spanish consciences to the plight of the natives. An indefatigable writer, he authored histories that brought such a tremendous backlash that there can be no doubt about his influence.[32]

Las Casas did not succeed in his efforts to halt the conquest or eliminate the *encomienda* system. Nevertheless, his plan for a peaceful evangelization of the inhabitants of the New World inspired some missionaries and natives to implement alternative modes of church development throughout the Americas.

Archbishop Toribio de Mogrovejo

Toribio de Mogrovejo, the patron of the Latin American bishops and the first bishop of Latin America to be canonized, is an outstanding but little-known figure in the history of colonial Latin America.[33] Named Archbishop of Lima in 1580, he was a thoroughly surprising choice for the office. The Archdiocese of Lima, rivaled only by Mexico, was one of the most important in the New World. When Toribio was named archbishop, he was not even a priest; in fact, he was the head of the Inquisition in Granada. Those details indicate that King Philip II named him in the hope that he would bring strict order to the Church of Peru.[34] If Philip's choice was originally a surprise to those who would have predicted episcopal appointments, Toribio's way of taking on the mission must have also surprised Philip.[35]

When Toribio began his tenure in 1581, he quickly mastered the indigenous language. Instead of administering his vast diocese from the capital city, he spent his career visiting the far reaches of his diocese. Of the twenty-five years that he served as archbishop of Lima, he spent a full seventeen on the road ministering to his people. Although Toribio left no record of having been influenced by the teachings of Bartolomé de las Casas, his mission style reflected Las Casas's ideals for a peaceful and dialogic approach to evangelization.

Toribio's correspondence with the king adds to the evidence that he was striving to implement a new style of evangelization. His formal reports, as well as those of other Spanish authorities in Peru, indicate that he found himself in constant conflict with civil and religious authorities whom he felt were abusing the people.[36] In regard to the reductions, Toribio not only refused to cooperate with their continued establishment, but within two years of beginning his ministry he wrote to the king:

> To reduce some of the native people to other towns can't be done because there is no desirable way to accomplish it. Also, bringing people from one town to another puts them in danger of death and takes them from their homes and fields. They lose everything and end up very poor. I supplicate Your Majesty to provide what serves our Lord in this. . . . I am afflicted greatly to see that I cannot remedy it and because I understand how many die now without the sacraments.[37]

Although far more subtle than Las Casas, Toribio worked for the same goals: an end to native suffering and the awakening of the Spanish conscience, which were the preconditions for an effective evangelization of the native people.

Throughout his time as archbishop of Lima, Toribio maintained a reputation for being the friend and advocate of the poorest of his people. Although he is perhaps most famous for being the administrator who first implemented the decrees of the Council of Trent in Latin America, his ecclesiastical legislation was marked by a profound desire to ensure that all of the people under his jurisdiction—native, Spanish, African, or *mestizo*—would receive authentic preaching of the Gospel and be allowed to live it under the conditions appropriate to them and the cultures from which they came.

Felipe Guaman Poma—Chronicler and Graphic Theologian

While Toribio was traveling through his vast archdiocese, Felipe Guaman Poma de Ayala, a native of Cuzco, traveled through the Andes, observing the life of his people and writing a very long report to the king of Spain about the conditions he found.[38] Guaman Poma's unique chronicle reports on everything he saw in those years with the intention of informing the king of the progress of the faith and the hope that the king would recognize that because the people had heard the Gospel, they would be allowed to live it in peace.

In his letter to the king, Guaman Poma described himself as a prince of the Andes. His writing, with frequent allusions to Spanish, Latin, and Incan traditions and literature, gives evidence that he was well educated and widely read. Making use of both Spanish and Incan modes of communication, he described the cataclysm of the conquest in prose and with graphic illustrations. His images powerfully conveyed the anguish and incredulity of a people who could not fathom the meaning of the events taking place in their midst. He vividly portrayed the native perception that under the announced pretext of bringing them faith and salvation, the European invaders scorned the people, decimated their population, and destroyed their cities and temples.

In what might be seen as sixteenth-century political cartoons, Guaman Poma detailed the contradictions, the mediocre endeavors, and the successes of evangelization in the Andes.[39] The commentary accompanying the three illustrations makes their import clear. The first (Figure 1) is labeled a "consideration," or a subject for meditation. Describing what has been called the "conquistador mentality," the text in the upper left reads:

Figure 1. "Consideration." Felipe Guaman Poma de Ayala, *Nueva Cronica y Buen Goberno* (1615), Edición de John V. Murra (Madrid: Historia 16, 1987).

How the Spanish priests and *corregidores* maltreated the poor Indians of this land. They are in their land without any consideration and they fear neither God nor the justice of His Majesty.[40]

The second illustration shows a priest preaching a text that is a purposely poor combination of Spanish and the native language

Sharing Faith Across the Hemisphere

Quechua (Figure 2). Even more strongly than the words, the illustration itself is a commentary on the work of the missionaries. While the priest is preaching, some of the congregation are listening and others sleeping, but the Spirit is coming in through the window, indicating that in spite of inadequate presentation of the Gospel, God will be present to the people.

The third illustration shows a native couple praying at home (Figure 3). The message is clear: Christianity has taken root in the

Figure 2. Illustration by Felipe Guaman Poma de Ayala.

Figure 3. Illustration by Felipe Guaman Poma de Ayala.

people, and married couples can establish Catholic homes and practice the faith, even in the absence of the clergy.[41]

Guaman Poma used an illustration of the crucifixion (Figure 4) to explain the meaning of the Christian message in his own time and culture. In his drawing, the sun and moon, previously revered by the native people, now represent the universe, which watched with the disciples as the Son of God gave his life on the cross.[42] The writing around the sketch made the simple and yet profound proclamation:

Figure 4. "The Crucifixion" by Felipe Guaman Poma de Ayala.

God died for the world and for the poor sinners, children of Adam and Eve, INRI, he was crucified for sins.

Using only a few words, Poma summarized two of the main theses of his work: *all* human beings are children of Adam and Eve, and Christ was crucified for sins. In the text that accompanies the illustration, Poma reminds the reader that God's concern for the poor will have eternal repercussions. He said:

Jesus went around, poor and persecuted. And after the day of judgment, he will come with majesty and glory and will bring . . . his blessed mother, Holy Mary, and all the saints, angels and joyful . . . to repay the poor and rejected.[43]

Guaman Poma wrote respectfully but truthfully. He had accepted the Christian message, but criticized the messengers who did not live according to the dictates of their faith. He understood Christian doctrine and the laws of the Spaniards well enough to state his case clearly to the king.

Guaman Poma composed his letter to the king to convey the message that he, like others in the realm, was a Christian prince with all the rights and responsibilities corresponding to that status. The Andean people had received the faith and were grateful for it. According to Guaman Poma, they were changed by the advent of the faith, and that change was positive. But once the faith had been imparted, the Spanish mission was finished. The Spaniards should return to their part of the world, leaving the Andes under the control of their rightful sovereigns.

Sharing Faith Across the Hemisphere

"It Was Not Necessary to Force These People to Abandon Their Idols. . . . They Did It for Themselves and Cleansed Their Hearts. . . ."

—Blas Valero, SJ

The Virgin of Guadalupe: The Mother of American Christianity

Gauman Poma's solution to the problems created by the conquest of America was impossible. However rationally it followed from the documents that authorized Spain's overseas expansion, motivations foreign to the spread of the Gospel had taken hold in America from the beginning; a peaceful withdrawal would not be countenanced even if the whole continent had become more thoroughly and deeply Catholic than Spain itself. But another more viable approach to the problems of evangelization in America had been proposed almost a century before Guaman Poma wrote his missive to the king. That happened not in the Peruvian Andes, but on the hill called Tepeyac outside Mexico City.[44]

According to the ancient story, on December 9, 1531, in an area where there had been a traditional shrine to Tonantzin, the Aztec virgin-mother of the gods, a native peasant named Juan Diego encountered a beautiful woman who identified herself as "the Virgin Mary, Mother of the true God through whom one lives, Mother of the Creator of heaven and of earth."[45] The woman sent him to Bishop Zumárraga to ask that a temple be built in her honor on the Tepeyac hill.

Juan Diego went to the bishop, who listened briefly to his story and told him to come back another day. Juan Diego reported this to the woman and, after begging her to send someone more worthy, someone important enough to require the bishop's attention, he obeyed her request to return

Our Lady of Guadalupe.

for a second audience in the episcopal residence. This time the bishop paid slightly more attention but asked him to return with a sign that would prove that the request was not just the idle invention of a simple Indian.

On December 12, when Juan Diego should have returned to speak to the woman and receive his sign, he was busy trying to care for his uncle who was at the point of death. Trying to avoid an encounter with the woman, he took an alternate route toward the city where he hoped to find a priest who would bring his uncle the last sacraments. Although he had tried to circumvent the place of encounter, the woman came to meet him and conversed with him. In reply to his concern about the uncle, she said:

> Listen, my littlest son, carry this in your heart. That which scares you, that which afflicts you is nothing. Do not let your face and heart be perturbed. Do not fear this illness or any other. . . . Do not worry about the illness of your uncle; he will not die from it. Be assured that he is now well.[46]

She then sent him to the top of Tepeyac hill where he found a glorious assortment of Castillian roses which he gathered and took back to her. She arranged the roses in his *tilma* (cloak) and sent him again to the bishop. Although the bishop's servants attempted to take the roses from him, he held them tight until he could unfold the *tilma* in front of the bishop. When he opened the *tilma*, the roses fell to the floor and exposed the image of the woman, now known as Our Lady of Guadalupe. The sign was sufficient.

Over the centuries, the appearance of the Virgin of Guadalupe has been interpreted by many as a divine intervention or sign in the history of Mexico and all of Latin America. Coming at a time when the native people, like Juan Diego's uncle, were at the point of death, she became an effective symbol of healing. When she assured Juan Diego that his uncle was healthy, her words were interpreted to refer not just to one old man, but to all of the New World inhabitants who had lost their sense of self-worth. Her appearance on the hill of Tepeyac held out the promise of an authentic, inculturated Christianity.

The woman who appeared to Juan Diego identified herself verbally as the "Mother of God, through whom one lives." That self-description blended the Christian tradition about Mary, the Mother of God, with the ancient Mexican traditions about Tonantzin, the goddess who was the source of life. So too, the image on the *tilma* combined the artistic expressions of the two cultures in a marvelous synthesis, neither Aztec nor European, that was a new creation born from the encounter between the two. Her words spoke to the Spaniards, who placed great importance on clear theological formulations. Her graphic image spoke the language of the natives, for whom symbolic expressions conveyed a depth that words could not approximate.

Theologically, Guadalupe symbolized the promise that a New World could be built, that resurrection was possible in spite of the perversions of Christianity that had brought about the nearly total destruction of native cultures. Neither fully native nor fully European, the Virgin of Guadalupe was an icon of future possibility, a sign that new life could arise from the ashes of death.

The story of Guadalupe spread like wildfire. Although the missionaries' opinion of the event ranged from tolerance to vehement opposition, there was no lack of people ready to spread the news. In an area where the process of conversion had been slow, nine million natives came into the Catholic Church in the six years that followed the apparition.

The Guadalupe event affirmed the native people like nothing else that had happened since 1492. Building something new on the basis of their traditions, it ratified their existing knowledge of God while teaching them that the mystery of God was larger and even more mysterious than their previous experience. The choice of a simple native as the person to bear a message to the bishop was a crucial element of the story. According to the account, when Juan Diego asked the Virgin to choose a more influential spokesperson, she responded:

> Listen, littlest of my children, and know for certain that I have no scarcity of servants and messengers whom I could charge with my comfort and my word so that they would carry out my will; but it is very necessary that you personally go and make the appeal, that through your intercession my desire and will be carried out.[47]

Highlighting Blessed Juan Diego as the chosen messenger of the Virgin Mary served as a sign that the natives had a dimension of truth to bring to the Spanish Catholic Church, just as that Church had a message for the natives.[48]

Understood as a revelatory experience, the message of Guadalupe denounced all those who would destroy or demean themselves or one another, whether they were rebels, conquistadors, paternalistic teachers, or natives who repudiated their own genuine heritage.[49] More visually than verbally, the Virgin taught that Christianity in America could be a new experience for everyone, native and Spaniard alike.

DISCUSSION QUESTIONS

1. Sixteenth-century Europeans experienced earthshaking changes in their understanding of the world and in the structures of society. Forty years after the invention of the printing press inaugurated one of the most significant communications revolutions in history, explorers brought the astounding news that a previously unknown continent and population inhabited the globe. Within twenty-five years, the Reformation split the previously united Church of the West. Are there significant parallels between the sixteenth century and our own from which we could learn?

2. Sixteenth-century missionaries worked from three distinct models of spreading the faith that can be summarized in the terms "conquest," "conversion," and "evangelization." In what ways might those still be operative today? How do the three models differ in their expression of mutuality of relationships among people of different backgrounds?

3. What experiences with or attitudes toward native peoples could have led some Europeans to take prophetic positions in defense of the natives? What efforts were made to awaken consciences?

4. Guaman Poma wrote to convince the Spanish king that native Americans could both accept and genuinely inculturate the Christian faith. How would his message be accepted today?

5. The verbal and visual message of Our Lady of Guadalupe symbolized the rich potential of the encounter between European Christians and Native Americans. In what ways has that potential come to fruition? What is still lacking?

Notes

1. Translated from Vargas Ugarte, *Historia de la Iglesia en el Perú,* 1511-1568, 5 vols. (Lima: Imprenta Santa María, 1953), 1:222-24.

2. *The Journal of Christopher Columbus,* translated by Cecil Jane (New York: Bonanza Books, 1989), 23.

3. Ibid., 24-26. Entry for October 13.

4. Ibid., 23.

5. Cardinal Jimenez de Cisneros spearheaded the reforms sponsored by Isabel. At the turn of the sixteenth century, Spain was among the intellectually most advanced and open areas of Europe. The reform was a major factor in avoiding the advance of the Reformation in Spanish territories.

6. For information about the diverse hypotheses that arose, see Lewis Hanke, *History of Latin American Civilization: Sources and Interpretations,* Vol. 1, *The Colonial Experience* (Boston: Little, Brown, and Co., 1973), 29-33.

7. Michel Paiewonsky, *Conquest of Eden* (Rome: Mapes Monde Ed., 1991), 76.

8. Pane, a Jeronomite friar, was originally open to the Amerindians and had taken great pains to learn their language and work toward their conversion. The murder of his first converts was such a shock that it changed his whole outlook on the possibilities of the mission. See Beatriz Charria Angulo, *Primera Comunidad Dominicana en América* (Bogatá: CELAM, 1987), 32.

9. See Hans Jurgen Prien, *La Historia del Cristianismo en América Latina* (Ediciones Sígueme: 1978), 163, 202.

10. For a thorough explanation of the rights and responsibilities of royal patronage as well as the eventual division of power between Spain and Portugal, see Pedro Leturia, *Relaciones entre la Santa Sede e Hispanoamérica* (Caracas: Sociedad Boliviariana de Venezuela, 1959) and Eugene Shiels, *King and Church: The Rise and Fall of the Patronato Real* (Chicago: Loyola University Press, 1961).

11. See Lewis Hanke, *All Mankind Is One* (DeKalb: Northern Illinois University Press, 1974), 74-75.

12. Oviedo, whom Las Casas called the "deadly enemy of the Indians," published his history in two parts between 1535 and 1547. He had a reputation for brutal treatment of the natives under his jurisdiction. See Hanke, *All Mankind,* 34, 37-42.

13. Hanke, *All Mankind,* 41-42, quoting Oviedo's *Historia General,* ed. Juan Perez de Tudela y Bueso, 5 vols. (Madrid: Biblioteca de Autores Españoles, 1959), 1:68.

14. There is a technical difference between the *repartimiento* and the *encomienda.* The former was a direct grant of labor while the latter was a reform measure in which the responsibility to see to the spiritual well-being of the natives was carefully spelled out. In practice, however, the distinction was negligible.

15. Columbus was the first to administer the *repartimiento* system in the New World when in 1498 he "divided the Indios living in each parcel of land among the receivers, like herds of sheep." See Prien, 164, 173-75.

16. Luis Rivera has described the devastating demographic results of the Spanish presence in America as a "holocaust." See Luis N. Rivera, *A Violent Evangelism* (Louisville, Ky.: John Knox Press, 1990), 170-79.

17. From a letter of Fray Pedro de Córdoba to King Charles V, written on May 28, 1517. See Gustavo Gutierrez, *Dios o el oro en las indias* (Lima: CEP, 1989).

18. For additional information about the work of reformers see the works of Lewis Hanke and Enrique Dussel, *El Episcopado Latinoamericano y La Liberación de los Pobres* (Mexico: Centro de Reflección Teológica, 1979).

19. Without knowing it, the Spaniards were aided in their conquest by the fact that many native people assumed that they were superhuman or sent by the gods. For an analysis of the differences between the Spanish and Native American cultures see Virgilio Elizondo, *La Morenita* (San Antonio: MACC, 1981).

20. One of the things that most shocked the natives was the blood shed by the Spaniards. Particularly among the cultures of Mesoamerica, the object of war was to strike the opponent and to take prisoners. The barbarism of the outright killing perpetrated by the conquistadors was incomprehensible to them. See Elizondo, 43.

21. For examples of the preservation of Mexican native faith, see Jacques Lafaye, *Quetzalcoatl and Guadalupe* (Chicago: University of Chicago Press, 1976), 20-21.

22. See *Ideología mesiánica del Mundo Andino: Antología de Juan M. Ossio A.* (Lima: Ignacio Prado Pastor, 1973), 83-95.

23. See John Leddy Phelan, *The Millennial Kingdom of the Franciscans in the New World*, 2d. ed. rev. (Berkeley: University of California Press, 1970), 5.

24. The 1986 film *The Mission* depicts life in a Jesuit reduction. As the film portrays what could be considered one of the best experiences of the reduction, it also brings out the opposition that missionaries faced from those whose interest was more in the labor of the natives than in their well-being.

25. The people of colonial Latin America could be classified by the circumstances of their birth: *peninsulares* were Latin American residents who had been born on the Spanish peninsula; *criollos* were the children of *peninsulares*, born in America; *mestizos* were the children of a person of Spanish background and a native; and natives or *indios* were the people of indigenous ancestry.

26. Garcilaso de la Vega is known as one of the original and best chroniclers of the history of Peru. His book *Royal Commentaries of the Incas and General History of Peru* is a classic interpretation of the conquest of Peru (Trans., Austin: University of Texas Press, 1966).

27. Alberto Flores Galindo, *Buscando un Inca* (Havana: Casa de las Americas, 1986), 54-59.

28. See Pablo Ricard, *The Spiritual Conquest of Mexico* (Berkeley: The University of California Press, 1966), 225.

29. Adapted from ibid., 226. Ricard adds: "They also objected that the knowledge of Latin would allow the natives to expose the ignorant priests."

30. Excerpted and translated from Gutierrez, *Dios o el oro*, 30-31.

31. The bibliography on Las Casas is massive. For an introduction see the works of Lewis Hanke, Helen Rand Parish, and Gustavo Gutierrez.

32. Las Casas's most infamous work was his *Very Brief History of the Destruction of the Indies*, which was supposedly written to awaken the conscience of the king, but which was found and published by Spain's European enemies and became the foundational document of the "Black Legend" of Spain's cruel New World policies. Under the rule of Francisco de Toledo, Las Casas's writings were banned in the Viceroyalty of Peru.

33. Because he was the first to implement Trent in America, St. Toribio of Mogrovejo was named the patron of the Latin American episcopacy in 1899. For more comprehensive information about Toribio see the works of Vicente Rodriguez Valencia (Madrid: Instituto Sto. Toribio de Mogrovejo).

34. When Philip named Toribio, Francisco de Toledo had just finished a long tenure as Viceroy of Peru. Toledo had ruled with an iron hand and brought order out of the chaos that had reigned in the area since its conquest in 1533.

35. See Mary M. McGlone, "The King's Surprise," *The Americas* L:1 (1993), and "Shepherd Against the Butchers," *The Journal of Hispanic-Latino Theology* 1:2 (1994).

36. In 1590, Viceroy Mendoza wrote to the king complaining that the archbishop did not spend enough time in Lima, but rather "spends all his time among the indios, eating the little that they have." The viceroy was no happier about the time that the archbishop spent in the capital; in the same letter he wrote: "he intervenes in everything that has to do with hospitals, the construction of churches and everything else that pertains to Royal Patronage. . . . It would be good if you would order him to go to Spain and assign a coadjutor here." See Emilio Lisson Chavez, *La Iglesia de España en el Perú* (5 vols., Seville: 1943-1956), 3:549-50.

37. Lisson Chavez, 3:36-37.

38. See Felipe Guaman Poma de Ayala, *Nueva Cronica y Buen Gobierno* (1615), Edición de John V. Murra (Madrid: Historia 16, 1987).

39. The artwork reproduced here is from Guaman Poma's *Nueva Crónica*, illustrations 922, 609, and 821.

40. Ibid., 1015.

41. Ibid., 482.

42. Ibid., no. 935, p. 1031.

43. Ibid., 1030.

44. For a general review of the sources of the Guadalupe event see León Lopetegui and Felix Zubillaga, *Historia de la Iglesia en La América Española Desde el Descubrimiento hasta Comienzos del siglo XIX, México, América Central, Antillas* (Madrid: BAC, 1965), 345-55. See also Jeanette Rodriguez, *Our Lady of Guadalupe: Faith and Empowerment among Mexican-American Women* (Austin: University of Texas Press, 1994) and reviews of her work in the *Hispanic American Historical Review* and the *Journal of Hispanic-Latino Theology*.

45. Long an important figure in the popular religiosity of Mexico, Juan Diego was recently beatified by Pope John Paul II.

46. Antonio Valeriano, *NICAN Mopohua: Narraciones de las Apariciones de la Virgen de Guadalupe*, translated into Spanish by Mario Rojas (Mexico: Librería de Clavería, no date), paragraphs 118 and 120.

47. *Narraciones*, paragraphs 58 and 59.

48. Juan Diego was beatified in December 1990.

49. This "understanding" goes beyond an investigation of the strictly historical data regarding the Guadalupe event; it pertains to the realm of the spiritual and to spirituality as a mode of understanding experience. In this sense, the "spiritual" is the invisible reality that mediates between ultimate reality and human experience. See Alex García-Rivera, "Creator of the Visible and the Invisible: Liberation Theology, Postmodernism and the Spiritual," *Journal of Hispanic-Latino Theology* 3:4 (1996): 35-56.

CHAPTER TWO

The Beginnings of the Church in the United States

Baron Baltimore's Instructions to the Catholic Colonists, November 13, 1633

His Lordship requires his said governor and Commissioners that in their voyage to Mary Land they be very careful to preserve unity and peace amongst all the passengers on Shipboard and that they suffer no scandal or offense to be given to any of the Protestants, whereby any just complaint may hereafter be made by them, in Virginia or in England, and that for that end, they cause all Acts of Roman Catholic Religion to be done as privately as may be, and that they instruct all the Roman Catholics to be silent upon all occasions of discourse concerning matters of Religion; and that the said Governor and Commissioners treat the Protestants with as much mildness and favor as Justice will permit. And this to be observed at land as well as at Sea. . . .

That by the first opportunity after their arrival in Mary Land they cause a messenger to be dispatched away to James town such a one as is conformable to the Church of England, and as they may according to the best of their judgments trust; and he to carry his Majesty's letter to Sir John Harvie the governor and to the rest of the Council there.

That when they have made choice of the place where they intend to settle themselves and that they have brought their men ashore with all their provisions, they do assemble all the people to gather in a fit and decent manner and then cause his Majesty's letters patents to be publicly read by his Lordship Secretary John Bolles and afterwards . . . either the Governor or one of the commissioners presently after make some short declaration to the people of His Lordship's intentions which he means to pursue in this his intended plantation which are first the honor of God by endeavoring the conversion of the savages to Christianity, secondly the augmentation of his Majesty's Empire and dominions in those parts of the world by reducing them under the subjection of his Crown, and thirdly by the good of such of his Countrymen as are willing to adventure their fortunes and themselves in it, by endeavoring all he can, to assist them, that they may reap the fruits of their charges and labors according to the hopefulness of the thing, with as much freedom comfort and encouragement as they can desire. . . . And that at this time they take the occasion to minister an oath of Allegiance to his Majesty unto all and every one upon the place, after having first publicly in the presence of the people taken it themselves; letting them know that his Lordship gave particular directions to have it one of the first things that were done, to testify to the world that none should enjoy the benefit of his Majesty's gracious Grant unto his Lordship of that place, but such as should give a public assurance of their fidelity and allegiance to his Majesty. . . .

That where they intend to settle the Plantation they first make choice of a fit place, and a competent quantity of ground for a fort within which or near unto it a convenient house, and a church or a chapel adjacent may be built, for the seat of his Lordship or his Governor or other commissioners for the time being in his absence.

"Be Very Careful to Preserve Unity and Peace. . . . Suffer No Scandal or Offense to be Given to Protestants"

—Cecil Calvert

Precarious Origins

Catholic beginnings in British and Spanish America could hardly have been more different. In the sixteenth century, the Spanish Catholics went to America with bravado, under the explicit protection of church and state. When Baron Baltimore, Cecil Calvert, invited people to populate his colony, the few British Catholics who ventured to America went as a persecuted, suspect minority who hoped to colonize a territory where they could develop their commercial interests, assume the rights of citizenship under Calvert governance, and be free to practice, though never flaunt, their faith. Thus, the tone of Calvert's religious instructions to the colonists was one of thorough conciliation.[1] The first Catholics to settle the Maryland colony knew well that they were starting at a disadvantage because of their faith.

Cecilius Calvert, Second Lord Baltimore and First Lord Proprietor of Maryland, 1657. Courtesy of the Maryland Historical Society.

The emigrants who set sail for Maryland under the auspices of Cecil Calvert were the products of one hundred years of official British hostility to Catholicism. In America, the already established English colonies were carrying on the traditions of the British homeland, including a strong anti-Catholic bias. The very idea of Maryland, an English colony open to Catholics and their faith, was a formidable innovation.[2] Nevertheless, on November 22, 1633, approximately two hundred colonists, including two Jesuit priests, a Jesuit brother, and at least sixteen Catholic families, embarked on ships named *The Ark* and *The Dove* and set sail for America.

Four months and two days later, they landed at the mouth of the Potomac River and began to settle in and around St. Mary's City.

Because they followed Calvert's instructions, religious differences were not a problem among the Maryland settlers, at least not at first. Serious problems arose twelve years later when Protestant Virginians, distressed about Jesuit mission work among the natives, the geographical proximity of prominent Catholics, and the fact that Maryland had given refuge to persecuted Puritans, attacked the colony. In 1645, Richard Ingle led an invasion, pillaged Catholic property, arrested two of the resident Jesuits and forced the others to flee.[3]

In 1649, after peace was restored, Cecil Calvert and his governing assembly drafted and passed the legislation called an "Act Concerning Religion." This act was not a new policy but rather a formal, legal statement of the religious tolerance on which the colony had been established. With the unquestioned expectation that toleration would extend only to Christian faiths, the act stated:

> And be it also further Enacted by the same authority . . . that whatsoever person or persons shall from henceforth upon any occasion . . . call or denominate any person or persons whatsoever . . . within this province . . . a heretic, schismatic, idolater, puritan, independent, Presbyterian, popish priest, Jesuit, Jesuited papist, Lutheran, Calvinist, Anabaptist, Brownist, Antinomian, Barrowist, Roundhead, Sepatist [sic], or any other name or term in a reproachful manner relating to matter of Religion, shall for every such offense forfeit and loose . . . ten shillings sterling or the value thereof. . . .
>
> And whereas the enforcing of the conscience in matters of Religion hath frequently fallen out to be of dangerous consequence. . . . And for the more quiet and peaceable government of this Province, and the better to preserve mutual Love and amity amongst the inhabitants thereof, be it . . . enacted . . . that no person or persons whatsoever within this Province . . . professing to believe in Jesus Christ, shall from henceforth be any ways troubled, molested or discountenanced for or in respect of his or her religion nor in the free exercise thereof.[4]

In spite of such attempts to ensure religious tolerance, life was never the same for Maryland Catholics after Ingle's invasion. In 1692, the

Calvert family lost their charter and Maryland became a royal colony. Among the first acts of the new colonial assembly was the legal establishment of the Church of England as the official church of the province. With establishment came a curtailment of Catholic civil rights and eventually a total disenfranchisement of the Catholic population: a state of affairs that would not be reversed until the time of the Revolutionary War.[5]

If Catholics did not fare well in "their own" colony of Maryland, much less could have been expected in other colonies. In reality, Catholics were almost nonexistent in much of the colonial territory. New York's brief moment of overt Catholic freedom and leadership came when James, the Duke of York, converted to Catholicism in 1672. He appointed several Catholics to official positions, and in 1683, Thomas Dongan, the Catholic governor of the colony, passed a bill that allowed freedom of worship. That freedom was short-lived. In 1689 a rebellion broke out, bringing a reign of terror for Catholics. Dongan was hunted, Jesuits were forced to flee the area, and within five years the Church of England and English penal legislation were firmly established in New York.

When new legislation barred the entry of priests into the colony, New York Catholicism went underground rather than die out. The Mass was secretly celebrated in private homes and a Catholic minority persisted, preserving their faith until the Revolution brought them the freedom to practice it openly.[6]

Once Maryland came under Puritan rule, the only haven left for Catholics was Pennsylvania, where the Quakers promoted both freedom of religion and civil rights for all citizens. As early as 1706, the Jesuits were able to open a mission near the Pennsylvania border, and by 1734 Fr. Joseph Greaton, SJ, opened a Catholic chapel in Philadelphia and became the first resident priest in Pennsylvania. Eventually, German Jesuits outnumbered their English-speaking confreres and ministered to German Catholic immigrants in the colony. But even in Pennsylvania, the imposition of English penal laws eventually curtailed the civil liberty of Catholics.

Throughout British America, the Catholic population was so small as to seem inconsequential. In 1756, a Pennsylvania census counted about 200,000 residents of whom 1,365 were Catholics. In 1765, Fr. George Hunter wrote to his Jesuit provincial that there were approximately 26,000 Catholics in the colonies of Maryland and Pennsylvania combined.[7] Limited numbers did not, however, imply insignificance—at least not in the eyes of those who feared that every "papist" was ultimately an agent of a foreign government and therefore incapable of patriotism. Because fidelity to the Catholic faith implied ties to Rome, Catholics were assumed to be open to "popish" plots and suspected of being agents of papal imperialism. Given the bitterness of the Reformation and Counter Reformation, combined with England's competition with Catholic Spain and France over American territories, it is perhaps understandable that the Protestant colonists would be suspicious of their Catholic neighbors.

Catholicism in the British colonies was born and grew in an atmosphere of uncertainty and persecution. The greatest advantages of the situation were that it led Catholics to develop a deep appreciation for religious freedom and an ability to live with religious pluralism, thus preparing them for life in the nation about to be born.

But the disadvantages were also great. Because they were denied the rights of full participation in the governance of their society, the Catholics could not adequately contribute their talents to the growth of the nation. The religiosity they developed in a situation of persecution led them to try to "fit in," sometimes at the cost of not being able or willing to take a public stand on moral issues that were as national as they were sectarian in nature.[8] More than anything else, the prohibition against official organisms and institutions of Catholicism meant that the Church could not begin to grow and develop naturally in the new soil of America.

Slow Stabilization

Because the Church was unable to operate as a fully established institution in British America, 155 years passed between the arrival of the first missionaries and the appointment of John Carroll as the first bishop in the country.[9] That meant that the Church was almost entirely dependent on missionary clergy—some of whom came from England, others from France, Germany, and other European nations.[10] The missionary character of the clergy did little to alleviate the Church's reputation for being "foreign," and, generous as they were, the immigrant priests were an important supplement but inadequate substitute for a native priesthood brought up in the culture of the country. The situation also implied that Catholics in the newborn United States had no experience of normal church government or organization when they did begin to exist in freedom and with civil rights.

Sharing Faith Across the Hemisphere

"Make Some Short Declaration of His Lordship's Intentions. . . . First the Honor of God by Endeavoring the Conversion of the Savages. . . ."

—Cecil Calvert

The Mission of the Church

Although the Maryland colony was first and foremost a commercial enterprise, the desire to freely practice and spread the Catholic faith made it unique among British colonies. The Jesuits who came to Maryland with the first expedition of settlers had every intention of dedicating themselves to the conversion of the natives. Like their French confreres who were already laboring in Canadian territory, Fr. Andrew White and his companions were willing to confront all the challenges of nature and language in order to evangelize the Indians. White, in particular, made excellent progress in the language of the Piscataway people and within a few years, the Jesuits could number their Indian converts in Maryland at about

Bishop John Carroll (1735-1815). Painting by Gilbert Stuart, circa 1808, from the Georgetown University Art Collection.

1,000.[11] That early progress was soon cut short by civil limitations put on the missionaries, anti-Catholic legislation, and conflicts with Cecil Calvert. After 1645, the Jesuits worked exclusively among the English colonists. Even that work became severely restricted through laws like Maryland's 1704 "Act to Prevent the Growth of Popery within this Province" which forbade priests to baptize the children of non-Catholics, to work for conversions, or even to celebrate the Mass in public.[12]

In spite of it all, Catholicism in British America survived and even grew. In 1784, John Carroll, then the Vatican-appointed superior of the Catholic mission in the United States, wrote a report to

Rome that included the following information about the state of the Church in the newly formed country.

> There are in Maryland about 15,800 Catholics; of these . . . 9,000 [are] freemen . . . about 3,000 [are children], and about that number of slaves of all ages of African origin. . . . There are in Pennsylvania about 7,000 . . . and the Catholics are less scattered and live nearer to each other. There are not more than 200 in Virginia who are visited four or five times a year by a priest. Many other Catholics are said to be scattered in that and other states, who are utterly deprived of all religious ministry. In the State of New York I hear there are at least 1,500. . . . As to the Catholics who are in the territory bordering on the river called Mississippi . . . this tract of country contains, I hear, many Catholics, formerly Canadians, who speak French, and I fear that they are destitute of priests. . . .
>
> In Maryland a few of the . . . more wealthy families still profess the Catholic faith. . . . As for piety, they are for the most part sufficiently assiduous in the exercises of religion . . . but they lack . . . fervor as many congregations hear the word of God only once a month, and sometimes only once in two months. We are reduced to this by want of priests. . . .
>
> There are nineteen priests in Maryland and five in Pennsylvania. Of these, two are more than seventy years old, and three others very near that age. . . . Of the remaining priests, some are in very bad health. . . .
>
> There is properly no ecclesiastical property here: for the property by which the priests are supported is held in the names of individuals and transferred by will to devisees. This course was rendered necessary when the Catholic religion was cramped here by laws, and no remedy has yet been found for this difficulty.[13]

Although he was not complaining, Carroll was explaining that he and his small Church had their work cut out for them. By 1789, when he was consecrated as the first bishop of the United States, the people under his jurisdiction numbered approximately 35,000, representing just under 1 percent of the total population of the country. They were served by about twenty-five priests, all of whom had been trained and ordained in other countries.

Obviously, native vocations were a priority. In 1791, French Sulpician priests fled France and opened St. Mary's Seminary in Baltimore. Although the response was not overwhelming, by 1829 St. Mary's had prepared fifty-two priests for ordination: twenty-one native born and the rest immigrants from Ireland, England, Germany, and France. An increased number of priests, both missionary and nationally trained, along with more freedom of religious expression, allowed for the type of institutional growth that had been impossible before the Revolution. More priests meant that more parishes could be established with the organizations of the laity and the range of services that come with parish organization.

Just before the foundation of the seminary, the first congregation of religious women was established in the United States by four Carmelites who came from Antwerp to Fort Tobacco, Md. Carroll obtained permission for them to be exempt from the restrictions of their cloistered rule and to teach, but they preferred to live a contemplative life and turned down his request that they open a girls' academy. In 1806, Elizabeth Seton, the famous Anglican convert who founded the first religious community for U.S. women, opened an academy for girls in Baltimore staffed by her Sisters of Charity.[14] This academy, along with a few others founded in the early 1800s, offered a good general education and replaced the "needlework" schools that had previously served the Maryland colony as secret centers for religious instruction.[15]

As the Catholic school system developed, it included academies, free schools in the cities, and by 1840, 200 parochial schools, half of which were west of the Alleghenies. The growing communities of women religious also provided the personnel necessary to staff Catholic hospitals and orphanages, thereby enabling the Church to make major contributions to the general welfare of the nation from the mid-nineteenth through the twentieth century.[16]

Becoming American Catholics

Aside from the chronic lack of clergy to provide regular sacramental ministry to the Catholic population, the biggest problems faced by the Church in the nineteenth century were the mutually related issues of immigration and nationalism. Already in 1818, Archbishop Marechal, the third Archbishop of Baltimore, wrote to Rome, "It is almost impossible to believe what large number of Europeans come to this country. It is estimated that during the present year about two hundred immigrants per day came to our shores from Europe. Among these were very many Catholics."[17]

Although the number of immigrants reported by Marechal would look paltry in the years to come, they were enough to add fuel to the fires of the already simmering "trustee crisis," a problem that pitted the authority of bishops against some local congregations. The central issue was whether the bishop or the parish trustees had the authority to appoint local pastors. A large part of the underlying problem was that pastors did not always share the language and cultural heritage of their parishioners. Complicating the whole issue was the fact that, in at least some states, the clergy could not hold property in their own name.

One of the first trustee-bishop conflicts happened in Pennsylvania in 1787, when the Germans of St. Mary's Church, weary of English-speaking priests, legally incorporated themselves and hired "a wandering German-born priest" without Carroll's approval.[18] While Carroll was happy to see congregations taking fiscal and planning responsibility for their churches, he stood firm in the conviction that canon law and basic Catholic church order demanded that clergy appointments remain under the ultimate jurisdiction of the bishop. To angry American Catholics and anti-Catholic Americans, that position sounded like a throwback to the royal authoritarianism against which America had fought her Revolution. Although the assertion of ultimate episcopal authority over congregations had every appearance of being anti-democratic, Carroll believed that the question had to do with the identity of the Catholic Church. Unwilling to accept the need to choose between "American" and "Roman Catholic," Carroll and the bishops who followed him forged a delicate balance of democracy and national identity while maintaining fidelity to the universal dimensions of church organization.[19]

The problem of trusteeism was particularly intense because it combined age-old Catholic tensions over church authority with questions of how Catholicism would take shape in the United States. Although the core question had to do with the model of Church that would take hold, it also highlighted the tensions among the different nationalities represented in the growing Church in the United States. The question seemed to be most intense among the German immigrants; they prayed and wanted preaching in their native language, and the parish church was the center of their religious identity. Trustee problems festered for years and were not resolved until the Third Plenary Council of Baltimore in 1884, when the bishops had won legal ownership of all parish property and could then promulgate appropriate ecclesiastical legislation. After nearly 100 years, the question of Catholic church governance was settled in favor of a hierarchical rather than a congregational model.

"Take the Occasion to Minister an Oath of Allegiance to All and Everyone. . . ."

—Cecil Calvert

From the seventeenth to the nineteenth century, to be Catholic in the United States meant to be caught in a confusing crossfire of demands having to do with attachment to national roots and culture, allegiance to the new nation, and fidelity to the Catholic tradition. Sometimes it seemed that Catholics were suspect to everyone but their closest companions. Nationalist loyalties and suspicion from Rome threatened the inner unity of the Church while the forces of bigotry attacked it from without. As the seventeenth-century Catholic minority grew to become the largest single denomination in the United States, Catholics struggled to integrate the diverse strands of their individual and collective lives into a coherent whole.

The Constitution of the United States guaranteed freedom of religious expression, and with that, the Catholic Church was finally free to organize itself institutionally. John Carroll was named the first bishop, and soon other bishops were named in large cities. But as Americans know well, legislation has little power to overcome prejudice. After the Revolution, the fledgling Catholic Church in the United States entered into a century and a half of difficult development in which it had to prove itself to both Rome and the Protestant majority in the country; at the same time it created a unified community from a fast-multiplying membership comprising multiple nationalities and economic backgrounds. Put simply, in the nineteenth century the Catholic Church of the United States had to forge its identity, and the trick was to make it both Catholic and authentically American.

Immigrants and "Foreigners"
The United States is primarily a land of immigrants. Unlike Latin America with its large *mestizo* populations, a very small percentage of U.S. citizens

can trace their family tree back more than two hundred years on American soil. After the Revolution, when Catholicism was emerging from legalized persecution, the Church was called on to respond to the needs of massive numbers of immigrants.

Between 1790 and 1850, 1,071,000 Catholics immigrated to the United States. They far outnumbered the already established Catholics, so that the Catholic Church, more than any other denomination, had to face the task of absorbing an enormous number and variety of newcomers. Of the 33 million immigrants to the United States in the century from 1820 to 1920, about one-third were Catholic. In 1820, the Catholic Church in the United States was dealing with members who spoke English, French, and German; by 1920, it was made up of people who spoke thirty-eight languages.[20] In the words of John Tracy Ellis, "Willy-nilly the American Church had become catholic in the broadest sense, and the problem of how best to mold the congeries of nationalities that composed its faithful into a stable element of the American population became its most pressing occupation."[21]

A majority of the Catholic immigrants were Irish. Although the Irish had been coming to America since colonial days, the real groundswell came with those who fled the ravages of the potato famines; in the five years between 1846 and 1851, more than a million Irish left their homeland, most of them young, single, and poor.[22] But if the Irish came in the greatest numbers, they had to deal with the fact that they were not the only immigrants to the United States, or even the only ones seeking the support of the Church. The next most populous group of Catholic immigrants were Germans. Along with them, there were also significant numbers of Poles, Italians, Portuguese, Austrians, and Czechs.

Most immigrants arrived on U.S. shores as semi-lost and vulnerable people. The traumas they had already passed through, and those they were about to face, were not unknown to the Church. In 1888, Pope Leo XIII wrote a plea on behalf of Italian immigrants, which began with a doleful description of the hardships that all immigrants endured:

How toilsome and disastrous is the condition of those who for some years have been migrating out of Italy to the regions of America in search of a livelihood. . . . It is to be deplored that so many unfortunate Italians, forced by poverty to change their residence, should rush into evils which are often worse than the ones they have desired to flee from. . . . At the outset, the emigrants' crossing itself is full of dangers . . . for many of them fall into the hands of avaricious men whose slaves, as it were, they become, and then herded in ships and inhumanly treated, they are gradually depraved in their nature. And when they have reached the desired land, being ignorant of both the language and the locale, and engrossed in their daily toil, they become the victims of the trickery of the dishonest or the powerful by whom they are employed. Those who by their own industry succeed . . . little by little lose the nobler feelings of human nature and learn to live like those who have set all their hopes and thoughts on this earth.[23]

As Pope Leo pointed out, the poverty of the immigrants was a total human poverty, a combination of the spiritual and the corporal. The Church that received those immigrants thus found itself called upon to meet their material as well as religious needs.

Pope Leo wrote, not just to remind the U.S. bishops of the needs of their people, but also to offer support and help. The "Propaganda," the mission office of the Church, had already been training missionary priests for the United States when Leo wrote. In 1888, Leo explained that he was personally supporting a foundation that would prepare Italian priests to minister to their compatriots in America. These priests, along with an abundant number of other European missionaries, helped provide for the "national" parishes that would be founded to meet the needs of the nineteenth-century immigrants.

Each of the immigrant groups arrived in the United States with a distinct language and culture. The immigrant Catholics among them soon made the surprising and disconcerting discovery that their particular experience of Catholicism was unique; each group brought with it national and regional traditions of piety and church organization. As strangers in the new land, they all looked to the Church to provide them with a touchstone, something familiar that could help them adjust to their new way of life.

In many cases, the poorer immigrants, those who remained in the cities as laborers, had more opportunity to find and identify with the Church than did their more prosperous brethren who could afford to buy land and begin farming. The city dwellers could usually find a parish, and the very fact that the church had a building and some modicum of organization was a comfort: something important from home existed in the new land and was legitimate and even powerful. The parish was a reminder that God had not abandoned them, and it was a sign that the Catholic faith was not confined by national boundaries.[24]

But the universality of Catholicism went only so far. Although the Catholic liturgy was celebrated in Latin and was equally familiar to immigrants from any country, preaching, teaching, patron saints, and popular religious devotions were another matter. It is no surprise that Catholic immigrants attempted to find or establish parishes based on their national origins. The importance of a culturally familiar faith community was well articulated by Rev. Peter Vay who visited a Hungarian parish in Chicago and spoke of the people:

> Set adrift in that great city, without knowing the language, without friends or any one to advise them, these poor folks are at the mercy of chance. . . . The church and the school are their only safeguards.[25]

Vay was particularly impressed with the love that the people had for their Hungarian parish and the sacrifices they had made to build it.

> The inauguration of that humble little church and its simple worshipers has left an indelible impression upon me. It was one of those never-to-be-forgotten scenes which, in spite of their apparent unimportance, form a page in the annals of history. This small beginning, representing the accumulated savings of those hardy workmen, is the center of new efforts and new struggles.[26]

As the Church attempted to assimilate the immigrants and to help them enter the mainstream of society, it also had to struggle through interior nationalistic rivalries that threatened to split it apart. The major discord was between the Germans and Irish, and the sources were many. Although they were often among the poorest of the immigrants, the Irish felt that they fit in more easily because of their command of the language and because their numbers made it easy for them to feel at home. The Germans, on the other hand, were not above conveying the idea that their language was superior to English, and that fact alone was enough to make up for their lack of English. In addition, the early German immigrants were generally not as destitute as the Irish, and rather than living in the big city ghettos, many of them had been able to purchase land and establish farming communities where they could also build their own churches. German Catholics were most concentrated either in rural areas or in the triangle of cities made up of St. Louis, Cincinnati, and Milwaukee. The Irish usually settled in major cities, particularly in the North, where they were able to find work.

The major tensions that arose had to do with the fact that the majority of the U.S. clergy and hierarchy had an Irish background. The Germans, in particular, resisted their "foreign" leadership and wanted to use the parishes as mechanisms to maintain their own culture as well as the faith. In some cases nationalist groups even attempted to separate themselves from the Church as a whole and establish an independent church structure within the country.

Nationalistic friction waxed and waned in the East and Midwest throughout the nineteenth century. In many respects, the nationalistic disputes were closely related to the "trustee controversy," especially in those parishes in which the laity had begun organizing and built a church even before they were able to procure a resident pastor. In brief, the proponents of national parishes wanted to maintain the practice of having distinct parishes for groups of people according to their national origin or mother tongue. Many of the bishops, anxious to see Catholics integrate into the mainstream of the culture and to make the most propitious use of their scarce resources, promoted the geographical parish model in which the dominant language for all would be English.

The issue came to a head when Archbishop Kenrick of St. Louis imposed previously promulgated legislation that ruled that national parishes did not have regular parish status. Although the statute was not carried out with any harshness, it wounded the pride of the German clergy who took their grievance to Rome. In the end, Rome decided that national parishes were valid and had irrevocable rights to exist, even when that would mean a surfeit of parishes in a particular locale.[27] National parishes, under the authority of the hierarchy, thus became a stable feature of the Catholic Church in the United States.

Parishes not only provided a locale for sacramental worship, but they were also centers for social life and welfare. The national parishes provided an almost ready-made group for newcomers and a strong community for old-time families. Parishes also served both informally and formally as social-welfare institutions; community members reached out to their neediest companions and formed charitable groups such as benefit societies and the St. Vincent de Paul Society to reach out to the poor. Finally, parish schools, which were almost mandatory for every parish after 1884, became key institutions through which the Church integrated immigrant families into American life and culture, preparing future generations to participate fully in the society.[28]

Beyond the parish level, church-sponsored hospitals and orphanages, which were usually staffed by women religious, cared for the most marginated casualties of what could often be a harsh society. Through the parishes, the services of religious communities, and diocesan organizations, the Church discovered and implemented a myriad of institutions designed to reach out to the immigrants and to build up the faith community.

Nativism and Anti-Catholicism

As if the challenges of weaving unity between old settlers and new immigrants were not enough, prejudice against Catholicism continued to plague the community through the whole of the nineteenth and into the twentieth century. In theory, all faith traditions in the United States were on an equal footing, but in attitude and practice, religious tolerance was frequently limited to Protestant denominations. Catholics seemed to be inevitably suspect in the eyes of the Protestant majority.

In a country that valued freedom and was struggling to forge a national identity, the Catholics' use of Latin for worship, their obedience to Rome, and accommodation, even if it was sometimes grudging, to a multitude of nationalities within their ranks, seemed dangerously un-American. Protestants shared a religious ideal of "voluntaryism," a belief that the faith community should never be beholden to or intimidated by any outside force in matters of faith. That principle seemed to be contradicted by almost every aspect of Catholic discipline.[29]

Suspicion of the Catholics grew as the number of Catholic immigrants increased. Even before the Civil War, Catholic immigrants were frequently labeled as dangerous agents of foreign powers. Some of the most renowned figures in U.S. history fit into the list of anti-Catholic propagandists, and their most eloquent spokesman was Rev. Lyman

Beecher who publicized his strong feelings in an 1835 essay called "Plea for the West."

> Clouds like the locusts of Egypt are rising from the hills and plains of Europe, and on the wings of every wind, are coming over to settle down upon our fair fields; while millions, moved by the noise of their rising and cheered by the news of their safe arrival and green pastures, are preparing for flight in an endless succession. . . .
>
> If they could read the Bible, and might and did, their darkened intellect would brighten, and their bowed down mind would rise. If they dared to think for themselves, the contrast of Protestant independence with their thraldom, would awaken the desire of equal privileges, and put an end to an arbitrary clerical dominion over trembling superstitious minds. If the pope and potentates of Europe held no dominion over ecclesiastics here, we might trust to time and circumstances to mitigate their ascendance and produce assimilation. But for conscience sake and patronage, they are dependent on the powers that be across the deep, by whom they are sustained and nurtured; and receive and organize all who come, and retain all who are born, while by argument and a Catholic education, they beguile the children of credulous unsuspecting Protestants into their own communion.[30]

Beecher's emotional invective against continuing immigration appealed to almost every traditional anti-Catholic prejudice. It painted Catholics in the United States as nothing more than the intellectually enslaved, advance troops of an invasion preparing to put an end to the American experiment. Because of their sheer numbers, as well as the "enthralling" powers of their "superstitions," Beecher would have had his readers believe that the pope himself was preparing to take a throne in the United States. The "nativism" promoted by such writings was to have a long life in America.

One of the most ironic aspects of Beecher's "Plea for the West" is the fact that at the very time he was crying out against a supposed foreign invasion, U.S. citizens were immersed in the process of settling and eventually usurping a vast portion of Mexico. From the time that U.S. settlers had been allowed to inhabit the area of Texas, there had been growing sentiment in favor of extending U.S. territory by taking at least the northern regions of Mexico. In 1836, with aid from the U.S. government, Texas broke away from Mexico and declared itself the "Lone Star Republic," a status it enjoyed until it entered the Union in 1845. In 1846, the United States declared a war on Mexico that concluded with the U.S. annexation of approximately one half of Mexico's territory, populated by slightly more than 75,000 people.[31]

Catholic Roots in the Southwest

Eighty years before the Maryland settlers brought Catholicism to the British colonies, Spanish missionaries had begun work in areas that would eventually include at least parts of the states of Florida, Arizona, Texas, New Mexico, Colorado, Kansas, and California. In 1539, Dominican chaplains accompanied Hernando de Soto and other Spanish explorers in the "borderland" territories of Florida and Arizona. In 1540, a group of Franciscans accompanied the Coronado expedition and one of them, Fray Juan de Padilla, remained among the natives in Quivira (Kansas); he died at their hands in 1544, becoming the first Catholic martyr in what is now the continental United States.

The Franciscans began their efforts in Florida in 1573, and by 1635, thirty-five friars were serving forty-four towns and a population of 30,000 inhabitants. Meanwhile, beginning in 1598, other Franciscans were preaching in what is now Colorado, New Mexico, and Arizona, where by 1750, they had administered 17,500 baptisms. The city of San Antonio was founded in 1718, and from there Franciscans, including the Blessed Fray Antonio Margil de Jesús, made converts among a variety of indigenous groups. The best known Franciscan effort was the establishment of the California missions. Beginning with the foundation of San Diego in 1769, Blessed Junipero Serra and his companions established a series of more than twenty missions along the California coastline, including San Francisco in 1776.[32] Some of these missions are the basis for parishes that are still active today.

Between 1614 and 1767, Jesuit missionaries concentrated their contribution to southwestern mission efforts in Northern Mexico and Arizona. The most eminent among the Jesuits, Eusebio Kino, combined the work of exploration with his missionary activities; from 1687 to 1711, he traveled through what is now Sonora, Ariz., and lower California, establishing missions and awakening interest in Christianity among the varied peoples of the region. When the Jesuits were expelled from Spanish-American territories in 1767, they left twenty-nine mission centers and sixty missions to be taken over by the Franciscans. Substantial mission activity continued until after Mexico won its independence from Spain. In 1828, the Franciscan missions were closed, ending a period of nearly three hundred years of the first phase of evangelization throughout the southern and western regions of what would gradually become United States territory.

As the United States took over vast portions of Mexico between 1836 and 1846, the Mexican inhabitants of the newly acquired territory unwittingly became U.S. citizens almost overnight. Unlike other Catholic newcomers to the nation, they had not chosen to cross any borders; rather, as Fr. Virgilio Elizondo is fond of saying, the border crossed them.[33]

The new "Mexican-American" population was as distinctive as its history. The newly acquired regions boasted a diverse population that included people of Spanish descent, Mexicans, and Native Americans. With a Catholicism implanted by the Spanish missionaries and cultivated through centuries of inculturation in native and *mestizo* populations, they had developed a unique spirituality that was difficult for the "Anglo" Church to understand and to which that Church was minimally prepared to respond.

Although there had never been an abundance of priests to evangelize the rural areas, after the 1828 closing of the Franciscan missions, Southwestern Catholicism maintained itself virtually without the benefit of priestly ministry.[34] Religious organizations among the laity, *cofradias*, took over the responsibility to perpetuate devotions to patron saints and the celebration of feast days. The passing on of religious instructions became primarily a task of the family. The religious faith and devotions that the people maintained through this process remained an integral part of the individual and communal life and became more and more marked by local and regional particularities as the people had less and less contact with formally trained ministers who represented the wider Church. The faith that emerged from this process was an integral component of family traditions and affected every dimension of life. From the perspective of the Mexican-Americans, the United States' hard-won ability to think of religion and culture as separable dimensions of life seemed heartless at best and more likely irreligious.[35]

After 1846, with almost no Spanish or Mexican priests to serve the population of the newly acquired territories, the Church of the southwestern United States came under the leadership of French, Italian, and Irish missionaries who were rarely able to appreciate the religiosity of the people. As Virgilio Elizondo describes the lamentable predicament of the people:

> Fundamentalists said that their Catholicism was pagan and superstitious; newly arrived . . . missionaries said that their Catholicism was savage, superficial, and "lacking faith." . . . Jansenistic Catholics imposed their religious convictions on the Mexican-American people. Culturally speaking, it is difficult to say which group did the most harm. . . . Mexican Catholics said that they had "forgotten" the true faith, and U.S. Catholics said they had never had the true faith![36]

In spite of such criticisms, Mexican-Americans refused to abandon their deep religious traditions.[37]

The Mexican-American people found themselves among the most displaced and disdained citizens of the country.[38] Their faith was culturally and religiously suspect, they had less motivation to "assimilate" than did immigrants, and, more than most other U.S. Catholic groups, they suffered the effects of racial discrimination. As other U.S. Catholics slowly climbed the social ladder, Mexican-Americans usually found themselves relegated to the bottom rungs. Although they represented the oldest expression of Christianity in America, their unique contributions would generally be ignored and rejected until the second half of the twentieth century. It was the British-bred experience of the colonial United States that would set the standard for U.S. Catholicism: a standard that seemed so incapable of embracing Latino spirituality that the oldest Catholic tradition in the growing nation would spend more than a hundred years being treated like a foreign element in its own birthplace. If Catholics in general were regarded as outsiders in the country, so much more so the Mexican-Americans and their descendants.

Words Turn to Violence

The anti-Catholic bigotry expressed by people like Lyman Beecher was not confined to words. As often happens, some of the first "nativist" violence was committed against those who were least capable of defending themselves. Catholic sisters became a special target of the anti-Catholic feeling. As a clearly identifiable group, the sisters seemed to typify all the "oddity" of Catholicism. They lived independently, defied the revered "womanly role" of being wife and mother, and dedicated themselves to a "mysterious" lifestyle. In 1834 a mob destroyed the Ursuline academy in Charlestown, Mass., and soon thereafter attacks followed in Baltimore, Frederick, St. Louis, Galveston, and other cities.[39]

In 1842, nativist riots broke out in Philadelphia, causing Bishop Francis Kenrick to flee the city until order had been restored. In 1844, Philadelphia rioters rose up again, this time burning two Catholic churches and leaving 13 dead and numerous wounded. In that same year, Bishop Hughes of New York was threatened with riots and responded less mildly than his Pennsylvania confrere; Hughes stationed armed guards around his city's churches and let it be known that if the churches were attacked, New York would be turned into "a second Moscow." When the mayor pleaded with him to restrain the Catholics, Hughes replied, "I have not the power; you must take care that they are not provoked."[40]

The one "anti-American" characteristic of the immigrants that Lyman Beecher did not underline or criticize was their poverty, but that too came into vogue as a complaint against the immigrant populations. The American myth held that the United States was the land of opportunity. The Protestant ethic taught that God helps those who help themselves: wealth was considered a blessing and poverty a curse. As industries grew and gobbled up the cheap labor of the immigrants, the poverty of the laboring masses appeared to be a blight on the national reputation and an affront to the American ideal. Ignoring the dependence of the wealthy classes on slave or near-slave labor, Henry Ward Beecher, Lyman's son, interpreted the Protestant ethic and taught that "no man in this land suffers from poverty unless it be more than his fault, unless it be his sin. There is enough and to spare thrice over; and if men have not enough, it is owing to the want of provident care, and foresight, and industry.[41] With sentiments such as this, class prejudice took its place in the motivations for anti-Catholic feeling, rhetoric, and activity.

Some form of anti-Catholic prejudice, whether or not it was formally called nativism, had been present since the first British settlements were founded in America. Calvert's instructions that the Catholic colonists should avoid scandal and work for unity were usually of little avail because the behavior of Catholics had little to do with the reactions that were unleashed against them. It was World War I that finally gave Catholics their best opportunity to demonstrate that, just like their Protestant compatriots, they were truly Americans at heart.

Entering the Mainstream

Although Catholics served in almost every capacity in the War between the States, the Church of the mid-nineteenth century did not take strong positions on the issues dividing the nation. The abolitionist movement, whose ranks included prominent anti-Catholic crusaders, was understandably unattractive to Catholics. Catholics served in the armies of both sides of the Civil War, but that service did little to enhance their social respectability. Catholic Americans had also demonstrated their national loyalty by supporting U.S. wars against the Catholic nations of Mexico in 1846 and Spain in 1898, but it was the "great War" that provided a defining moment.[42]

When the United States finally entered World War I, the U.S. Catholic Church was composed of immigrants and their descendants from all of the warring European nations. This was the moment for them to prove themselves—and the hierarchy led the way. In 1916, Archbishop John Ireland urged Catholics to follow their president: "Years ago it may be that we were Irishmen, Germans, or Frenchmen. Today we are Americans."[43] If Ireland's words were more hope than reality in 1916, the Church was prepared to solidify the structures that would make them come true during and after the war.

The major step in this process, and the one which would have the most long-lasting consequences, was the establishment of the National Catholic War Council in 1917. The council coordinated the U.S. Catholic war effort at home and abroad. It advanced the task of "Americanizing" the immigrants by encouraging local parishes to offer language and civics classes and to help their people attain U.S. citizenship. The council evolved to become the National Conference of Catholic Bishops, the permanent and highly respected organization of the U.S. hierarchy. Although struggles against bigotry did not end with the war, by the early twentieth century U.S. Catholics had a new confidence about themselves as both Catholic and patriot—and, in the long run, that self-concept was perhaps as important as the cessation of hostilities from without.

Sharing Faith Across the Hemisphere

Relationships with Rome

As the Catholic Church in the United States slowly gained national prestige, it also grew in the estimation of the Vatican. In the eyes of European Catholicism, the U.S. experiment with the separation of church and state had at first appeared to be a hazardous innovation. The U.S. refusal to establish or endow any religious tradition was interpreted as a contemptuous indifference to religion itself.[44] The Church that bishops like John Carroll and John England envisioned, one in which

Cardinal James Gibbons. Photo: Sulpician Archives, Baltimore.

there was an English language liturgy, an ecumenical spirit, and freedom from foreign interference, was unacceptable to Rome and thus impossible to establish in eighteenth- and nineteenth-century America. But acceptance of Roman models of church authority did not alleviate the suspicions of the Vatican about the American experiment nor quench the democratic spirit of the Americans.

From the time of John Carroll on, the bishops of the United States approved of the separation of church and state. For the most part, they defended the policy through private conversations, but in 1887, Cardinal James Gibbons used the occasion of his elevation to the rank of cardinal to preach a sermon that explained and extolled the U.S. experience to European and Vatican hierarchical officials. He quoted Leo XIII to remind his listeners that the Church is not tied to any particular political expression:

> Our Holy Father . . . in his luminous encyclical on the constitution of Christian States, declares that the Church is not committed to any particular form of civil government. She adapts herself to all; she leavens all with the sacred leaven of the gospel. She has lived under absolute empires; she thrives under constitutional monarchies; she grows and expands under the free republic.

Then, combining national pride with an exhibition of ecumenical spirit he said:

For myself, as a citizen of the United States, without closing my eyes to our defects as a nation, I proclaim with a deep sense of pride and gratitude . . . that I belong to a country where the civil government holds over us the aegis of its protection without interfering in the legitimate exercise of our sublime mission as ministers of the Gospel of Jesus Christ. Our country has liberty without license, authority with depotism. . . .

Our Holy Father has been graciously pleased to exalt [me] to the dignity of the purple. For this mark of exalted favor I offer the Holy Father my profound thanks in my own name and in the name of the clergy and people under my charge. I venture also to thank him in the name of my venerable colleagues, the bishops, the clergy, as well as the Catholic laity of the United States. I presume to thank him also in the name of our separated brethren of America who, though not sharing our faith, have shown that they are not insensible to the honor conferred on our common country, and have again and again expressed their warm admiration of the enlightened statesmanship, the apostolic virtues and benevolent charities of the illustrious Pontiff who now sits in the Chair of Peter.

Rome accepted the U.S. policy of separation of church and state, but only gradually. In 1895, when Pope Leo XIII wrote an encyclical to the Church of the United States, he praised U.S. national progress and commended the fact that the U.S. form of government did not hinder the work of the Church.

That your Republic is progressing and developing by giant strides is patent to all; and this holds good in religious matters also. For even as your cities, in the course of one century, have made a marvelous increase in wealth and power, so do we behold the Church, from scant and slender beginnings, grown with rapidity to be great and exceedingly flourishing. . . .

The main factor, no doubt, in bringing things into this happy state were the ordinances and decrees of your synods. . . . But moreover . . . thanks are due to the equity of the laws which obtain in America and to the customs of the well-ordered Republic. For the Church amongst you, unopposed by the Constitution and government of your nation . . . is free to live and act without hindrance.[45]

But, lest America be seen as a model for the rest of the world, Leo continued:

Yet, though all this is true, it would be very erroneous to draw the con-clusion that in America is to be sought the type of the most desirable status of the Church, or that it would be universally lawful or expedient for State and Church to be, as in America, dissevered and divorced. The fact that Catholicity with you is in good condition, nay, is even enjoying a prosperous growth, is by all means to be attributed to the fecundity with which God has endowed His Church, in virtue of which unless men or circumstances interfere, she spontaneously expands and propagates herself; but she would bring forth more abundant fruits if, in addition to liberty, she enjoyed the favor of the laws and the patron-age of public authority.[46]

Things would get worse before they would get better in terms of the re-lationship between the Vatican and the Church in the United States. The most serious source of conflict between the two arose in relation to what was called "Americanism." As it was described, "Americanism" can be summarized as a school of thought that taught that "the Church should adapt itself to modern civilization, relax its ancient rigor, show indulgence to modern theories, de-emphasize religious vows and give greater scope for the action of the Holy Spirit on the individual soul."[47] Rome interpreted such thinking as heretical because it seemed to strike at the heart of the Church's right and responsibility to teach about doctrine and morals.

In reality, the "Americanism" controversy surged from cultural as well as strictly theological issues: from efforts to inculturate Catholicism in the context of U.S. democracy and religious pluralism. Much of what Rome specifically condemned as heretical was actually derived from a poorly translated book about Fr. Isaac Hecker. Although some U.S. bishops re-joiced at the condemnation of "liberals" in their midst, Cardinal Gibbons spoke in the name of the hierarchy saying: "This doctrine, which I deliber-ately call extravagant and absurd, this Americanism as it has been called, has nothing to common with the views, aspirations, doctrine and conduct of Americans."[48] Rather than become embroiled in a worthless dispute, the U.S. bishops who might have supported what they saw as a "legitimate Americanism" simply joined Rome in condemning the distorted teachings that were attributed to them.[49]

Although it had serious repercussions for the future of theology in the United States, the Americanism controversy did not cause a serious rift between the papacy and the Church in the United States.[50] A few years later, Leo would write the U.S. bishops with high praise for their Church, its contributions to the faith, and its support of the papacy itself. In that letter he also positively applauded the U.S. government, which, in his estimation, was then more a friend of the Church than were some European governments:

> The voice . . . of the Bishops and the faithful of the United States of America brings us special joy, both on account of the conditions which give your country prominence over many others and of the special love We entertain for you. . . .
>
> We . . . confess that Our pleasure [with you] has increased from day to day by reason of the increase of Catholicity among you. The cause of this increase, although first of all to be attributed to the providence of God, must also be ascribed to your energy and activity. You have . . . promoted every kind of catholic organization with such wisdom as to provide for all necessities and all contingencies, in harmony with the remarkable character of the people of your country . . . we have found your people . . . endowed with perfect docility of mind and alacrity of disposition. *Therefore, while the changes and tendencies of nearly all the nations which were Catholic for many centuries give cause for sorrow, the state of your churches, in their flourishing youthfulness, cheers Our heart and fills it with delight. True, you are shown no special favor by the laws of the land, but on the other hand, your lawgivers are certainly entitled to praise for the fact that they do nothing to restrain you in your just liberty.*[51]

If Pope Leo did not retract his earlier criticisms of the relationship between church and state in the United States, this letter demonstrates that he certainly had come to a new appreciation of the possibilities offered by the American experiment.

In 1908, Pope Pius X issued the encyclical *Sapienti Consilio*, which declared that the Church in the United States had been removed from the jurisdiction of *Propaganda Fide*. No longer considered a mission territory, the United States was recognized as a mature Church, on an equal footing with the ancient churches of Europe. The accumulated experience of more than two-and-one-half centuries had born its fruit. The U.S. Church facing the decade of the 1920s was very different from what it had been a century or even a few decades before. The Church had gained recognition on both the national and international levels as a strong, autonomous, and productive institution. U.S. Catholics, immigrants and their descendants, were poised to begin to play a full and even prophetic role in shaping the future of their nation and the world. The Church was in a position that Cecil Calvert could not have imagined and of which John Carroll would have dared to dream.

DISCUSSION QUESTIONS

1. Catholicism in the United States began as the tradition of a minority of "outsiders." How has that status affected the character of Catholicism in the United States?

2. The U.S. separation of church and state seemed to be an innovation that was difficult for Rome to understand. In the end, however, Pope Leo XIII affirmed the U.S. tradition. What are the unique strengths that the U.S. democratic tradition can bring to the Church?

3. In spite of the traumas they suffered, including a forced change of nationality and a lack of sufficient clergy who understood and appreciated their cultural traditions, Hispanic Catholics in the United States have maintained their deep faith through family and communal traditions. What does their experience offer to the rest of the Church in the United States today?

4. The ethnic diversity of its members has brought unique challenges to the Church in the United States. In what ways does that diversity strengthen Catholicism in the United States?

5. In what ways does the Church still need to broaden and deepen its appreciation for ethnic diversity?

Notes

1. The instructions excerpted at the beginning of this chapter can be found in full in John Tracy Ellis, *Documents of American Catholic History* (Milwaukee: Bruce, 1956), 100-2.

2. Evidence that the project faced opposition in England is found in a pamphlet published by the Calvert family. The pamphlet defended the project against allegations that include the supposed danger that British Catholics would form a traitorous alliance with France or Spain. In response to the supposed danger that Catholics would overtake the Protestant colonies, it points out that there were already more Protestants in America than there were Catholics in all of England. See Edwin S. Gausted, *A Documentary History of Religion in America* (Grand Rapids, Mich.: Eerdmans, 1982), 1:109-12.

3. The arrested Jesuits, Andrew White and Thomas Copley, were sent to England and then charged with violating the English laws that no priest ordained in another country was allowed to come into England. They were released when they pleaded that they had not come to England freely, but as prisoners. See Thomas T. McAvoy, *A History of the Catholic Church in the United States* (Notre Dame, Ind.: University of Notre Dame Press, 1969), 13.

4. Maryland's Act of Religious Toleration, April 21, 1649. See John Tracy Ellis, *Documents*, 115-17.

5. An Act of Toleration was passed in 1702, but it extended only to dissenting Protestants, not to Catholics. McAvoy, 21.

6. See Charles H. Lippy, et al. *Christianity Comes to the Americas, 1492-1776* (New York: Paragon House, 1992), 358-60.

7. John Tracy Ellis, *American Catholicism* (Chicago: University of Chicago Press, 1956), 29.

8. In spite of urgings from Rome, U.S. bishops found it difficult to protest U.S. involvement in the Spanish American War. When the United States went to war against Mexico in 1846, Abraham Lincoln spoke out far more forcefully against U.S. aggression than did the Catholic Church.

9. It is interesting to note that when England won Quebec, there was a possibility that Quebec's French bishop could serve the English colonies, but laymen from Maryland feared how such service would be seen by the Protestants, and they even made a petition to Rome that no bishop be appointed for them. See McAvoy, 34.

10. In the nineteenth century, U.S. bishops were known to beg for European missionaries. Not only did they receive a response from Rome and European religious communities, but lay-directed societies for the Propagation of the Faith contributed funds to help the overseas missions. See James Hennesey, *American Catholics* (New York: Oxford University Press, 1981), 112.

11. See Jay Dolan, *The American Catholic Experience* (New York: Image Books, 1985), 78-79.

12. Ibid., 84.

13. John Carroll to Cardinal Antonelli, March 1, 1785. See Gausted, *A Documentary History,* 1:303-6.

14. See Sr. Mary Agnes McCann, "Religious Orders of Women of the United States," *Catholic Historical Review* (New Series) 1(Oct. 1923): 316-29.

15. See James K. Kenneally, *The History of American Catholic Women* (New York: Crossroad, 1990), 5.

16. The first Catholic hospital was founded in St. Louis by the Sisters of Charity with the help of a generous endowment from the Catholic layman, John Mullanphy. See Ellis, *American Catholicism,* 57.

17. Archbishop Marechal's Report to Propaganda, October 16, 1818. Ellis, *Documents,* 214.

18. Ellis, *American Catholicism,* 45.

19. See Dolan, 105-18.

20. For statistics and additional information on the immigrants, see Dolan, 127-57.

21. Ellis, *American Catholicism,* 51.

22. Dolan, 128-29.

23. Pope Leo XIII, "Plea for the Italian Immigrants in America," December 10, 1888. This letter set the stage for the foundation of the "Scalabrini" priests, a group of Italian missionary priests who would minister to the immigrants in America and for the Missionary Sisters of the Sacred Heart of St. Francesca Cabrini. Ellis, *Documents,* 482-85.

24. See Oscar Handlin, *The Uprooted* (Boston: Little, Brown, 1973).

25. Rev. Peter Vay, 1905; Ellis, *Documents,* 571-75.

26. Ibid.

27. McAvoy, 270-74.

28. After years of debate and experimentation, the bishops meeting at the Third Plenary Council of Baltimore, under instructions from Rome, made the establishment of Catholic schools mandatory in every parish. See McAvoy, 255-62.

29. See Franklin H. Little, "The Churches and the Body Politic," *Daedelus* (Winter 1967): 22-42.

30. Quoted from *Eerdmans Handbook to the History of Christianity in America* (Grand Rapids, Mich.: Eerdmans, 1983), 236.

31. The treaty of Guadalupe-Hidalgo, signed in February 1848, ceded the area now composed of the states of California, Arizona, and New Mexico and sections of Nevada, Utah, and Colorado. New Mexico, with 60,000 inhabitants, had the greatest population at the time, followed by California with 10,000, Texas with nearly

4,000, and Arizona with 2,000. See Matt S. Meier, "Mexican Americans in the Southwest," in *Catholics in America* (Washington, D.C.: United States Catholic Conference, 1976), 107-10.

32. Junipero Serra was beatified in September 1988.

33. For a theological interpretation of the Mexican-American experience, see Virgilio Elizondo, *Galilean Journey: The Mexican American Promise* (New York: Orbis Books, 1983).

34. See Hennesey, *American Catholics*, 135-36.

35. See Orlando O. Espín, "Popular Religion as an Epistemology of Suffering" in *Journal of Hispanic/Latino Theology* 2(2): 65, note 17.

36. Elizondo, *Galilean Journey*, 22.

37. See Elizondo, *Galilean Journey*.

38. A rare exception to the dominant prejudice of "Easterners" against the Hispanics was Herbert Vaughan, an English Catholic who remarked on the distinction between the two groups, saying:

> Consider the ways in which the two cultures treat the Indian, then decide which is superior. The Spaniards went with the tenderest devotedness to serve and save the Indian . . . the Yankee came, straining every nerve and energy in the pursuit of wealth. . . . The Indian was . . . fair game, just as bear and elk were, and men would shoot them by way of pastime. . . . Murder became thus a relaxation. . . .
>
> Then regard the names which Anglos and Hispanics give to their respective towns. The latter bestow such dignified titles as Jesus Maria, Buena Vista and Nuestra Señora de Soledad, while the former afflict their settlements with such labels as Bloody Run, RatTrap Slide and Jackass Gulch. Let any fair-minded person decide which civilization considered all men and all races as people of God and which endeavored to give a Christian flavor to all they discovered and explored and inhabited.

39. Joseph M. White, *Catholic Religious Life: Selected Historical Essays* (New York: Garland, 1988), 17.

40. Ellis, *American Catholicism*, 68.

41. See Sydney Ahlstrom, *A Religious History of the American People* (New Haven, Conn.: Yale University Press, 1972), 789.

42. In both the War with Mexico and the Spanish American War, Catholic chaplains served the U.S. troops and sisters operated hospitals for the wounded. In the aftermath of the Spanish American War, Archbishop Ireland did warn the United States that it would not be prudent to send Protestant missionaries to Cuba, Puerto Rico, and the Philippines. See Gausted, *A Religious History of America*, 224.

43. *New York Times*, Feb. 5, 1916, cited in Richard M. Linkh, *American Catholicism and European Immigrants (1900-1924)* (New York: Center for Migration Studies, 1975), 136.

44. See Thomas T. McAvoy, *The Great Crisis in American Catholic History, 1895-1900* (Chicago: Regnery Co., 1957), 5-6.

45. Leo XIII, "Longinqua Oceani." Ellis, *Documents*, 515-27.

46. Ibid.

47. Ellis, *American Catholicism*, 121.

48. Ellis, *Documents*, 2:538.

49. For an overview of the state of the question of Americanism, see *U.S. Catholic Historian* 11, 3 (Summer 1993). The entire issue deals with scholarly assessments of the Americanist controversy.

50. For Americanism's effects on theology, see Hennesey, 203.

51. Leo XIII, April 15, 1902, in Ellis, *Documents*, 2:547-49. Emphasis added.

CHAPTER THREE

Collaboration Among the Churches of America During the First Half of the Twentieth Century

Negotiations in Mexico City, May 18, 1928

The Mexican Government had taken over all the churches and, as a result, the Mexican Church was on strike. The "Cristero" guerrillas were rampaging through the Mexican countryside to defend the faith while "up North," the Knights of Columbus were pressing the U.S. army to intervene to end religious persecution in Mexico. Those were just a few of the specters in the background as representatives of the Catholic Church and the governments of Mexico and the United States sat down around a negotiating table at Chapultapec Castle in Mexico City.

The fact that they were there at all might have seemed like a miracle. Serious church-state conflicts had been festering in Mexico for seventy years and the last fifteen years had seen them explode into bloody violence.

The U.S. representatives, Ambassador Dwight Morrow and Fr. John Burke of the National Catholic Welfare Council, had themselves been involved in delicate negotiations to get the U.S. government to support their efforts to mediate the conflict. Perhaps the fact that Morrow was a Protestant added to his credibility with the Mexican government officials—at least they knew that the government he represented was adamant about the separation of church and state. And Burke, perhaps more than anyone else, represented U.S. Catholics with a voice of diplomatic moderation. The meeting might never have happened except for the efforts of these two men.

The atmosphere was tense. President Calles refused to look Archbishop Ruiz in the face, and Ruiz believed that Calles and President-elect Obregon represented the work of the devil in his homeland. Nevertheless, the combination of civil violence and international pressure led the government officials to be willing to barter about an agreement; the image of a Catholic nation with no church services so haunted the bishops that they were willing to compromise.

Long discussions, secret letters of intent, and careful diplomacy finally brought the main parties to agree on the main terms of a modus vivendi *through which the Catholic Church could recommence its ministry in Mexico. Even though thirteen months would pass between this meeting and a final agreement, by the end of the day, the foundations had been laid.*

Although the "final agreement" came ostensibly without the aid or intervention of U.S. diplomats, the process that led up to it was extremely important for the Church. Through years of expressing solidarity and protest, the Church in the United States had learned that to help a sister church, it first had to listen carefully and follow its advice.

Latin American Independence—State and Church

In 1804, Haiti became the second American colony to attain independence from a European colonizer, in this case, from France. In 1810, almost simultaneously, citizens in Mexico, Venezuela, and Argentina rose up against Spain. By 1826, Spain and Portugal had lost control of the vast majority of their American territories.[1]

Freedom from European colonial rule was one thing, the formation of stable governments and social structures was quite another. With the exception of Haiti's slave rebellion, Latin American independence was generally a project of the *criollos*, American-born and well-educated people of Iberian heritage, who rebelled because they were fed up with their second-class status in relation to Iberian-born governmental and church leaders. In social terms, Latin American independence was not so much a revolution as a changing of the guard. The *criollos*, and in some cases *mestizos* (people of Spanish and native heritage), took charge of the new nations. Meanwhile, the situation of indigenous peoples remained the same or even worsened as a result of the loss of Spanish paternalism. Far from solving the social or economic problems of the area, independence simply made them more local.

Although it was not a religious conflict, the struggle for independence divided the Church as well as civil society. Both royalists and revolutionaries evoked religion to support their causes. The higher ranks of the clergy tended to be royalists, supporting the government that had placed them in power.[2] Mirroring their civil counterparts, the *criollo* clergy were more likely to be revolutionaries. Resentful that by mere accident of American birth they were excluded from the highest offices in the Church, it was natural that lower clergy would take leadership roles and encourage the masses to support the cause of independence. Clergy who promoted the cause of independence received an uneven response to their political positions. Fr. Miguel Hidalgo, the priest who led the opening movement of Mexican independence, was excommunicated before he was executed, but a Colombian priest, Juan Fernandez de Sotomayor, who wrote a popular catechism that legitimized the struggles for independence, was not only tolerated but eventually became the first bishop of his new nation.

Just as church opinion about independence was divided in America, Rome was uncertain about how to respond to developments in the Americas.[3] As early as 1811, the first government of New Granada (later Colombia) began attempts to obtain recognition from the Vatican and to establish the rights of patronage for the new nation. The request put Rome in a quandary: dealing directly with the revolutionary governments would appear to imply recognition of their legitimacy and therefore alienate Spain; refusal to deal with them would leave the territories in question without church leadership. In 1816, Pope Pius VII took the royalist side and wrote an encyclical asking the American hierarchy to urge the faithful to stop their disorder and sedition.

In 1823, after the Spanish colonies had virtually won their independence, Cardinal Consalvi told Pope Leo XII that a refusal to recognize the new governments could cause serious problems including, he said, "exposure to Methodists, Presbyterians and even sun worshipers."[4] Disregarding the cardinal's counsel, Leo issued an encyclical asking Latin Americans to return to allegiance to King Ferdinand VII. In the uproar that followed the encyclical, the new governments sent clerical ambassadors to Rome to plead that the pope listen to the American version of the situation. They were successful. Rome established ecclesiastical relationships with the new nations, named bishops for the vacant sees in Colombia, Mexico, Argentina, and Chile, and began the process of creating new dioceses respectful of the new national borders.

Much to the chagrin of the new governments, Rome's establishment of relations and eventual recognition of their legitimacy did not include the concession of church patronage to the new nations. Throughout the course of the Iberian conquest and colonization, the rulers of Spain and Portugal had exercised the privileges of "royal patronage," an arrangement that gave them virtually total control over the Church in their territories. In addition to granting the monarchs or their delegates the authority to name bishops, patronage allowed the governments to censor all correspondence between Rome and Spanish America and to control every aspect of missionary activity from the approval of catechisms to the establishment of missions and reductions. While patronage relieved Rome of considerable financial burdens and administrative labor, it also made the Church a virtual arm of the state. The cultural dialogue promoted by people like Las Casas, Toribio, and Guaman Poma was abandoned; the government curtailed the work of missionaries and effectively prevented the development of native clergy.[5] Rome's refusal to concede patronage to the new Latin American countries signaled a clear determination to free the Church from control by the state.

New Patterns of Church-State Relationships

When the patronage system no longer structured the relationship between church and state, the question of the power and influence of the Church became a bone of contention with some of the new governments. As the century wore on, struggles between political conservatives and liberals came to have serious repercussions for the Church. Conservative governments were generally content with the religious *status quo*; Catholicism remained the official state religion, there were open lines of communication between ecclesial and civil leaders, and the clergy maintained a significant degree of moral and even economic influence. Liberals, on the other hand, wanted a clear separation of church and state and worked to diminish the power and independence of the Church. As liberals became more and more anti-clerical, the hierarchy generally looked to conservatives for support, thus playing into what would become a long-standing and vicious cycle of antagonism between the Church and political liberalism.

The situation of the Church was different in each nation—in reality, with each change in national government.[6] In Haiti, Argentina, and Paraguay, independence had relatively little effect on the power of the Church. At the other extreme, with Mexico as the outstanding example, governments would do everything in their power to disestablish the Church and decimate its economic and social power and prestige.

Even in the best of political circumstances, the Church in the independent states faced a mammoth task of organization. In the space of a few years, churches, no longer defined by relationships with Spain, became national churches relating independently and individually to Rome, and were defined in terms of new and sometimes uncertain national borders. Whereas a centralized authority had previously overseen church governance, missionaries, and the relationships between local clergy and religious orders, now the bishops of each country had to establish their own patterns and recruit and support their own clergy. Spain had intentionally made local churches dependent. When Spain was removed from the picture, the local clergy was inadequate in both numbers and preparation even to maintain the organization that was left in their hands. To make matters worse, national populations were growing and immigrants were arriving without the support of accompanying priests. The Church suffered from a lack of resources, and the brunt of it fell on distant, rural areas. The worst hit were the missions among indigenous peoples, which were all but totally abandoned within fifty years after independence.[7]

With independence, the situation of the Church in Latin America had changed radically. In many ways, the new problems it faced were similar to those with which the Catholic Church in the United States had been dealing since the 1600s. Although Catholicism would remain the dominant faith tradition throughout Latin America, independence brought heretofore unimaginable ideological challenges and shortages of personnel that had to be dealt with at the local level. Throughout the century following independence, the churches in Latin American nations deveoped relatively independently of one another and thus became characterized by a diversity that was the result of each one's episcopal leadership, the number and activity of its clergy, and the relationship of each to its own national government. It was not until the end of the nineteenth century that Latin American bishops would meet formally in anything like a plenary council. Then, in 1899, Pope Leo XIII called the Latin American bishops to Rome to celebrate the fourth centenary of the "discovery of America" and to work together on questions of the unification of ecclesiastical discipline. Although that meeting stimulated a sense of international cooperation, more than fifty years would pass before the Latin American bishops would set up an effective organization for international pastoral cooperation.

The U.S. Church in the Early Twentieth Century

While the Latin American Church was going through its period of radical change and loss of privilege, the Church in the United States was growing in strength and self-confidence. Internal developments and organization were preparing it to reach out beyond its national borders. By the early twentieth century, the Church had been removed from the status of being a mission territory, dioceses and parishes had developed a significant degree of structure, the bishops had organized the National Catholic War Council (NCWC), and a great variety of lay groups were becoming active on the parish, local, and even national level. All in all, U.S. Catholicism was fast moving out of defensiveness and dependency, into a role of activity, and toward world leadership.

Two important signs of the Church's growing maturity came even before the foundation of the NCWC. Although still rightly concerned about sufficient pastoral care for the immigrants and urban masses, the Church in the United States demonstrated its readiness to look beyond those pressing concerns by founding two "mission" enterprises: the Catholic Church Extension Society in 1905 and, in 1911, the Catholic Foreign Mission Society of America, better known as Maryknoll. The former organized church outreach to underserved areas of the rural United States and the latter was the first official Catholic organization founded to send U.S. missionaries to the rest of the world.[8]

It was Cardinal Gibbons of Baltimore who asked the U.S. hierarchy to approve the Maryknoll project. The letter he wrote on behalf of the society expressed the purpose of Maryknoll and the reasons why he thought it was an important step forward for the Church. Using an astute mixture of nationalism, Catholic loyalty, and evangelical zeal, Gibbons solicited the bishops' support for Maryknoll by telling them that it was a matter of religious pride as well as a measure for the preservation and promotion of the faith in the United States. He wrote:

Venerable Brethren:

At the request of His Excellency, the Apostolic Delegate, I submit to your consideration a plan to establish an American Foreign Mission Seminary.

That such a Seminary is needed, and urgently, seems daily more evident. The prestige of our country has become wide-spread; and Protestants, especially in the Far East are profiting by it, to the positive hindrance of catholic missioners. I understand that even the educated classes in China, misled by the almost complete absence of American Catholic priests, believe that the Church of Rome has no standing in America.

The priests of the U.S. number more than 17,000, but I am informed that there are hardly sixteen of them in the foreign missions. This fact recalls a warning which the late Cardinal Vaughan gave in a kindly and brotherly letter . . . urging us American Catholics not to delay participation in foreign missions *lest our own faith should suffer*. . . .

With pleasure, therefore, acting on His Excellency's request, I submit the following outline of the plan. . . .[9]

As expected, the bishops approved his request and authorized the Maryknoll plan.

According to the plan, Fathers James A. Walsh and Thomas F. Price were named as the founders of a seminary to train U.S. priests for service in the foreign missions. Maryknoll was to be a society of secular priests rather than a new religious order, and it would be directly responsible to Rome's office for the Propagation of the Faith. Although numerous reli-

Rev. James Walsh (*left*) and Rev. Thomas Price (*right*), founders of Maryknoll. Photos: Maryknoll Missioners.

gious congregations who worked in the United States already had missionaries in other countries, Maryknoll was the first group founded in the United States specifically for the missions. Maryknoll began its work in the Orient, and later expanded to Africa and South America. Maryknoll would soon become the United States' best known missionary society.

Organizing the National Church—the NCWC

At the time that the United States entered World War I, the Catholic Church was growing in both numbers and national respect but, like a garden sown by the wind, its 20,000,000 members were divided into 100 independent dioceses, and individual Catholics could belong to one or more of 15,000 different Catholic societies and organizations. Some of those organizations, like the Knights of Columbus, could boast of impressive national membership rolls; others were local, perhaps under the direction of their local bishops and perhaps autonomous.[10] At the hierarchical level, although there were annual informal meetings of the archbishops, the U.S. bishops had not met in a formal session since 1884.

Sharing Faith Across the Hemisphere

When President Wilson called on the whole country to support the war effort, the bishops, individual Catholics, and multiple lay Catholic organizations were anxious to do their part but lacked a mechanism through which to coordinate their efforts. Rev. John J. Burke, CSP, then the editor of *The Catholic World*, believed that the war presented the Church with an almost overwhelming challenge and a tremendous opportunity. The country desperately needed moral guidance as it entered the war; creating effective means to provide that guidance would call forth a hitherto unknown unity among the Catholic institutions and organizations of the nation. Burke explained his assessment of the situation in an editorial in *The Catholic World*:

> In the calling of hundreds of thousands of young men from . . . the normal paths . . . of life, our country faces a grave crisis. . . . The event . . . is pregnant with enduring consequences of good or evil for the future generations of America. . . .
>
> But to think that this . . . [crisis can be met] without the aid of religion is equivalent to thinking that one can keep the ocean's tide from rising or falling. Those who are conversant with the moral history of great armies . . . who know the history of some of our own divisions in the recent encampment on the Mexican border, know well the fearful danger that faces the flower of our American manhood today. . . .
>
> In this work every Catholic society, every individual may wholeheartedly join. For the national need demands that we think nationally and act as one country-wide united body. . . .
>
> As Catholics we must . . . realize the gravity . . . of the danger both for Church and for country. . . . United as one body, we must give our hearts and our hands to tangible work within our reach for the religious, spiritual and moral welfare of Catholic soldiers and sailors. . . .[11]

Burke asked Cardinal Gibbons to take the lead in building the necessary unity by calling representatives of dioceses and lay organizations to the task of national coordination. Gibbons agreed and garnered the support of fellow bishops.

On August 11 and 12, 1917, one hundred and fifteen delegates met at The Catholic University of America. Although the opening session has been described as "a medley of misconceptions, zeal for vested interests and contentions," Burke had the ability to inspire unity. Before the two days were over, the diverse factions came together and formed the National Catholic War Council.[12] Burke described it all in the September 1917 issue of *The Catholic World*:

> On August 11th and 12th there was held at the Catholic University at Washington D.C. a conference called by the authority of their Eminences James, Cardinal Gibbons, John, Cardinal Farley and William, Cardinal O'Connell, which included representatives from 58 dioceses throughout the country, representatives of all the leading Catholic societies of the country, both men and women and representatives of the Catholic press. The conference met to consider the problems which the War has obliged American Catholics to face; to decide how in the work common to all, unity of action and aim: the full coordination of all our societies might be secured. The conference unanimously agreed upon a national organization which . . . should . . . study to cooperate and coordinate the work of every Catholic society. This was the unanimous decision of all the representatives and the societies present, and it is hoped that the vast, generous agencies of Catholic activity will thus be made more efficient, saved from loss of effort and money caused by overlapping, and enabled to work together under the hierarchy with a common purpose for a common end.[13]

Although the war precipitated the formation of the NCWC, Burke described it in such a way that unity of action seemed to be its major purpose.

When the war ended in November 1918, the NCWC could have faded out of existence, remembered only as a flash of Catholic unity in response to a national emergency. But men like Gibbons and Burke believed that too much had been accomplished to allow that to happen. The NCWC had succeeded in much more than a simple coordination of Catholic war activity. Through it, U.S. Catholicism had developed a credible voice with which to speak for the Church to the government and society.[14] The continuation of the NCWC had great potential—its promoters needed only the opportunity to get the rest of the hierarchy to share their enthusiastic vision.

That opportunity came in February 1919, when seventy-seven bishops gathered at The Catholic University to celebrate Cardinal Gibbons's golden jubilee. Pope Benedict XV used the occasion to send a representative

Sharing Faith Across the Hemisphere

with an official message for the U.S. bishops. In a formal address, Archbishop Bonaventura Cerretti told the bishops that the Holy Father desired to establish some form of organization that could effectively further the cause of peace and promote education in Catholic principles of social justice, and he wanted their help. Gibbons immediately called for a committee to respond to the pope's request. The next day the archbishops met and recommended that the entire U.S. episcopacy begin to meet in formal annual assemblies that would allow them to function in a unified manner. In April of that same year, Gibbons received a letter from the pope congratulating him on his successful efforts.

In September 1919, ninety-two of the nation's one hundred and one bishops met at The Catholic University to inaugurate the National Catholic Welfare Council. Cardinal Gibbons described the need for the organization, saying: "Our diocesan units are well organized. But the Church in America as a whole has been suffering from the lack of a united force that might be directed to the furthering of those general policies which are vital to all."[15] The National Catholic War Council had been voluntarily formed to respond to the crises of World War I; through it the Church in the United States began to exercise its public voice. The bishops founded the National Catholic Welfare Council as a voluntary organization through which bishops could exert influence in matters of national and international concern.

The council did not swing into action without some controversy and conflict. Early on, it ran head-on into the Knights of Columbus, one of the most powerful lay organizations in the country. In 1921, Fr. Burke, the general secretary of the council, wrote to NCWC vice president, Archbishop Hanna, complaining that the knights were representing themselves in Washington as the official voice of the Catholic Church, and as a result, when he spoke to government officials, they treated him "as if I were the head of some sodality."[16] For years to come, incidents such as this would lead Burke to use all his diplomatic genius to ensure that the NCWC would be publicly recognized as the authoritative voice of the Catholic Church in the United States.

Clashes with lay organizations were not the only problem faced by the nascent council; there were also bishops who objected to its perceived imposition of authority over that of the local ordinary. As a result of their protests in Rome, the council was temporarily suppressed in February

1922. The matter was quickly resolved, and in June 1922, the NCWC was again approved with the conditions that it should change its name, that it was not required to meet annually, and that its decisions would have no binding force. The new organization, the National Catholic Welfare Conference, had weathered its first major storm and was poised to lead the Catholic Church in the United States.[17]

International Relations

Religious Crises in Mexico—1910-1940

The National Catholic Welfare Conference had been born as the Church's response to international crisis. It was hardly established when it was called upon to make its voice heard in regard to another problem beyond its borders—this time in Mexico.

Like many other Latin American nations, Mexico's independence had not brought radical change to the structures of society. But in 1857, anti-clerical reformers promulgated a new constitution that officially separated church and state and brought an end to the Church's privileged position. The Mexican Constitution of 1857 prohibited the Church from owning any property that was not used for worship, a provision that undercut all of the Church's institutions of social service. Between 1857 and 1867, the country was wracked by war, bishops were banished, and the Church lost parishes, seminaries, monasteries, and land.

Political instability and violence reigned until Porfirio Diaz's thirty-four-year "presidency" established a dictatorial peace in the nation and brought economic growth to the wealthy classes.[18] Although Diaz did not repeal the anticlerical decrees of the 1857 Constitution, neither did he enforce them. Under Diaz's rule the bishops returned to the country, seminaries and Catholic schools were re-opened, and new dioceses were established. In spite of the Church's tenuous legal standing, the number of priests in the country grew to 5,000 and lay associations prospered. All of that would change drastically after 1910 and the Mexican Revolution.[19]

Mexico began its process of anticlerical reforms in 1833, and they were made stronger in the Constitution of 1857. Nevertheless, although the separation of church and state was official, the laws were not effectively enforced during the nineteenth century.

The Revolution and the U.S. Response

Although the revolution began as a movement for free elections, serious repression quickly became part of the program. Foreign religious were expelled from the country, and many of them either fled to the United States or passed through it on their way to Europe. Their stories of persecution and sacrilege found ready audiences among U.S. Catholics. As a result, some clerics and lay groups began to pressure President Woodrow Wilson to invade Mexico and restore religious freedom.[20] Others, with Cardinal Gibbons at the forefront, responded with more moderation. In 1914, Gibbons wrote President Wilson saying, "Just one word from you to [the Mexican leaders] would have a great effect and would relieve the sad conditions." Wilson wrote back saying, "I am sorry to say that it is not true . . . for I have spoken that word again and again. My influence will continue to be exerted in that direction. . . . Apparently we shall have to await the subsidence of the passions which have been generated by the unhappy condition of the country."[21]

Whether or not Gibbons believed that the president sincerely supported the Church's cause in Mexico, he was absolutely convinced that some Catholics were going too far in their criticism of the U.S. government. When Fr. Francis Kelley, editor of the *Extension* magazine, accused the United States of making the religious persecution possible, Gibbons reproached him saying, "This is a serious charge, and one that has been felt keenly at Washington. It is one that can be made only after very careful investigation and with sufficient proof."[22] Gibbons was willing to exert pressure on the government, but only when he thought it might have some measure of success; he refused to jeopardize the hard-won reputation of the Church by making unfounded accusations or futile demands. Referring to Kelley and others like him, he worried aloud that "the effect of this ceaseless harassing might probably result, not in securing any assistance in our cause, but in setting the entire Administration against us."[23]

The problems of the Mexican Church would grow worse before any kind of solution would be worked out. The 1917 Mexican Constitution strengthened the 1857 Constitution's limitations on church activity. Under the rubric of separation of church and state, the new constitution actually attempted to establish state control over the Church. While proclaiming "freedom of education," it forbad religious instruction in primary schools and banned religious congregations. It nationalized all ecclesiastical property and prohibited worship outside church buildings, thus putting all worship directly under state control. Priests were stripped of political rights, their education was denied official recognition, and their freedom of speech was restricted. The framers of the new constitution designed it to wipe out the Church's influence in Mexican society.[24]

The promulgation of Mexico's 1917 Constitution coincided roughly with the U.S. entry into World War I. Wartime activity suddenly supplanted the close attention that sectors of the U.S. Church had previously devoted to Mexico. But in 1926, when the government of President Plutarco Calles intensified enforcement of the anti-church legislation, the Church in the United States, now including the NCWC, was prepared to respond.

The 1926 crisis began with a war of words. The Mexican bishops announced a plan to stage a formal protest against increasing government harassment. Then the aging archbishop of Mexico City, José Mora y del Río, said in a newspaper interview that the Mexican hierarchy did not recognize those articles of the constitution that were contrary to liberty and religious dogma.[25] The government accused the Church of trying to overthrow the revolutionary government and then launched a fresh assault on the Church. Priests and religious were again expelled from the country, religious schools were closed, and all priests were ordered to register with the local government to receive permission to continue in their ministry.

Registration of the clergy became the key to the conflict. If the priests registered, they were in fact recognizing that the state had authority over their ministry. If they did not, the state would not allow them to function. State governments took advantage of the moment and set ridiculously low limits on the number of priests allowed to function within their borders.[26] Although local enforcement of the restrictions varied, church authorities throughout the country lived in a constant state of tension, knowing that at any moment they could be cut off from their ministry.

In response, lay groups began an economic boycott designed to paralyze the economy of the country. Boycotters refused to purchase anything that was not absolutely necessary for daily sustenance—no new clothes, specialty food items, or entertainment or lottery tickets, and women dressed in mourning as a sign of their support for the Church. The boycott succeeded in antagonizing the government and gaining international attention, but its economic effects were limited; the majority of the population had no money to spend on luxuries. When boycott organizers were arrested and repression intensified, the option of violent resistance became more attractive to groups of citizens and even to some of the hierarchy.[27]

The Church Strike

The situation came to a head on July 2, 1926, when President Calles tightened the enforcement of restrictions on the Church and actually carried the repression further than was constitutionally mandated. The presidential legislation forbade foreign clergy to carry out any religious functions, prohibited any religious education in primary schools, outlawed monastic life, and gave free rein to officials who were enforcing the restrictions on priests.[28]

On July 24, 1926, the bishops published a pastoral letter explaining that, in light of the governmental restrictions and their own rejection of armed rebellion, the only alternative left for them was a total suspension of church services throughout the entire country until the government relented in its antireligious policies. In their letter, the bishops explained that until the decree of July 2, "our conduct has been one of prudent silence, because the antireligious articles were not applied up to the point of making impossible the life of the Church." But the most recent decree was so restrictive that "it would be a crime for us to tolerate . . . the impossibility of practicing our sacred ministry." Therefore, they said, "after having consulted with the Most Holy Father . . . and with his ratification, we order that after July 31, until we order otherwise, all religious services requiring the intervention of priests shall be suspended in all the churches of the country."[29] The bishops' decree was read in every church that was still functioning throughout the country, and the following week an unprecedented number of people flocked to the churches.[30]

In addition to their participation in the frenzy of religious devotion, some activists decided that the time had come to join in armed rebellion against the government. The Cristeros, a rag-tag movement that fought in the name of Christ the King, began guerrilla-style activities throughout the country. Short on everything except the willingness to die for their cause, they carried on bitter combat against the federal troops, and sometimes against civilian targets. Although the national hierarchy did not officially support them, neither did they condemn them.[31]

U.S. Reaction

Meanwhile, U.S. national publications such as *America*, *Commonweal*, *The Catholic World*, and *Extension* thrust the Mexican religious conflict before the public eye and fired up the demand for a U.S. response. Believing that the secular and Protestant press downplayed Mexican persecution of religion, Catholic journals made a cause of presenting the other side of the story. In their attempt to rally support for the persecuted Mexicans, they were not above exploiting deep-seated prejudices. An anonymous article published in *America* aroused Catholic defensiveness by implying that Protestants were behind the religious persecution. The article said in part:

> In all this witches' cauldron of pillage and destruction there has been a strong flavor of Protestant seasoning. Protestant missionaries have before this been eager to lend their aid to revolution in the hope of being able to reap a harvest from the seeds of dissension thus sown, and the liberal revolutionaries have always been eager to seek such an alliance for the valuable assistance it has given in propaganda among Americans, and influence at Washington. . . .[32]

In August 1926, *America* printed an article by William Lonergan, SJ, entitled "Is there Religious Persecution in Mexico?" Using emotion-laden language and mocking restrictions against women religious, Lonergan said

> Calles and his satellites in their pride and bold audacity have not hesitated to strike the church simultaneously at every point of vantage. . . . The first line of attack is always the schools. . . . The second . . . the Religious Orders. . . . It is hard for the impartial observer to understand just what political significance the garb of a Sister of Charity can have in the public streets, especially in a Catholic country. One curiously asks, what danger the government . . . has to fear from the teaching nuns of Mexico and from the devoted women that minister to the orphans and homeless, and care for the sick and suffering in hospitals?. . . But these good women must disband because a Government sedulously interested in safeguarding human liberties has discovered that their vows of poverty, chastity and obedience are contracts which imply a surrender of inalienable rights![33]

This article was published just weeks after Pope Pius XI drew world attention to the Mexican situation by declaring August 1, 1926, the Feast of St. Peter in Chains, as World Day of Prayer for Mexican Catholics.

NCWC Involvement in the Mexican Crisis

As conditions worsened, the Vatican began to look to the Church in the United States to help mediate the Mexican religious crisis. That appeal would draw on the good reputation and experience that the Church had gained through the war and would again test the NCWC's diplomacy over and against the more extreme strategies of some U.S. clergy and lay groups.

In 1926, the administrative committee of the NCWC commissioned Notre Dame professor Charles Phillips to confer with the Mexican bishops. Reporting back to the NCWC, Phillips said that the Mexican bishops, recognizing the fierce nationalism of their government, had advised against U.S. protests, fearful that they would only hurt the Church's cause. But not all U.S. Catholics agreed. Archbishop Curley of Baltimore called for nationwide protest against the government of Mexico and charged that the U.S. government was derelict in its duty. Francis Kelley, former editor of *Extension*, now Bishop of Oklahoma City, agreed and called for public outcry against the Mexican government. The Knights of Columbus began a million dollar campaign "to the end that the politics of Soviet Russia shall be eliminated and the ideals of liberty of conscience and democratic freedom may extend to our afflicted fellow human beings beyond the Rio Grande."[34] All in all, while the NCWC obeyed the request of the Mexican bishops and advised moderation, some U.S. bishops and lay groups were calling for public protests and asking Congress to break diplomatic relations with Mexico. The U.S. government, unwilling to risk a war over religious issues, maintained an official policy of refusing to intervene in Mexico's domestic affairs.[35]

In an attempt to focus the situation, the NCWC prepared a long pastoral letter on Mexico. Published on December 12, 1926, it was the first letter of the U.S. hierarchy devoted completely to a problem beyond the U.S. borders. The bishops defended the integrity of the Mexican Church, listed its contributions to Mexican society, and lamented the injustice and irrationality of the persecution. The bishops took pains to make it clear that they were not asking for political intervention, but simply trying to explain the truth and asking for prayers on behalf of their suffering brothers and sisters in Mexico. Although the letter did not seem to have any immediate political effects, it was a strong statement of solidarity that heightened worldwide concern about Mexico.[36]

The situation grew even more volatile in 1927 when a Jesuit priest, Fr. Miguel Pro, was falsely accused of attempting to assassinate former Mexican President Alvaro Obregon. Pro was arrested and executed without a trial. The story and pictures of his martyrdom were published throughout the world, further inflaming the passions of those who condemned the Mexican government.[37]

In that same year, Dwight Morrow became the U.S. ambassador to Mexico, and NCWC representatives asked him to use his influence to resolve the Mexican religious crisis. In 1928, Morrow asked Fr. Burke to join him in Mexico City for negotiations with President Calles. With the support of the NCWC and Archbishop Pietro Fumasoni-Biondi, the apostolic delegate to the United States, Burke accepted the invitation.

In April 1928, Burke and Morrow met with Calles. The president stated that if a Mexican were named as apostolic delegate to the country, the bishops could return and be free to minister in the country. Burke communicated this to the Mexican bishops in exile, and they agreed to write to Calles suggesting a similar plan. In May, Archbishop Ruiz y Flores, spokesman for the Mexican bishops, joined Burke in a secret meeting with Calles, and the two sides exchanged letters of agreement. Then, just before they could approve a formal settlement of the conflict, the church negotiators were called back to the United States. For unknown reasons, the Vatican had put the negotiations on hold and the Burke-Morrow negotiations seemed to be a lost cause.

A long-awaited breakthrough finally came in 1929, when Calles' successor, President Portes Gil, issued a public statement saying that, if there were good will on both sides, the religious problem could be resolved. Archbishop Ruiz immediately issued a statement commending Gil and saying that the Church would demand only religious toleration, not a change in the constitution. Ruiz was then appointed apostolic delegate and on June 21, 1929, he, Archbishop Diaz, and President Portes Gil agreed to a *modus vivendi* that allowed the Church to resume its ministry in the country. The agreement was essentially the same as that which had been worked out thirteen months earlier by Calles, Ruiz,

Morrow, and Burke; the only significant difference was that the final agreement had the public appearance of being instigated, negotiated, and signed without foreign influence—a particularly important detail to the nationalistic Mexican government.

The Conflict Revisited

The 1929 truce between church and state had more importance as a model than as a permanent solution. Contrary to the agreements made in the *modus vivendi*, many of the Cristero rebels who accepted the truce were executed. Violent oppression erupted in 1931 at Vera Cruz; churches were systematically raided, and, in a well-publicized attack, Fr. Dario Acosta was shot and killed while teaching religion to children in his own parish.[38] The states again imposed absurdly restrictive limitations on the number of priests who could function. The bitter enmity that had marked the Calles era had revived, and once again the eyes of U.S. Catholics turned to Mexico.[39]

As before, the Catholic press, the Knights of Columbus, and individual U.S. bishops called for severe sanctions against Mexico.[40] In January 1933 the NCWC issued a protest against the renewed persecution in Mexico. Although the bishops called for all Americans, regardless of creed, to help end the persecution, there was little reason to hope that the U.S. government would make an important issue of religious liberty in Mexico.

Nevertheless, President Franklin Roosevelt respected Burke's reputation and looked to him as an advisor on national and international Catholic affairs. In response to Roosevelt's position on non-intervention, Burke met with him in 1934 and explained that the persecution was worse than ever. Perhaps more importantly, Burke pointed out that as Mexico continued to exile hundreds of Catholics, the U.S. spirit of hospitality was beginning to be replaced by resentment as the numbers of refugees grew overwhelming.[41] Roosevelt kept up informal pressure on the Mexican government.

As had been demonstrated in 1929, outside support might strengthen the Mexican Church's bargaining position, but only the Mexicans themselves could ultimately resolve their church-state conflicts. The persecution and harassment began to diminish around 1935 during the term of President Lázaro Cárdenas. In 1940, President Avila Camacho, like some of his more moderate predecessors, tried neither to change the constitution nor to strictly enforce its restrictions on the Church. That sort of *modus vivendi*, a winking toleration of formally "illegal" church activity, would continue for the next fifty years.[42]

In the meantime, the U.S. bishops maintained their concern for the problems in Mexico. In November 1935, in order to sidestep the restrictions imposed on the Mexican Church, the NCWC set up a committee to help establish a seminary for Mexicans in the United States. Although the seminary committee did not function precisely as the bishops had hoped, they did indeed raise the necessary money. In September 1937, the Montezuma Seminary opened near Las Vegas, N.M. Over the years, the seminary provided a much-needed opportunity for Mexican seminarians to prepare for the priesthood, and its alumni included numerous bishops.[43]

Throughout the years of crisis, Burke had stood between rabid reactionaries and political isolationists. Through him, the NCWC influenced U.S. diplomats to steer a course that maintained sufficient pressure on Mexico without the appearance of interventionism. In the long run, the Mexican government was aware that its anti-religious activity would not be passively ignored, and the Church of Mexico knew that it had faithful allies in the United States. At the same time, Burke's diplomacy and sage advice helped strengthen the informal ties between the U.S. government and the NCWC. The Church had maintained its credibility, and the NCWC gained recognition among both Catholics and Protestants as the voice of the Catholic Church in the United States.

The Church in the United States and Latin American Missions

The Mexican crisis made U.S. Catholics more aware than ever before of their brothers and sisters to the south. Although U.S.-born members of religious congregations had been ministering in various Latin American countries since before the Civil War, the Church's major pastoral efforts had been necessarily directed to needs at home. In 1919, U.S. bishops had written a long pastoral letter that contained only a few paragraphs on the missions. At that time, the bishops called on Catholics to pray for missionaries and for vocations to the missions, and in an almost direct reference to the recently founded Maryknoll society, they said, "We bless with cordial approval the efforts of those who . . . develop this apostolic spirit . . . for the distant parts of the vineyard." One statement from the letter stands out as uniquely relevant to the relationship beween the U.S. Catholic Church and the Church in Latin America:

> Let it not be said, to our reproach, that American commerce has out-stripped American Catholic zeal, or that others have entered in to reap where Catholic hands had planted, perchance where Catholic blood had watered the soil.[44]

That one sentence reminded Catholics in the increasingly prosperous United States that they had an obligation to subjugate economic gain to the demands of faith and to support the Church in areas where it would be challenged by other religious or philosophical traditions. With that re-minder, the bishops, without knowing the full implications of their state-ment, pointed the way for future relations between the United States and Latin American Churches.

The Seeds of Involvement—The 1940s
Until World War II, U.S. Catholics did not think of Latin America as mis-sion territory; talk of "U.S. missionaries in Latin America" generally re-ferred to Protestants. There were, to be sure, some religious congregations in the United States that had Latin American missions, but Latin America's high percentage of Catholics, especially when compared to the United States, prevented most from thinking of it as a Catholic mission field.[45] Typ-ical of this mindset was a 1943 mission study book that said that Central American bishops were asking U.S. Catholics for help, not by sending per-sonnel, but through stemming the flow of Protestant missionaries and U.S. moving pictures into their countries. According to the bishops, Protestant missionaries "ordinarily come armed with hatred . . . and contempt for our Holy Catholic religion and our clergy," and the movies were "conducive to sin" and "de-Christianizing our faithful people."[46] The predominant idea was that Catholic Latin America needed not missionaries, but help in de-fending itself from anti-Catholic values, be they in the form of anticlerical politicians, proselytizers, or cultural invasions. What no one seemed to be looking at was Latin America's amazingly small ratio of priests to Catholics.

Then came Fr. John Considine, a Maryknoller who recognized, publi-cized, and instigated an enormous response to that problem. Considine de-voted his entire career as a journalist and organizer to making world mission

Rev. John Considine's book, *The Call for Forty Thousand*. Photo: Robert Pelton, CSC.

a clear and important part of every Catholic's consciousness.[47] Through his writings, his travels, and his influence on church leaders, he became one of the most important figures in U.S. mission history. Of his many books, *The Call for Forty Thousand* is the one that perhaps best captures the thrust of his vision. Writing in a style that might be called a religious travel-log, he startled his readers into understanding Latin America's clergy shortage by quoting a conversation he had with Bishop Larraín of Talca, Chile. He said,

> "In the United States . . . we have one priest for every six hundred and fifty Catholics. How does this compare with the average here?"
>
> He [Larraín] smiled ruefully. "We have barely two thousand for a population of five million. . . . In other words, three million of our people are without adequate priestly care."[48]

Considine went on to cite statistics from around Latin America, demonstrating that Chile, so far below the U.S. ratio, still had a relatively strong priest population when compared to other countries. According to Considine, another bishop told him:

> Were such a situation suddenly to develop in the United States, there would be grave danger of all of you losing your faith, for in North

Sharing Faith Across the Hemisphere

America you do little without the leadership of your priests. With us in Latin America it is different. It has to be, for we have suffered from this malady for generations and we have built up a certain immunity to its evils. In Latin America it can be said that millions of us have learned to live a certain form of catholic life without priests.[49]

Writing in 1946, Considine had no idea how that story would sound fifty years later when U.S. Catholics look to Latin American base communities and active laity as examples of how to maintain a strong faith in spite of a shortage of priests. *The Call for Forty Thousand* was Considine's opening volley in a campaign to move vast numbers of U.S. clergy to serve the Latin American Church. The campaign would grow, change shape, and eventually transform the U.S. Church by leading it into a new relationship with Latin America.

His extensive travels and conversations with Latin American church leaders had convinced Considine that Latin America's single greatest religious need was for more clergy and religious. Regarding his conjecture that the need was for 40,000, he said, "Perhaps it would be too few . . . perhaps 25,000 would be abundantly adequate. But for our purposes, it is enough to know that the needs run into the tens of thousands."[50] Although he was by no means suggesting that 40,000 missionaries should immediately embark for Latin America, he did not hesitate to say that "our present diminutive contribution of 571 priests and Brothers and 531 Sisters in all Latin America is much too small."[51]

While Considine worked to increase the number of missionaries to Latin America, another U.S. church movement, the National Catholic Rural Life Conference, became involved in a complementary process of raising international awareness and building relationships between the North and South. Founded by Edwin V. O'Hara in 1923, the Rural Life Conference, with its concern for the land and the welfare of those who work it, had an immediate and natural bond with similar groups in Latin America. Through the 1940s, U.S. rural life leaders visited Latin America; by the 1950s they were able to sponsor international conferences in Colombia, Panama, Venezuela, and Chile. These conferences not only helped rural Americans from both hemispheres become more aware of their common bonds and concerns, but the U.S. bishops involved in them developed an awareness of Latin America that would continue to grow in the future.[52]

Development Through the 1950s

CELAM

Without a doubt, the most important event to take place in the Catholic Church in America during the 1950s was the meeting at which the Latin American bishops organized CELAM, the Latin American Episcopal Conference.[53] Taking advantage of the large number of bishops who would be attending the International Eucharistic Congress in Rio de Janiero during July 1955, Pius XII called the meeting and prepared its agenda. The ninety-seven bishops who attended were mandated to construct a pastoral program to deal with the most pressing needs of the continent: the priest shortage, religious education, and the needs of indigenous peoples. CELAM was their response to that challenge.

The bishops designed CELAM to fulfill four specific functions: to study the problems facing the Latin American Church, to coordinate activities, to promote and support Catholic charitable agencies, and to prepare further conferences. They also appointed a highly capable staff to work under the general secretary, Archbishop Dom Helder Camara of Brazil. Beginning in 1956, CELAM held annual assemblies in which the bishops worked together on themes chosen to help them achieve their organizational and pastoral goals. Through those annual assemblies the bishops also begin to develop the continental unity and common methodology that would prepare them for active participation in Vatican II and the changes that would come in its wake.

CAL: The Pontifical Commission for Latin America

Vatican concern for Latin America did not end with the formation of CELAM. In 1958, Pius XII founded the Pontifical Commission for Latin America, commonly known as CAL. CAL's mandate was to support the work of CELAM, to study the fundamental problems of Catholic life in Latin America, and to encourage close cooperation among the Roman congregations working with Latin America.[54] Because it was both a supportive and a coordinating agency, CAL's possibilities were literally endless. As it turned out, its two most important contributions to the Latin American Church were the appointment of Antonio Samore as its vice president and, through him, its call for regular inter-American bishops meetings.

Since 1959, the inter-American bishop meetings have provided an annual opportunity for bishops from Canada, Latin America, and the United States to discuss matters of international cooperation and concern. Under the leadership of Cardinal Cushing, the first meeting resulted in the recommendation that the United States initiate a million dollar campaign for the Church in Latin America and that the NCWC establish a formal Latin American bureau to administer that collection and to educate the U.S. Church about Latin America. With John Considine as its first director, the bureau quickly became a driving force in the U.S. Church, fostering the growth of new relationships and deeper understanding between the Churches of the North and South.

New U.S. Responses to Latin America

Even before the foundation of CAL, the United States had become more aware of the real needs of the Latin American Church. By 1955, of the 4,755 U.S. priests and religious serving as foreign missionaries, a full third were working in Latin America.[55] At the same time new models of mission were beginning to develop. One of those new models, the diocesan mission, seems to have been born almost fortuitously at a lunch table in St. Louis.

St. Louis, like Boston and a few other U.S. dioceses, had an abundance of priests. Thus, Archbishop Umberto Mozzoni, the papal nuncio in Bolivia, must have thought that it would be a good place to turn for help. As the story goes, in 1956, Mozzoni wrote a letter asking the Archbishop of St. Louis to send some of his priests to Bolivia. When Archbishop Joseph Ritter received the request he was not only surprised, but ready to dismiss the petition. Nevertheless, he casually mentioned the letter at a lunch, and some of his staff suggested that rather than reject it out of hand, he should see if there would be any volunteers. When he did so, he found that two-thirds of the priests who met the eligibility requirements actually offered to spend five years working in Bolivia. As a result, the first U.S. diocesan mission in Latin America was born.[56]

Two years later, in 1958, Cardinal Cushing of Boston announced his new plan to support Latin American missions. More than a diocesan mission, Cushing wanted to establish a society for diocesan priests who would serve temporarily in the missions. Formally named "The Pious Society of St. James the Apostle," the St. James Society was a project for continental

Priests from the St. James Society, which was founded by Cardinal Richard Cushing, have ministered in Latin America for nearly four decades. The society coordinates the work of priest missionaries from throughout the United States. Photo: St. James Society.

apostolic coordination. St. James priests, drawn from any dioceses willing to participate, would serve areas with a large number of Catholics and a shortage of priests—a precise description of Latin America.

According to Cushing, the effort would not be for the sole benefit of Latin America. Like Cardinal Gibbons a half-century before him, Cushing had an intuition that mission work would benefit more than the receiving countries. "It is my opinion," he said, "that the church of this country needs a challenge not only to help foreign and home missions but to save the faith in countries where it needs to be revivified."[57] In that seemingly simple statement, Cardinal Cushing was describing a future that he could hardly have imagined. The sixties would see a burgeoning of mission activity, the long-term result of which would include an extraordinary impact on the faith of the Church in the United States.

Sharing Faith Across the Hemisphere

DISCUSSION QUESTIONS

1. During the first two decades of the twentieth century, the Church in the United States emerged from the designation of being a mission territory, established the NCWC as a national organization, and founded its first indigenous foreign mission society. Some national organizations and local bishops resisted the formation of the NCWC, seeing it as a threat to their autonomy. Could the Church in the United States have exercised credible national and international influence without it?

2. What was the message behind Cardinal Gibbons's suggestion that the faith of the Church in the United States would suffer if it did not become involved in the missionary endeavor? How would the Church benefit from the mission outreach?

3. During the period of intense persecution of the Mexican Church, the Catholic press kept U.S. readers aware of the events unfolding to the south. In what ways was such publicity helpful or harmful on both sides of the border?

4. Throughout the years of the Mexican church-state crisis, Catholic leaders and organizations in the United States offered to help or even demanded that their government intervene. What can be learned about how to manage U.S./Latin American relations from Fr. John Burke's diplomatic career?

5. In 1919, the U.S. bishops challenged the Church to be as zealous for evangelization as the United States was for commerce. What would be necessary for that challenge to be met? In what ways should zeal for evangelization resemble commerce? In what ways must it be different?

Notes

1. For a general introduction to Latin American history, see E. Bradford Burns's *Latin America, A Concise Interpretive History*, and John A. Crow, *The Epic of Latin America* (Berkeley, Calif.: University of California Press, 1992).

2. This loyalty was, no doubt, influenced by the events of provincial synods which Spain called in 1771. At the Mexican synod, the assembled bishops approved the points presented by the government, and then they added provisions that called for the excommunication of anyone who resisted a royal decree. When Bishop Diaz Bravo of Durango objected, he was put on trial and removed from office. He set off for Spain to defend himself, but died en route (see Hubert Jedin, ed. *History of the Church* [New York: Crossroad, 1980-1982], VI:268).

3. See Carlos Castenada, "Social Developments and Movements in Latin America" in Joseph Moody, ed., *Church and Society: Catholic Social and Political Thought and Movements, 1789-1950* (New York: Arts, Inc., 1953), 746-47.

4. Castenada, 748.

5. See Jedin, VI:236-42.

6. National governments have had a tendency to change frequently in Latin America. There have been more than 180 different constitutions promulgated in the Latin American nations since independence. Venezuela, the record holder, has had 22 constitutions since 1811 (Burns, 90).

7. Jedin, VIII:150.

8. The foundation of Maryknoll was preceded by the opening of a mission seminary for the Society of the Divine Word in 1909 and was quickly followed by the 1921 opening of a seminary, St. Columban's Foreign Mission Society. But Maryknoll is the only one of these to be a U.S. foundation.

9. John Tracy Ellis, *Documents of American Catholic History* (Milwaukee: Bruce, 1956), 592-96.

10. The statistics and much of the following information is based on John B. Sheerin, CSP, *Never Look Back: The Career and Concerns of John J. Burke* (Mahweh, N.J.: Paulist, 1975).

11. Editorial, *The Catholic World* 105 (Aug. 1917): 711-12.

12. Sheerin, 41

13. Ibid., 862-63.

14. Another strong promoter of the NCWC, Bishop Patrick Muldoon of Rockford, emphasized its potential to help the Catholic press, teachers, and clergy know how to think critically about issues of national concern. See Elizabeth McGowan, "The National Bishops' Conference, An Analysis of its Origins" in *Modern American Catholicism, 1900-1955, Selected Essays*, Robert Kantowitz, ed. (New York: Garland Publishing Inc., 1988), 48.

15. Ibid., 50.

16. The issue at stake was Hoover's thirty-three-point program for European relief work. The knights had publicly proclaimed their support for it, but NCWC felt that it was apt to be carried out as a proselytizing effort. As a result of the incident, Burke outlined a policy to help lay organizations collaborate with the bishops in speaking on public issues. See Sheerin, 64-65.

17. Sheerin, 60-82.

18. Diaz ruled from 1876 to 1911. At the end of his regime, 95 percent of the rural population was landless, and fewer than 200 families owned one-fourth of the land while foreign investors owned another fourth. See Burns.

19. Mexico began its process of anticlerical reforms in 1833, and they were made stronger in the Constitution of 1857. Nevertheless, although the separation of church and state was official, the laws were not effectively enforced during the nineteenth century.

20. Wilson had intervened a short time before by sending troops to help defeat Victoriano Huerta. In 1914, those troops still occupied Veracruz. See Robert E. Quirk, *The Mexican Revolution and the Catholic Church, 1910-1929* (Bloomington, Ind.: Indiana University Press, 1973), 62.

21. Quirk, 61-62.

22. Quirk, 66.

23. Quirk, 64.

24. See Enrique Dussel, ed. *The Church in Latin America: 1492-1992* (New York: Orbis, 1992), 125-26.

25. Mora y del Rio was accused of sedition, and when he said that his health would not allow him to appear in court, the judge came to his home to take testimony. The archbishop denied that he had made the statements that were attributed to him. See Quirk, 150-53.

26. Colima, which had 62,000 inhabitants, allowed for 26 priests; Nuevo Leon limited the number to one priest for every 2,500 inhabitants; Tamaulipas, 13 for 350,000; Aguascalientes, 1 for 50,000; and the Federal District, 140 priests for 1,000,000 people.

27. Following the counsel of the Vatican, the bishops officially rejected any idea that the Church should organize violent rebellion. Nevertheless, individual bishops held diverse opinions about the groups who organized themselves, and the bishops actually provided official chaplains for the Cristero rebels who fought throughout this period.

28. Quirk, 168. The anti-monastic legislation stipulated that any person who returned to religious life after a community had been dissolved would be liable to one or two years in prison.

29. Quirk, 173.

30. Quirk, 179, recounts a dramatic description of the activity published by the *New York Times*, July 25, 1926, 2:5.

31. Some individual bishops openly supported the Cristeros. Others, including Archbishop Diaz, believed that they could never be successful. Ironically, in 1927, Diaz was arrested and exiled for alleged complicity in anti-government military activity. He then took up temporary residence in New York where he hoped to gain the ear of U.S. government officials. See Quirk, 188-208.

32. "Tyranny in Mexico" by an anonymous "American residing in Mexico," *America* 34 (Feb. 27, 1926): 471.

33. *America* 35 (Aug. 28, 1926): 468.

34. Sheerin, 113-14.

35. When Burke asked President Coolidge to pressure Calles, Coolidge said that he didn't think Calles would listen to him and that strong U.S. reaction could precipitate war with Mexico. Sheerin, 118.

36. See *Pastoral Letters of the United States Catholic Bishops*, Vol. 1. (Washington D.C.: United States Catholic Conference, 1993).

37. Miguel Pro was beatified in November 1988.

38. See "Bolshevism in Vera Cruz," *America* 45 (August 15, 1931): 437.

39. See Douglas J. Slawson, "The National Catholic Welfare Conference and the Mexican Church State Conflict of the Mid-1930s: A Case of Deja Vu," *The Catholic Historical Review* 80:58-96. For an example of the U.S. Catholic press approach to the conflict, see Carleton Beals, "Mexico's New Religious Conflict" in *The Commonweal* 15 (March 2, 1932): 483-86.

40. It was to expose and protest this phase of persecution that Bishop Kelley published his *Blood Drenched Altars* and Wilfred Parsons, SJ, the editor of *America,* published the book *Mexican Martyrdom.*

41. Sheerin, 163.

42. See Gerald Fogarty, *The Vatican and the American Hierarchy from 1870 to 1965* (Wilmington, Del.: Michael Glazier, 1985).

43. See Slawson, 85-91.

44. See *Pastoral Letters*, vol. 1, 1919 letter, articles 50 and 53.

45. It is nearly impossible to get an accurate count of the early U.S. contribution to Latin American missions because many congregations worked in Latin America, especially in Mexico, Cuba, and Puerto Rico, as a part of the normal work of their U.S. provinces. Among the first U.S. congregations on record as serving in Latin America are the Benedictines, who began work in the Bahama islands in 1891, and the Jesuits, who took responsibility for a large mission in British Honduras in 1893.

46. James A. Magner, *Latin America Pattern* (Cincinnati: Catholic Students Mission Crusade, 1943), 93.

47. Shortly after his ordination, Considine began work for the Roman Congregation for the Propagation of the Faith; he started the "Fides" news service, wrote numerous books, and served on the Maryknoll General Council. The last job of his career was as the founding director of the NCWC's Latin American Bureau.

48. John J. Considine, *Call For Forty Thousand* (New York: Longmans, Green & Company, 1946), 9.

49. Ibid., 10-11.

50. Ibid., 14.

51. Ibid., 15-16. Considine's numbers are higher than those listed in the *Catholic Almanac* for 1945, which said that there were 504 priests and brothers and 242 sisters working in Mexico and Central and South America. The *Almanac* also reported that there were 281 priests and brothers and 435 sisters serving that year in the West Indies.

52. O'Hara, later named Bishop of Kansas City, and his protégé, Bishop Joseph Marling of Jefferson City, would be among the leaders in establishing diocesan missions to Latin America. See Gerald M. Costello, *Mission to Latin America: The Successes and Failures of a Twentieth Century Crusade* (New York: Orbis, 1979), 28-29.

53. See Emile Poulat, "The Path of Latin American Catholicism," and Francois Houtart, "CELAM, The Forgetting of Origins," in Dermot Keogh, ed., *The Path of Latin American Catholicism* (New York: St. Martin's Press, 1990).

54. Costello, 41.

55. According to the 1955 *Catholic Almanac*, there were 1,780 priests, sisters, and brothers serving in South and Central America and the West Indies.

56. Costello, 74.

57. Joseph Dever, *Cushing of Boston: A Candid Portrait* (Boston: Bruce Humphries Publishers, 1965), 188.

CHAPTER FOUR

Mission Surge of the 1960s

August 17, 1961, Notre Dame, Indiana, USA

The priests, brothers, and sisters gathered to hear the speaker from Rome had no idea what was about to hit them. The audience, made up of the major superiors of both the women's and men's religious communities in the United States, was about serious business, but only a few like Maryknoll Fr. John Considine could have imagined that this speech and their responses would dramatically affect the future history of the Church throughout America.

The speaker, Msgr. Agostino Casaroli, represented the most beloved pope of recent history, and he counted on John XXIII's popularity to add weight to his message. Casaroli quickly went to the heart of the issue:

> *I appeal to you in the name of the Holy See in favor of Latin America. You well know that dangers to the Christian life in such an important*

sector of the Church represent a serious menace, while progress there represents a bright promise.

Latin America, so heroic in times of persecution, so strongly resisting internal insufficiencies and dangers from without—yet suffers from perilous elemental weaknesses of structure. These weaknesses are manifested by the well-known lack of apostolic workers in Latin America, a lack which is aggravated by the greater menace of the enemies of Catholicism including the inroads of Protestant sects, secularization, the menace of Marxism, and a disquieting practice of spiritism.

Of course, the Holy See is quite well aware of all that American religious communities, with approximately 2,700 members now in Latin America, are already doing in this sense. But the need is felt to request yet more from your generosity.

What aid does the Holy See expect for Latin America from the religious communities of the United States? I spoke earlier of a plan. . . . That which the Church feels it necessary to do for Latin America cannot be done through isolated and uncoordinated efforts. The field is so vast, the urgency so great, and the danger so real, that all efforts must be added together. The basic solution would be that Latin America succeed in being self-sufficient for its own needs and, we may add, capable also of giving a full and valuable contribution towards the progress of the universal church.

Interpreting the mind of the Pontifical Commission, I offer you an ideal—that each religious province aim to contribute to Latin America in the next ten years a tithe—ten percent—of its present membership. The judgment is left to you.

With that prayer, the Holy Father includes his gratitude and his benediction upon all those of his children who give a generous response.

The crowd immediately applauded Msgr. Casaroli, but more than that, the U.S. response to the call would come in the form of personnel and funds. In the next thirty-five years, thousands of priests, religious, and laity would serve in Latin America, and the Church in the United States would collect more than $72 million to support the endeavors of the Latin American Church. And all of that would be only the beginning.

The Revolution of the 1960s

The 1960s was a time of overwhelming vitality—changes that had previously been the stuff of dreams, and sometimes nightmares, were exploding on the horizon. Latin America found itself in the throes of the astounding awakening of the poor, most potently symbolized by the Cuban revolution. The United States was embarking on its "Camelot" era under the leadership of John F. Kennedy. U.S. Catholicism was strong, and vocations to the priesthood and religious life were growing prodigiously. Although Europe still seemed to be the center of the Catholic world, Latin America had begun to burst into church consciousness and the United States was suddenly recognizing the political and economic importance of its southern neighbors. With Pope John XXIII's call for *aggiornamento* or renewal of the Church and adaptation to the modern world, the stage could not have been more perfectly set for an appeal to U.S. Catholics to reach out to Latin America.

Msgr. Casaroli's talk to the U.S. religious superiors had been carefully prepared behind the scenes.[1] As early as 1955, Bishop Manuel Larraín had said: "We must pass from a level of national isolation to one of inter-American cooperation. Latin America is on the threshold of immanent and radical reform."[2] While the Church in Latin America was strengthening its multinational organization, Fr. John Considine had supplemented his writing about Latin America's needs with careful work among both Roman and U.S. church leaders. Although he never touted it, Considine himself most likely instigated the call to the U.S. religious, and he was certainly the moving force behind the Papal Volunteers for Latin America (PAVLA).[3] But other actors on the scene, especially church leaders and social science researchers, also played their respective parts to encourage the sudden surge in missionary interest in Latin America.

In 1961, the "plan" to which Msgr. Casaroli referred was far from a detailed project. In reality, it might have been more aptly understood as a "wild dream" and a hope. The "wild dream," the contribution of 10 percent of U.S. religious to Latin America, never came true. But something of the hope became a reality. Missionaries and their Latin American hosts, building on enthusiastic generosity and warm hospitality, would eventually develop patterns of shared reflection, evaluation, and action. The results would have transforming effects on them and their respective societies.

Fundamental Weaknesses of Structure

Latin America in the Early 1960s

The Church's turn toward Latin America represented the fruition of seeds planted during the previous two decades. In 1955, a Jesuit from the Gregorian University, Prudencio Damboriena, published a report on the extraordinary growth of Protestant groups in Latin America.[4] Suddenly there was a flowering of efforts to assess the real situation of the Church in that enormous area traditionally considered a Catholic stronghold. The results of the studies were startling. Although the vast majority of the Latin American population was Catholic, a chronic shortage of priests, especially in rural areas, had produced a Catholicism with precious little sacramental practice.

The most thorough investigators of the Latin American Church scene were the scholars who joined together in FERES (the International Federation of Institutes for Socio-Religious Research). Under the leadership of Louvain sociologist Francois Houtart, the European and Latin American scholars who collaborated at FERES centers in Bogatá and Rio de Janeiro produced studies that brought to light a new picture of Latin American Catholicism.[5] According to their research, the Latin American population had changed substantially over the past century: indigenous peoples had fallen from 35 percent to a mere 8 percent of the population; people of African descent had doubled as a proportion of the population, from 4 to 8 percent; the *mestizo* population had grown from 27 to 38 percent; and, due to massive immigration, people of European descent now comprised 44.5 percent of the total Latin American population. That majority group was transforming social structures and providing the basis for a new urban middle class.[6]

In addition to the changes caused by immigration, improved health care and new scientific discoveries had helped bring about a population increase of 50 million people in the decade from 1950 to 1960. Because neither agricultural food production nor land distribution matched the needs of the increased population, the strains on rural society led to massive migrations to the cities and the creation of high-density population centers where the inhabitants found themselves far removed from their rural origins and marginalized in their new social setting.[7] Because of that double displacement and their often-frustrated hope for social advancement, the migrants were often receptive to new political ideologies. With such a combination of population increase, immigration, internal migration, and social unrest, it is no wonder that Barbara Ward referred to these times as "the most catastrophically revolutionary age that men have ever faced."[8]

The simple example of how a *campesino* experienced the multifaceted "communications revolution" can illustrate the Latin American implications of Ward's statement. A rural villager who took his first bus trip over newly constructed roads not only traveled an unbelievable fifty or one hundred miles in a single day, but also traversed some 400 years of technological progress as he left a village just like that of his ancestors and arrived in a modern city. If he returned home with a transistor radio, the twentieth century came back with him—with all of its advertising, its music and information, its potential for education and political involvement.[9] People who had lived in a culturally isolated world could suddenly drink Coca-Cola while they listened to news about local and world events.

For the *campesino*, as much as for the rest of the world, the 1960s became an age of rising expectations—a time of confusing secularism and growing materialism. The communications revolution proposed new dogmas to replace ancient religious and political belief systems. Scientific progress brought in its wake new and disturbing questions about God and the human endeavor; mass communications promoted new beliefs about equality together with a near divinization of material progress and the goods it promised. Few in the Latin American Church could even imagine the magnitude of the changes facing them.

The Religious Scenario

In 1960, there were approximately 37,600 priests in Latin America or 5,420 Catholics per priest.[10] The figure has even more critical implications when one takes into account that a good number of those priests were involved in works other than full-time catechetical and sacramental ministry. Given those statistics, it is hardly surprising that only about one-third of Latin America's Catholics could participate regularly in the sacramental life.[11] Using formal religious education, participation in parish structures, and reception of the sacraments as the standard measure of active and authentic religious practice, the Latin American delegates to a 1953 Inter-American Catholic Action Week described their situation:

The average person in Latin America receives only an appalling minimum of religious instruction, and is a nominal Catholic for that reason. . . . He inherits a traditional and devitalized form of Catholicism, often with a curious mixture of religious sentiments and practices that bear no relation to the real substance of his Faith. His religion is thus an external ritualism of routinized practices.[12]

The situation was most critical in rural areas where more than 50 percent of the population lived in small and often very remote villages. There, where a priest might visit only once or twice a year, the faith life of the people centered on a popular religiosity that focused on patron saints and traditional practices in the home, which outsiders initially perceived as having little connection to the core message and practices of Catholicism.[13] According to the Catholic Actionists,

Indian and European civilization and culture have remained largely incompatible during four centuries. The colonizing of the country, and the accompanying missionary work did leave the sierral Indians with a religious sediment of sincere faith. . . . Nevertheless, grave deformations and deviations have been produced . . . due in part to scarcity of clergy—a scarcity that resulted in the virtual abandonment of those people since the time of the independence era. . . .[14]

In spite of what would later appear to be hasty judgments, the delegates who produced the Catholic Action report made two very important contributions to understanding the religious situation of Latin America. First, they underlined the problems suffered by a local church with an insufficient number of clergy. Second, although inadvertently, they made it clear that there was a widespread lack of understanding of the religious depth and truth found in "popular religiosity," those practices that had been developed by rural people as a means of preserving the faith in areas where the structures of the institutional Church were weak or virtually absent. The Church would deal with both of those issues in the coming decades as local and international missionaries directed their efforts to marginalized areas and, in the process, gained a greater understanding of and appreciation for the traditional religious practices of the people they served.

In addition to a lack of clergy, beginning in the middle years of the twentieth century, the Catholic Church in Latin America found itself increasingly challenged by missionary activity on the part of Protestant denominations. Latin American Protestantism, although still clearly a minority, was experiencing growth of geometric proportions. Between 1938 and 1961, Protestantism grew from representing .49 to 3.84 percent of the population. The FERES researchers attributed that rise to a number of different factors. First, with World War II, Latin America replaced Asia as a major field for Protestant proselytism. Perhaps more significantly, Protestant groups that could prepare their ministers in a short amount of time were able to develop an indigenous clergy to the extent that by 1961, 84 percent of Protestant ministers in Latin America were native and each of them had responsibility for approximately 482 church members.[15] With its lack of ministers and large geographical areas lacking adequate pastoral attention, there is little doubt that the Latin American Catholic Church did, as Msgr. Casaroli so bluntly stated, suffer from "fundamental weaknesses of structure."[16]

The Resources of the Church of the United States

The U.S. Catholic Church in the 1960s

The summons to Vatican II provided the U.S. bishops with an opportunity to assess the Church they would represent at the council. In August 1962, the NCWC issued a statement on the ecumenical council that included a general description of the state of the Church in the United States:

> We are a new and recently cultivated part of Christ's vineyard. We cannot boast the saints that have arisen in the churches of Europe. . . . [We have] not produced the number of profound scholars and brilliant writers who adorn some of the older centers of Christian culture.
>
> Undoubtedly, we bear the imprint of our past—of a Church which was born and has grown to maturity in an atmosphere not always friendly, which has had to struggle almost every step of the way to produce the institutions necessary for its preservation and development, whose people are sprung from ancestors, many of whom . . . came to this country unlettered and in great poverty. It has had to struggle against an excessive preoccupation with material things,

occasioned not only by its needs but also in part by the very wealth our country has produced, and against a public philosophy strongly affected by a special kind of secularism. The marks of our origin and history are certainly upon us.

But whatever the limitations of the Church in this country . . . we know, first of all, the advantages which we have . . . from living and growing in an atmosphere of religious and political freedom. The very struggle which the church here has had to face has been responsible in large measure for the vitality which it has developed as it grew to maturity, unaided by political preference but unimpeded by political ties. Our lay people, both men as well as women, are to an extraordinary degree active. . . . Devotion to the Mass, love for the Eucharist . . . active participation in every kind of parochial, diocesan and national Catholic life—these are the signs of religious vitality which so often impress visitors to our shores.

[Other signs of vitality include] the vast educational system . . . growing enthusiasm for the liturgy . . . an intense desire for a rich spiritual life . . . the successful efforts of the Church in charitable works, in the constant concern for the spread of the Gospel in other lands through increasing missionary activities, and in the manifestation of love for our brothers of all races and nations which energizes our Catholic Relief Services and similar organizations.[17]

The bishops described a Church that was clearly aware that it had come into its own. Recognizing its youth and cherishing its vigor, the difficulties of the past were understood as trials that had strengthened it, and the current preoccupation of the Church would focus on the newfound prosperity and materialism of the culture. The Church in the United States felt strong and prepared not only to reach out, but to lead others.

The Menace of Marxism

Cuba Focuses Attention on Latin America
If the Church in the United States felt prepared to make an impact on the world, Cuba epitomized the dangers lurking throughout that world. Fidel Castro's revolution galvanized the attention of the whole

Church, and particularly that of the United States, moving Latin America toward center stage in terms of international awareness and concern.

Until 1959, Cuba, like many Latin American countries, had lived under dictatorships that favored the oligarchy-military alliance and kept the majority of the people, if not quiet, at least under control.[18] In 1959, the Cuban Church, one of the institutionally weaker Churches in Latin America, reportedly had only 681 priests and 1,872 sisters ministering to a population of nearly 6 million.[19] The United States had watched with mildly supportive interest as Castro and his guerrilla army gradually worked their way from mountain hideouts toward the nation's capital.[20] That support soon waned and then turned to bitter antagonism as Castro included U.S.-owned assets in his program of nationalization.

After Castro's victory, news about Cuba became a constant feature in both the secular and religious press in the United States. Although much of the publicity did little more than denounce the abuses of the Castro government, some authors made a concerted effort to understand both the events and their wider implications. Opinions about Cuba ebbed and flowed in response to what could be known about events on the island.[21]

In general, the Church and government in Cuba coexisted in an uneasy peace until 1961. Then, after the Bay of Pigs invasion, Castro announced his intention to expel foreign priests (approximately 70 percent of the priests in the country), to confiscate their property, and to severely limit religious activity on the island. As a result, hundreds of priests and religious emigrated to other countries. Then, between July and September 1961, the government and Church entered into a series of open conflicts, resulting in the deportation of one bishop and 145 priests—nearly half of the active clergy remaining on the island.

In October 1961, John Leslay wrote an article for *America* magazine that tried to report objectively about events on the island, and interpret their meaning for the rest of both hemispheres. Leslay praised Castro's literacy campaigns but commented that Castro had lost control of his revolution and was losing popular support because of his persecution of the Church. Refusing to get caught up in polemics about Castro, Leslay's main point was that the Cuban Revolution was a *fait acompli*, which, more than anything else, called the United States to be serious about reaching out to the rest of Latin America:

The chief lesson to be drawn at this moment does not concern Cuba, but the other Latin American countries. Just as the Marshall Plan in 1947 came too late to save Eastern Europe, . . . so the Alliance for Progress program . . . will not pull Cuba back into the Western fold . . . but it may help some of the other Latin American nations to resist the terrible stress and temptation they are now facing. . . .

Let us be perfectly clear. . . . If no other solution is proposed now—and rapidly—then the temptation to try communism will grow stronger in all the underdeveloped countries. . . . My own conclusion is that probably the situation created by the Castro regime and the Cuban power grab by the communist party is something that is here to stay, at least for a long time. But the drama of Castro and Cuba may yet help us to draw some badly needed lessons for other countries and other continents.[22]

Theologian Leslie Dewart expanded on that last idea by suggesting that Cuba's revolution was a sign of the newest development in an evolving world—the appearance of post-western civilization. He said:

The problem that the Universal Church is ever increasingly pressed to meet is not essentially different from that which was faced in Cuba. The problem may be formulated as follows: How shall the Body of Christ as it ages and matures, and as it finally comes to its childhood's end, adapt to an emerging world-wide civilization. . . .

The Church is faced with an unprecedented, extremely rapid, and radical change on a multitude of planes and on a world scale. It must cope with socio-politico-economic problems of the emerging post-Western contemporary world. To reduce it to the dimensions of how to cope with Russian imperialism and the appeal of Marxism-Leninism reveals a failure of imagination to comprehend the range and magnitude of the problem.[23]

Castro's Cuba served as a wake-up call to the Church and to the United States. Too close for comfortable armchair philosophizing, and full of portentous possibilities, it urged a response. The Vatican call for help in Latin America seemed to be a response to "the signs of the times," even before Vatican II made the phrase popular.

U.S. Response to the Call

The Religious

When Msgr. Casaroli addressed the men and women religious in 1961, he may have been preaching to the choir, but he was asking them for more than they had already given, and undoubtedly more than they thought they could give. Nevertheless, the religious of the United States responded to the call with extraordinary enthusiasm.

In 1995, the National Conference of Catholic Bishops surveyed all the dioceses, religious congregations, parishes, and Catholic colleges and universities in the country about their involvement with Latin America over the past thirty-five years.[24] According to their responses, religious communities felt that they had made a very positive response to the original call to mission; 68 percent of religious communities, more than any other surveyed group, felt that their support of the call to mission had been good or very good (Figure 1). The language with which the respondents described their reaction is full of enthusiasm, giving witness to the extraordinary optimism that characterized religious life in the 1960s. Typical commentaries indicated that it was a "peak" time of concern for Latin America, that

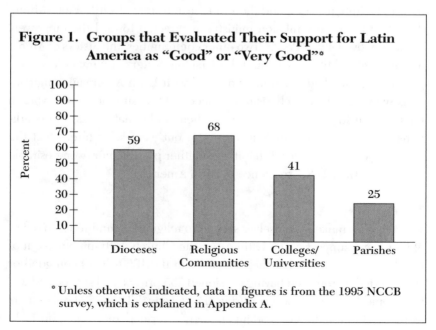

Figure 1. Groups that Evaluated Their Support for Latin America as "Good" or "Very Good"*

* Unless otherwise indicated, data in figures is from the 1995 NCCB survey, which is explained in Appendix A.

"Pope John's call awakened a burst of support, zeal and enthusiasm" among religious and their lay supporters.

With the strength of their community life and the warmth they felt for John XXIII as a backdrop, the religious of the United States genuinely welcomed the invitation to reach out to Latin America and quickly responded with personnel and resources. According to their survey responses, U.S. religious communities missioned 570 priests, 171 brothers, 1,776 sisters, and 32 lay people to Latin America during the 1960s. Those 2,547 newcomers served in a variety of settings, from establishing new individual or collaborative "missions," to helping their own already existing provinces and founding new Latin American provinces of their communities.[25]

The vast majority of the communities who described their first ministries in Latin America said that they became involved in schools, hospitals, clinics, orphanages, social work, and parish ministries—works that generally mirrored their traditional apostolates. Nevertheless, two communities reported that they assumed new types of ministry that became prototypes for much of what would develop toward the end of the decade. The Eastern Province of the Holy Cross priests and brothers reported that they left wealthy foreign plantations to begin direct involvement with the poor in Chimbote, Peru, and the Franciscan Sisters of Little Falls, Minn., described their early mission ministry as directed toward the empowerment of native laity in Peru.[26] Two other communities, the Sisters of Mercy of Farmington Hills, Mich., and the Ursuline Sisters of New Orleans, reported that they had taken in or merged with Latin American congregations who shared their charism and needed their support. Even when a mission ministry seemed to continue their traditional works, the conditions under which the religious carried it out were so different that the U.S. religious soon realized that it was neither possible nor even desirable to replicate their U.S. experience in Latin America.

The Dioceses
U.S. dioceses ranked themselves second to religious communities in terms of their early support of the Latin American Church. Fifty-nine percent of the dioceses reported that their response in the 1960s had been good or very good; they reported having missioned 255 priests, 249 sisters, and 217 lay people to Latin America during the decade.[27] Those 721 missioners were most often found working in newly formed diocesan efforts as

PAVLA volunteers or as members of the St. James Society.

Far and away, the greatest number of diocesan priests to serve in Latin America have gone under the auspices of the St. James Society; as early as 1963, 78 St. James priests had begun their mission work—and half of them were from the Archdiocese of Boston.[28] Among the earliest U.S. dioceses to establish formal and long-lasting ties with their Latin American counterparts were St. Louis in 1956; Spokane in 1961; and Cleveland, Kansas City-St. Joseph, Jefferson City, and New Ulm in 1962.[29]

The Laity

Less than half of the Catholic colleges and universities responding to the survey indicated that they had attained a good level of involvement in Latin American concerns in the 1960s. A few began exchange or volunteer programs; some began or intensified their Latin American studies offerings; and others supported the mission efforts of their sponsoring religious congregations by offering courses to prepare missionaries or beginning English as a Second Language programs at home and abroad. Nevertheless, in general, student and faculty involvement in the mission to Latin America would begin through campus cooperation with programs sponsored by dioceses or other organizations.[30] Essentially the same thing could be said for the parishes.[31]

After the publication of the papal appeal, lay organizations, some of them formed for that specific purpose, joined in the intensified outreach to Latin America. The best known of them, the Papal Volunteers for Latin America, was founded in May 1960 to encourage U.S. lay missionary activity and the development of leadership in the Latin American Church. Thus, PAVLA's charter stated the following:

> It is of paramount importance that laymen be made to understand the necessities of the Church in Latin America and the many problems involved. For the Latin American countries, when restored to the ancient vigor of their Catholic life, will become a reservoir of spiritual energy that will meet not only their own needs but those of many other parts of the world.[32]

Through the decade of the 1960s, approximately fifty dioceses participated in the program, recruiting and sponsoring almost one thousand volunteers to represent them in mission to Latin America.[33] In addition to PAVLA, many smaller lay programs developed and often met with significant success in the dual goals of increasing awareness of Latin America and helping to develop the undertapped resources of the Latin American Church. AID, the Association for International Development, founded by Gerald Mische and John S. Connor in 1957, promoted U.S. awareness of conditions in Latin America and recruited sponsors and volunteers to support economic development projects throughout the Third World.[34] The stories of the contributions make by groups like the Grail, organizations of lay women, and projects like the Jesuits' recruitment of St. Louis laity to serve in British Honduras have yet to be collected.[35] Finally, some diocesan mission teams, pioneering the concept of team ministry, included laity from the beginning, thus leading the way into new forms of shared ministry for both the United States and Latin America.[36]

All in all, the U.S. response to the appeal for Latin America implied much more than the original participants could have imagined. First, and most obviously, it required the funding and sending of personnel, lay as well as religious. And in that, the Church did admirably well. Without counting private contributions to particular mission efforts or the annual collection for the Propagation of the Faith, in recent years the national bishops' collection for the Church in Latin America has brought in up to $4.3 million annually.[37] In addition, thousands of U.S. Catholics have left home to offer their time and talents to their Latin American brothers and sisters. In 1940, there had been 489 U.S. missionaries in Latin America; in 1958, there were 1,767; and at the peak, in 1968, there were 4,589 U.S. priests, sisters, and lay people actively offering their service to the Church throughout Latin America.[38]

More important than sheer numbers, the mission implied the hidden and subtle costs of sending people into new cultures to work under new circumstances and often in a collaborative and multicultural style that they had not experienced in the United States. Traditionally apostolic communities had to develop a missionary dimension, diocesan priests who had rarely expected to serve more than two hundred miles from home were suddenly ministering in a distant and unfamiliar culture, and, as team ministries developed in the missions long before they had become in vogue at home, the ministers—priests, religious, and lay—found themselves relating both to one another and to their work in unbelievably new ways.

A Plan

Missionary Training in Language and Culture

Obviously, finding mission personnel was only the beginning. The new missionaries would need help to assimilate the shockingly new experiences that came their way.[39] The people to be sent needed language training and orientation. As director of the newly formed Latin America Bureau of the NCWC, Fr. John Considine saw adequate preparation for missionaries as one of his top priorities. The man he turned to for help was Ivan Illich, a European priest who had already favorably impressed Cardinal Spellman with his ability as an educator and his success in ministry among Puerto Ricans in New York. Considine asked Illich to choose a locale for a mission training center, and he settled on Cuernavaca, Mexico. There, in March 1961, under the academic auspices of Fordham University, and with funding from the Latin American Bureau, he opened the Center for Intercultural Formation (CIF).[40]

Illich and his program were well known, confrontational, and controversial from the start. CIF offered a four-month course that emphasized intercultural communication and spiritual formation along with intensive language study. Like similar centers in Puerto Rico, Brazil, Bolivia, and San Antonio, Tex., the idea behind the program was to prepare prospective missionaries not just to speak a language but to develop an appreciation of cultural differences and a mission spirituality open to diverse expressions of Catholicism.[41]

Rev. John Considine, MM, first director of the Bureau for Latin America. Photo: Maryknoll Missioners.

While programs like PAVLA had the organizational structure and funding to provide an intensive preparation for their personnel, many of the new missionaries, particularly the priests and religious, received little or no special formation before their arrival in a mission country.[42] For a time, that lack of training caused some tension and mistakes, but as the missionaries worked with seasoned missioners and their Latin American counterparts, they learned new skills, developed new models for pastoral reflection, and began to experience an unprecedented level of collaboration among diverse groups.

Describing not only the naive approach with which the Sisters of St. Joseph began their work in Peru, but also the tremendous advantage of inter-community collaboration, Sr. Rosemary O'Malley said,

> In 1962 . . . we were very green and our preparation was minimal. Eight of us did go to St. Louis University and took a course in global awareness—and a very little Spanish. . . . It wasn't sufficient. . . .
>
> Back in '62, if you can believe it, we didn't know the importance of spending five hours a day studying language. There were fourteen of us at the time, whether finances had anything to do with it, I don't know. . . . When I look back now, I realize that the community was overwhelmed.
>
> When we were living in Lima, a Maryknoller, Fr. Vincent Mallon, came in and he really gave us a sense of Peru, the sense of the clergy and religious . . . popular religiosity . . . the situation here . . . the poverty, the economy, all of that. That was probably the best introduction that we had.
>
> Maryknoll did a great job in orienting the new people. The sisters as well—Sr. Barbara, a Maryknoll sister, was principal at St. Rose of Lima grade school in Lima. At any moment we could call and go and observe the classes. They reached out in any way that they could. . . .
>
> The Immaculate Heart of Mary Sisters from Philadelphia who were at Villa Maria in Lima were very good too. . . . [Their] service was to reach out to every religious that ever hit Lima.[43]

The mutual help, communal reflection among both foreigners and nationals, and solidarity with which the new arrivals began their missions introduced them to a pattern that would extend beyond the boundaries of nationality and become a cherished characteristic of their Latin American experience. That sort of collaboration not only helped to involve the U.S. missionaries in the communal spirit that dominated Latin American culture, but became the mode through which they participated in the radical changes that characterized the end of the 1960s.

A New Era Engenders New Approaches

The Ecclesiology and Missiology of Vatican II

The mission surge to Latin America came just as Catholicism entered into the dramatic period of renewal begun by Vatican II. The council transformed the self-concept of the Church and reemphasized long-dormant dimensions of its theology in both theory and practice. Whereas Catholics in recent centuries had held a predominantly institutional-hierarchical ecclesiology, Vatican II accentuated the dynamic character of the Church as People of God. Moreover, it called ordinary Catholics to assume the mission of being a sacrament for the world.[44] All across the world, the People of God heard the same poetic and prophetic challenges put before them:

> The joy and hope, the grief and anguish of the people of our time, especially of those who are poor or afflicted in any way, are the joy and hope, the grief and anguish of the followers of Christ as well. Nothing that is genuinely human fails to find an echo in their hearts. . . . That is why Christians cherish a feeling of deep solidarity with the human race and its history.[45]

In calling the People of God to an all-embracing human solidarity, the council underlined the importance of being deeply involved in the events of history. Vatican II reminded all the faithful of their vocation to know the world, to interpret human events, and to offer concrete responses to the world's questions and hopes:

> At all times the Church carries the responsibility of reading the signs of the times and of interpreting them in the light of the Gospel, if it is to carry out its task. In language intelligible to every generation, she should be able to answer the ever recurring questions which men ask about the meaning of this present life and of the life to come, and how one is related to the other. We must be aware of and understand the aspirations, yearnings, and the often dramatic features of the world in which we live.[46]

Insisting that missionary activity is essential to the very nature of the Church, the Decree on Missionary Activity, *Ad Gentes*, underlined the primacy of the value of witness and dialogue:

> All Christians by the example of their lives and the witness of the word, wherever they live, have an obligation to manifest the new man which they put on in baptism, and to reveal the power of the Holy Spirit by whom they were strengthened at confirmation, so that others, seeing their good works, might glorify the Father and more perfectly perceive the true meaning of human life and the universal solidarity of mankind. In order to bear witness to Christ fruitfully, they should establish relationships of respect and love . . . should be familiar with . . . national and religious traditions and uncover with gladness and respect those seeds of the Word which lie hidden among them. They must look for the profound transformation which is taking place among nations and work hard so that modern man is not turned away from the things of God by an excessive preoccupation with modern science and technology, but rather aroused to desire, even more intensely, that love and truth which have been revealed by God. Just as Christ penetrated to the hearts of men and by a truly human dialogue led them to the divine light, so too his disciples, profoundly pervaded by the Spirit of Christ, should know and converse with those among whom they live so that these men might learn of the riches which a generous God has distributed among the nations.[47]

As Vatican II urged Catholics to become ever more creatively involved in the world, it also called individuals and nations to the mutual relationships that would strengthen them as members of the one body:

> In virtue of its catholicity each part [of the Church] contributes its own gifts to other parts and to the whole Church, so that the whole and each of the parts are strengthened by the common sharing of all things and by the common effort to attain to fullness of unity. . . . Finally, between all the various parts of the Church there is a bond of close communion whereby spiritual riches, apostolic works, and temporal resources are shared.[48]

These texts undergird a renewed theology of mission. According to the teaching of Vatican II, an appreciation for and sharing of everything that is truly human is the basis of the deep solidarity possible among all peoples. At the same time, to adequately preach the truth about Jesus Christ, the Church must read the signs of the times; it is part of the Church's vocation to analyze and direct contemporary movements in the light of the Gospel. Reiterating the teaching that the whole Church is missionary, Vatican II not only calls religious and laity into "foreign missions," but tells Christians that they are called to be missionaries wherever they find themselves and reminds them that dialogue, not one-sided proclamation, is the mode through which disciples of Jesus carry out their vocation. Finally, while the council did underline the unique identity of local, national, and regional Churches, it also taught clearly that no single unit was sufficient unto itself; each needed the strengths of the rest. This turn to the world, responsibility for history, and missionary vocation to build solidarity were

Rev. Albert Nevins. Photo: Maryknoll Missioners.

not new, but Vatican II gave them an emphasis and a centrality they had not enjoyed for centuries. These theological emphases were going to shape the development of the theology of mission and the spirituality undergirding missionary practice.

A New Mission Reality

In 1965, Maryknoll's Fr. Albert Nevins wrote that he was seeing the "End of an Era" in the missions.[49] His point was that traditional missions, what he called "the orderly, simple and uncomplicated life that . . . missioners once knew" had disappeared. Missioners were, he said, "caught up in a social, political and technological revolution that undermines the very foundations of their vocations and which challenges the existence of the Church itself." Perhaps the most startling aspect of Nevins's article was that he placed responsibility for the upheaval in mission not on communism, materialism, and paganism, the traditional enemies of faith, but rather on the approach taken by the missionaries themselves:

> They did not know it, but among the things that [the missioners] took with them was a heritage which held within it the seeds of their defeat. They were proud of their own cultures and wanted others to be as blessed, and so they Francized or Anglicized or Gaelicized the people among whom they worked. They built little islands of their homelands on the outposts of the world. Without meaning to, they patronized those among whom they had come to work.[50]

Although the examples in his article came from Africa, Nevins was describing precisely the situation in which many missioners to Latin America were finding themselves. In fact, a few years later CELAM convened its first meeting on missionary pastoral work and restated Nevins's critique in slightly more theoretical terms:

> Many missionaries are pained to see that the Church sometimes appears excessively weighted down with the sociocultural patrimony of the Western world—both in the formulation of her dogmas and in her institutions and discipline. The concepts and formulations of her preaching and catechesis generally follow the mental and philosophical frames of the Greco-Latin world. Her sacramental discipline and her liturgical forms, despite the reform process under way, still basically preserve structures that correspond to a different ecclesial environment and a different culture. The uniform formation, life-style, and bearing of her ministers do not take adequate account of the distinctive social configuration of different communities, and this poses obstacles to the fostering of native vocations. Thus the normal development of these communities is impeded.[51]

According to both Nevins and the Latin American bishops, the crusade outlined by Msgr. Casaroli in 1961, designed to combat the dangers of Protestantism, Communism, and spiritism, was not turning out as the missioners

Sharing Faith Across the Hemisphere

had expected. A major problem, whether in Africa or Arica, Peru, was that in their generous attempts to help, the missionaries were often involved in unconscious practices of cultural insensitivity and/or paternalism.[52]

Msgr. Sandheinrich, director of the St. Louis office for the Propagation of the Faith, described the learning process that the St. Louis archdiocesan missioners went through in their early years in Bolivia:

> When we began, we worked with the Sisters of the Precious Blood from O'Fallon. They ran a school. Then they saw that they were trying to relocate the St. Louis church in Bolivia and they handed the school over to *"Fe y Alegría"* and began to do social service in the parishes.[53]

Many missioners in the 1960s had gotten caught in the same trap that snared their sixteenth-century counterparts: they had not learned to differentiate sufficiently between the core of faith and its cultural expressions. The difference was that in the late-twentieth century, critiques of mission methods were becoming more insistent and, under the influence of Vatican II's call to renewal, the Church was giving them very serious attention.

Evaluation of the Mission Effort

The Critique
From the beginning, educating the Church in the United States about Latin America and its various cultures was one of the major goals of the Latin American Bureau of the NCWC. CICOP, the Catholic Inter-American Cooperation Program, became the centerpiece of that educational effort. In a series of annual meetings between 1964 and 1973, the national CICOP gatherings brought Latin American church leaders and theologians together with their U.S. counterparts for a few days of intensive encounter, debate, and, most of all, consciousness raising. Inevitably controversial, the CICOP conferences provided a forum for new ideas in missiology and for serious critiques, not only of U.S. mission practices, but also of the objectives and results of U.S. government projects and policies in Latin America.[54]

When it came to offering a critique of mission practices, no one could outshine Msgr. Ivan Illich. In 1967, on the eve of the annual CICOP meeting, he published the best remembered attack of his career, an article entitled "The Seamy Side of Charity."[55] True to his reputation for conflictive techniques, Illich garnered into this one article "all the ideological missiles he had been launching for a decade."[56] In spite of all the publicity, Illich's message was not news, it was merely a strident repetition of critiques that had already been discussed by missionaries themselves and by bishops from both the United States and Latin America.

At a 1966 CELAM meeting at Mar del Plata, Argentina, Dom Helder Cámara had evaluated Latin America's missionary receiving experience. Cámara's constructively critical approach can be summed up by his statement that "he who hides the truth is no friend. Neither is he who blurts out the truth without any heartfelt concern for proper remedies and the opportune moment."[57] With that characteristic combination of integrity and gentleness, Cámara pointed out the weaknesses of mission efforts and offered positive suggestions for improvement.

Without a doubt, many missionaries had gone to Latin America with more zeal than preparation. As a result, too often they lacked the adequate tools for a deep understanding of the cultures in which they were ministering. In relation to that, the very generosity that impelled them could also be expressed or interpreted as an attitude of cultural superiority. Recognizing that these weaknesses were not new, nor even solely a problem of "foreigners," Cámara used the problems to set a humble and ambitious pastoral agenda:

> The church cannot allow the authentic values of our culture, which she helped to create, to be deprecated and ground under. . . . Even more importantly, she is obliged to condemn the collective sin of unjust and anachronistic structures—not as if she were some innocent outside observer but fully acknowledging her own share of responsibility and guilt. She must be courageous enough to admit her solidarity with the past and to acknowledge her responsibility to the present and the future.[58]

Then, emphasizing the fact that a recognition of weakness is not a condemnation but an invitation to grace and conversion, he said,

> Whatever the course of past history may have been, the Church today is truly present to our developing Latin America. The human aspects of

this society in crisis call for her attention, and a decisive effort to help the continent achieve its liberation from underdevelopment.[59]

Thus, through admitting past mistakes and emphasizing the importance of genuine respect for cultures, Cámara plotted a future direction for pastoral ministers in Latin America, whether foreign or native.

Along with deficiency in cultural understanding, another major criticism of mission practices was that when missionaries gave material aid— whether it came from church or governmental sources—the assistance could have the double effect of creating dependence in the receivers while simultaneously salving the conscience of the givers. Cámara again turned critique into pastoral agenda by proposing that aid should be carefully used and understood, not as a solution, but as a doorway to the conscience of affluent donors. He said,

Another delicate question with both positive and dubious aspects is *the surplus food that is sent to us from affluent nations*. There can and must be improvements in the way it is offered to us, and alterations in the propaganda that is now attached to it.

We realize the necessity of taking due account of those who aid us, and of the propaganda element involved in this aid. Clearly the food-stuffs offered must be production surpluses (in terms of the national economy of the donor nation), and they must not compete with the local products of the receiver nation.

Given the growing rate of hunger, the underdeveloped world cannot indulge in the luxury of rejecting the food-stuffs sent to it. We will accept

Archbishop Helder Cámara. Photo: CELAM Archives.

them. But in so doing, we shall point out in a friendly and fraternal way that they are *surpluses* after all. We shall do this delicately, of course, but in such a way that the donors do not feel they have discharged their obligations to conscience or that the problem of justice has been resolved.[60]

He took a similar approach to the problem created by the fact that many volunteers had been sent to the missions without a clear task or the most needed skills. In this case, Cámara suggested that Latin America could provide an educational experience which those volunteers could fruitfully apply when they returned to their home country:

Another issue is the *pros and cons of accepting volunteer workers from foreign countries.* When an affluent country wishes to give us more than money, when it offers us its experts and its young volunteers, we would be ungrateful and discourteous not to accept them. . . .

So let us welcome the volunteers, without giving way to mistrust or fears of dangerous infiltration. If we have had some experience with these volunteers . . . we know that they often lack experience and proper acculturation even though their preparatory training is better than it used to be. But we also know that they evince generosity and a capacity for self-sacrifice. A problem is often created when these volunteers return to their own country, for the impact of the substandard conditions they have seen often has revolutionary implications. So we shall accept these volunteers, at the same time letting them know in a nice way that their presence does not get at the root of the matter.[61]

Whereas radicals like Illich were calling for a moratorium on all mission-sending activity from the First World to Latin America, Cámara suggested the following:

The churches of Europe and the United States could set a good example. Improvements in the objectives and methods of international cooperation, which is being provided in a dedicated way, could have positive repercussions on the whole problem of relations between the developed and underdeveloped worlds. The idea would be to discover the most appropriate way to contribute to development in close

Sharing Faith Across the Hemisphere

collaboration with national organisms. Evaluation of proper aid priorities should be made by national groups that are in closer contact with the real situation and that are working for human betterment.[62]

According to Dom Helder, Latin Americans themselves bore the responsibility to "explore our own problems and work out our own solutions" so that all international aid could be "truly integrated into the overall framework required by international justice."[63] Where Illich seemed to be saying, "It didn't work, so go home," Cámara offered a much more profound challenge. By saying in effect, "Come, and stay to learn *from and with us,*" Cámara was inviting the missionary Church to join Latin America in a movement of graced conversion.

Response to the Critique

Whether the missionaries and their supporters were hearing the radicals or Dom Helder, the truth in the critiques was hard. Without a doubt, U.S. missionaries had brought a variety of gifts to the mission experience. No one could deny that their pragmatism had contributed to make pastoral planning more effective, vital, and concrete. They worked indefatigably to foster local vocations and brought special organizing skills to every field they entered. Nevertheless, criticisms of mission efforts addressed crucial issues. In reality, weaknesses in preparation and mission practices had created a situation which, as Fr. Nevins said, undermined the vocation of the missioners. In spite of good intentions, they had made serious mistakes. They had too often failed to recognize and appreciate Latin American cultural values; in many cases neither their personal nor financial generosity had been well enough directed to make a significant impact on the existing problems; and they were typically neophytes when it came to understanding political and economic systems.[64] Some of the missionaries came to the conclusion that it had all been a misguided effort.

Among these, a significant number, like their brothers and sisters in the United States, left the priesthood or religious life. Others left mission work and returned home.[65] Those who stayed, and those who continued to come after them, could not afford to ignore either the critique or the invitation to conversion. Individually and collectively they entered into a new, serious, and ongoing process of theological reflection to renovate their mission theology and practice.

Growth of Theological Reflection

The theoretical tools for a renewed theological reflection were close at hand. In addition to the documents of Vatican II, papal encyclicals like *Mater et Magistra, Pacem in Terris,* and *Populorum Progressio* offered the theological background for a revitalized pastoral approach to the Church of Latin America.

Throughout his pontificate, Pope John XXIII had tried to encourage and give direction to the First World's response to the needs of the Third World. In 1963, writing *Pacem in Terris,* he made the same points as did Dom Helder in regard to donors' responsibility to respect and foster the self-determination of receiving cultures:

> It is never sufficiently repeated that [international] cooperation . . . should be effected with the greatest respect for the liberty of the countries being developed, for these must realize that they are . . . the principal artisans in the promotion of their own economic development and social progress. . . .
>
> It is vitally important, therefore, that the wealthier states, in providing varied forms of assistance to the poorer, should respect the moral values and ethnic characteristics peculiar to each, and also that they should avoid any intention of political domination.[66]

Underneath problems of justice and development, there seemed to be a problem of faith. Speaking equally to the First and the Third World nations, Pope John lamented a widespread breach between the religious faith and professional work of Christians:

> It is clear that today, in traditionally Christian nations, secular institutions, although demonstrating a high degree of scientific and technical perfection, and efficiency in achieving their respective ends, not infrequently are but slightly affected by Christian motivation or inspiration. . . .
>
> How does one explain this? It is our opinion that the explanation is to be found in an inconsistency in their minds between religious belief and their action in the temporal sphere. It is necessary, therefore, that their interior unity be re-established, and that in their temporal activity Faith should be present as a beacon to give light, and Charity as a force to give life.[67]

According to Pope John, international relations, particularly among Christians, needed to be increasingly marked by the mutual respect that could only flow from shedding the light of faith on the whole of life. Pope Paul VI built upon John's message and strengthened his teaching about Christian responsibility to the poor. In his 1967 encyclical *Populorum Progressio*, he wrote:

> The development of peoples has the Church's close attention, particularly the development of those peoples who are striving to escape from hunger, misery, endemic diseases and ignorance; of those who are looking for a wider share in the benefits of civilization and a more active improvement of their human qualities. . . . Solidarity in action at this turning point in human history is a matter of urgency. . . .
>
> Today the peoples in hunger are making a dramatic appeal to the peoples blessed with abundance. The Church shudders at this cry of anguish and calls each one to give a loving response of charity to this brother's cry for help.[68]

The theoretical teaching of the popes and the council was clear. Solidarity among nations, and particularly between the rich and poor, was a Christian responsibility that had to be carried out in a spirit of profound mutual respect, free from all attempts of manipulation. John XXIII called the Church to repair the modern rift between spirituality and temporal activity so that faith would guide the actions of persons, institutions, and nations. Finally, Paul VI made it clear that the cries of the poor were those that made the most urgent demands on the Church.

Although applying that theory was the task of the People of God in each particular locale, in *Mater et Magistra*, John XXIII proposed a methodology designed to ensure the union of faith and life. The methodology he recommended was a serious examination of the actual situation, an evaluation of it in the light of the Gospel, and finally, a decision or planning process "in order that the traditional norms may be adapted to circumstances of time and place."[69]

This process of analysis-reflection-planning mirrored the "see, judge, act" methodology of Catholic Action groups, a methodology that would eventually be promoted by liberation theologians. Applicable to everyone from the simple people who formed basic Christian communities to more sophisticated groups of students, intellectuals, and pastoral workers, the core of the method was that it began with a serious examination of the most pressing problems of a given situation. Only after the problems had been seriously analyzed could solutions be proposed, and those solutions would be characterized by the fact that, directed by the light of the Gospel, they responded, not to symptoms, but to what Dom Helder called the "root" of the problems.[70] This approach to theological reflection and pastoral planning, following the approach and the mandates of *Gaudium et Spes*, eventually incorporated people from every level of the Latin American Church in a process of renewal that would continue for decades to come.

When they did this type of reflection and planning together with other pastoral workers and ordinary people from their host nations, the missionaries entered into the type of collaboration that the popes and Dom Helder Cámara had been promoting. Through that sort of shared reflection and planning, they helped build up the Church that had been symbolized by Our Lady of Guadalupe and envisioned by Guaman Poma and Bartolomé de Las Casas.

The revolution of the 1960s did not end with the close of the decade. As a matter of fact, many would say that it only began in 1968. That was the year when the Latin American bishops met at Medellín, Colombia, for their Second General Assembly, which focused on "The Church in the Present-Day Transformation of Latin America in the Light of the Council." The title was long, the resulting document was comparatively short, and the results would be genuinely transformative.

DISCUSSION QUESTIONS

1. In the 1960s the Church in the United States seemed uniquely prepared to respond to Pope John XXIII's request to reach out to Latin America. What combination of factors in Latin America and in the United States allowed for such a sudden growth in mission activity? In what ways is the Church today more or less prepared for such a challenge than it was in the 1960s?

2. Some of the mission efforts of the 1960s prospered while others did not. What can be learned from both those that grew and developed and those that seemingly died out?

3. In *Mater et Magistra,* Pope John XXIII espoused a method for theological reflection and pastoral planning that included a serious examination of a given situation, an evaluation of it in the light of the Gospel, and a concrete pastoral strategy designed to bring a Christian remedy to urgent needs. Is that method still valid for pastoral planning? In your experience, what step is most often overlooked?

4. As U.S. missioners to Latin America responded with enthusiasm and generosity, they also discovered that they had much to learn about cross-cultural evangelization. As more U.S. Catholics become involved in outreach to Latin America, what can they learn from that previous mission experience and how might that change their current outreach? To what degree might authentic dialogue between the sending and receiving communities have been a factor contributing to the growth or decline of the mission efforts?

Notes

1. The full text of the talk can be found as an appendix in Gerald M. Costello, *Mission to Latin America: The Successes and Failures of a Twentieth Century Crusade* (New York: Orbis, 1979).

2. See Robert S. Pelton, CSC, "Vatican II and Latin America: An Example of Inter-Regional Church Cooperation" in *International Papers in Pastoral Ministry* (Notre Dame, Ind.: Helen Kellogg Institute for International Studies, 1996), VII:1.

3. See Costello, 47, 90; and Edward L. Cleary, *Crisis and Change, The Church in Latin America Today* (New York: Orbis, 1984), 9. For further information on the history of U.S. mission activity, see Angelyn Dries, OSF, *U.S. Catholic Mission History,* to be published in 1997 by Orbis Press.

4. See Marina Herrera, "The Context and Development of Hispanic Ecclesial Leadership" in *Hispanic Catholic Culture in the U.S.: Issues and Concerns*, eds. Jay P. Dolan and Allan Figueroa Deck, SJ (Notre Dame, Ind.: University of Notre Dame Press, 1994), 180.

5. Over the years, FERES became increasingly international, with additional affiliated research centers in Latin America as well as in Europe. See Considine, *The Church in the New Latin America* (Notre Dame, Ind.: Fides Publishers, Inc., 1964), 38, 52; and Cleary, 27-28.

6. See Francois Houtart, *The Church and the Latin American Revolution* (New York: Sheed and Ward, 1965), 44-45.

7. Houtart notes that those urban populations formed a very heterogeneous social group. Whereas the upper classes had generally received a similar "classic" education, village people tended to retain traditions that were local and unique. Ibid., 59.

8. Joseph B. Gremillion used this and other citations to Barbara Ward's work in a talk reprinted in *The Christian Challenge in Latin America* (New York: Catholic Foreign Mission Society of America, 1964), 13.

9. Juan Luis Segundo analyzes this process in *The Hidden Motives of Pastoral Action* (New York: Orbis, 1978).

10. Houtart (154-57) makes the point that many of these priests were missionaries, primarily from Spain and Italy, but also from other European countries and the United States. Two years later, another statistical study stated that there were 37,842 priests in Latin America, or one to every 4,700 Catholics. That figure compared to a ratio of one for every 835 Catholics in the United States. See Considine, *The Church in the New Latin America*, 91.

11. According to a review of Gary McEoin's book *Latin America: The Eleventh Hour*, the percentage of Latin American "practicing" Catholics was between 15 and 30 percent. It is important to note that the designation "practicing" was based on a perspective that measured active practice through regular reception of the sacraments and participation in a parish or other forms of institutional church life. Naturally, this definition is lacking, wherein it does not consider the profound integration of faith found in cultural and familial life in the region. See *The Catholic World* 96 (Nov. 1962): 119.

12. This evaluation was made by Catholic actionists representing twenty Latin American countries at a meeting held in Chimbote, Peru. The two-pronged task of the delegates at that meeting was to conduct a self-study of the Church in Latin America and, on the basis of that, to plan a more modern and efficacious lay apostolate. The documents produced at that meeting served as a basis for the next two Latin American Catholic Action conventions. See William Coleman, MM, *Latin American Catholicism: A Self Evaluation* (Maryknoll, N.Y.: World Horizon Reports, 1954), 21.

13. In later years, pastoral workers learned to view indigenous expressions of religiosity and spirituality with greater understanding and respect. See the Puebla documents on the topic of popular religiosity.

14. Coleman, 28.

15. Houtart, 154.

16. For a thorough Latin American assessment of the missionary structures of the Church in Latin America, see the final document of the CELAM meeting on missionary pastoral work, held in Melgar, Colombia, April 20-27, 1968. The document is translated in *Between Honesty and Hope* (New York: Maryknoll Publications, 1970), 97-112, especially the section entitled "Training Ministers and Shaping Pastoral Structures" (109-11).

17. "Statement on the Ecumenical Council," Aug. 19, 1962, nos. 10-13, *Pastoral Letters of the United States Catholic Bishops* (Washington, D.C.: United States Catholic Conference, 1983), III:11-16.

18. Fulgencio Batista, the dictator Castro ousted, had governed the country from 1933 to 1944, and then again more brutally from 1952 until his overthrow in 1959.

19. The statistics are from a report made by the Cuban bishops to the 1955 meeting of Latin American bishops at Rio de Janeiro. According to the same report, approximately 30 percent of the sisters and 19 percent of the priests were Cuban by birth. Two communities of brothers, the Christian Brothers and the Marists, had novitiates on the island with a total of seventeen candidates preparing for ministry. See Raúl Goméz Treto, *The Church and Socialism in Cuba* (New York: Orbis, 1988), 10-12.

20. Just after Castro's victory, *Time* magazine wrote: "The face of dictatorship in Cuba was the padlock on Havana University, the bodies dumped on street corners . . . the arrogant functionaries gathering fortunes from gambling, prostitution and a leaky public till. In disgust and shame, a nearby band of rural guerrillas, aided by angry Havana professional men . . . started a bloody civil war. . . . Last week they smashed General Fulgencio Batista's dictatorship" (*Time* 73 [Jan. 12, 1959]: 32).

21. See Jedin, *History of the Church*, X:723-727 and articles in *America* 105 (May 13, 1961): 264 and (Sept. 30, 1961): 814. While a careful reading of the sources reveals some discrepancy in the reported numbers of clergy and religious, all the reports coincide in reporting a calamitous decline in the numbers of clergy and religious able to remain in active ministry following the events of 1961.

22. John Leslay, "Fresh Look at Cuba" *America* 106 (Oct. 28, 1961): 115-17.

23. Leslie Dewart, "The Church in Cuba: A Universal Dilemma," *Commonweal* 79 (Oct. 11, 1963): 67.

24. The survey, which will hereafter be referred to as the NCCB survey, is described and summarized in appendix A.

25. The data reported in the surveys do not always coincide with the statistics published by the U.S. Catholic Mission Association. In addition to the fact that not every congregation responded to the survey, congregations that were active in Latin America sometimes considered such ministry as a part of the regular apostolate of the congregation or one of its provinces rather than specifically "missionary" activity. Some of the survey statistics are therefore more valuable as indicators of perceived involvement rather than as absolute numbers. See appendix A for an explanation of the survey and its results.

26. Unless another source is cited, the individual information reported comes from the narrative responses on the NCCB survey. Particular communities are mentioned only when the text refers to their particular experience.

27. The numbers listed by decades come from the diocesan surveys and are limited to those diocese that responded. Although precise statistics may not exist, the annual *Catholic Almanac* (St. Anthony Messenger Press) published annual statistics and is the best available source for comparatives figures.

28. Costello, 58.

29. The list, compiled from the survey responses, includes only the dioceses that indicated that they began a mission relationship in the very early 1960s that continued through 1995. All told, eighty-five dioceses reported having sent priests to Latin America during the thirty-five years covered by the survey. Numerous dioceses have had shorter-term projects in Latin American dioceses.

30. According to the 1966 *Catholic Almanac*, Fr. Louis Colonnese sponsored one such program when he organized 270 students from 47 colleges to do summer work in Mexico.

31. The parish surveys reported very little in the narrative sections reflecting the 1960s. Those that did offer information generally said that they supported the collections, diocesan missions, or the missions of priests or religious related to the parish.

32. From the PAVLA charter as quoted in Costello, 89.

33. Although many of its volunteers had very successful and rewarding experiences and some later joined other missionary programs or continued to serve Latin America through ministries in the United States, the PAVLA program closed at the end of the 1960s. According to Fr. Frederick McGuire, Considine's successor in the Latin American Bureau, one of PAVLA's weaknesses was that John Considine's key criteria that volunteers be placed to fulfill specific requests from Latin America was not consistently put into practice; thus some of the recruits went to Latin America without a clear task or the necessary skills to serve the needs they encountered. See Costello, 89-102.

34. Costello, 85. See also Gerald Mische, "Aid Goes to Latin America" in *America* 107 (May 26, 1962): 298-330; and "Aid Means Service" in *America* 113 (Aug. 28, 1965): 197-98.

35. According to Msgr. Bernard Sandheinrich, director of the Society for the Propagation of the Faith in St. Louis, in an effort to give local teachers the opportunity to study in the United States, the diocese recruited volunteers from local colleges and universities to teach in Jesuit schools in British Honduras (later Belize) while the teachers came to the United States.

36. Fr. Denis St. Marie, the first Cleveland missioner to go to El Salvador, commented that one of the strongest features of the Cleveland mission is that it included lay people from the very beginning. Ms. Rosemary Smith, a community organizer, formed part of the first Cleveland mission team. The Chicago diocesan program in the parish of San Miguelito in Panama also served for many years as a model for lay involvement. Under the leadership of Fr. Leo Mahon, a group of Hispanic laymen from Chicago, *Los Hermanos de la Familia de Dios*, were pioneers in the development of lay missionaries.

37. The million dollar figure refers only to the special collection for Latin America that began in 1966. A more accurate figure would include previous donations from the U.S. bishops as well as such collections as those for the Society for the Propagation of the Faith, diocesan missions, the Mission Co-op program, and the support given to individual missionaries and religious congregations.

38. These figures are based on information from annual editions of *The Catholic Almanac*.

39. According to Sr. Karen Kennelly, "Initial culture shock centered around the educational and health care ministries undertaken by the women, and the conditions of extreme poverty and ways of expressing religious belief they encountered among the people" (Karen Kennelly, CSJ, "Foreign Missions and the Renewal Movement," *Review for Religious* [May-June, 1990]: 454).

40. CIF eventually changed its name to CIDOC, the Center of Intercultural Documentation. See Costello, 105-9, and Joseph P. Fitzpatrick, "Training Center at Cuernavaca" in *America* 106 (Feb. 24, 1962): 678-80.

41. Illich had previously helped form the center at Ponce, Puerto Rico, which was connected with The Catholic University. The center at Anapolis, Brazil, was effectively the Portuguese-language division of Cuernavaca. The Instituto de Idiomas in Cochabamba, Bolivia, founded by Maryknoll in 1965, had a similar focus on language and culture studies. Like the programs offered in Latin America, for many years, the Secretariat for Latin America sponsored a mission-training program in conjunction with the programs offered at the Mexican-American Cultural Center in San Antonio, Tex. Religious communities and educational institutions founded other centers, large and small, such as the St. James Society's language school in Lima.

42. In the early 1960s, a frequent, naive assumption was that priests and religious were prepared for the missions by the training they had received in the seminary and novitiate. Preparing the laity received more attention because of the newness of their role and the diversity of their backgrounds. According to Rev. Joseph Fitzpatrick, formation for Latin America should include an understanding of the nature of culture, skills for intercultural communication, spiritual formation, and an understanding of the deep religious spirit of the indigenous people. In spite of that list, he could still say, "The religious is backed up by years of training for teamwork . . . lives in community . . . and the rule provides a familiar and well-tried life that supports him wherever he goes." Religious would soon learn that they needed as much orientation and preparation as their lay counterparts. See Fitzpatrick, "Training Center."

43. Sr. Rosemary O'Malley, CSJ, who served in Peru from 1962 to 1977, currently works in Los Angeles with the Columban Fathers' Global Education program.

44. These are major themes in *Lumen Gentium*, which specifically states, "The Church . . . is in the nature of sacrament—a sign and instrument of communion with God and of unity of all people" (no. 1). It goes on to say, "The faithful are appointed by their baptismal character . . . they must profess . . . the faith they have received from God . . . [they are] strictly obliged to spread the faith by word and deed" (no. 11).

45. *Gaudium et Spes*, no. 1.

46. *Gaudium et Spes*, no. 4.

47. *Ad Gentes*, no. 11.

48. *Lumen Gentium*, no. 13.

49. See Albert Nevins, "End of an Era: The Missions Reappraised," *The Critic* (March 1965): 32-37.

50. Ibid., 34.

51. See the "Final Document" of the CELAM meeting on missionary pastoral work, *Between Honesty and Hope*, 98.

52. As the first Maryknoll missioners prepared to leave for Latin America, Bishop James E. Walsh, the Maryknoll superior general, alerted them to the dangerous potential of such attitudes. In his departure ceremony homily, later published in *Maryknoll Magazine* (May 1942), Bishop Walsh said,

> We are going to South America as missioners, but we are not going as exponents of any so-called North American civilization. We will endeavor to preach the Catholic Faith in areas where priests are scarce and mission work is needed; but, as regards the elements of true civilization, we expect to receive as much as we have to give.

53. *Fe y Alegria* is a school project begun by the Jesuits that demands high involvement and personal investment on the part of the parents of the students. Beginning as a local phenomenon, it has grown throughout the Latin American continent.

54. The full history of CICOP remains to be written. More information can be found in Costello.

55. See *America* 116:88-91. *America* took pains to indicate that Illich's article appeared in a column that was "an occasional feature that offers an outlet for varied opinions" and that the "thoughts expressed do not necessarily represent the opinions of the editors."

56. See Joseph P. Fitzpatrick's response to Illich, "What Is He Getting At?" *America* 116:444-49. Considine, 127-36, reports that the publication of the article infuriated Cardinal Cushing, who denounced it in the opening address of the CICOP conference.

57. Helder Cámara, "The Church and Modern Latin America," *Between Honesty and Hope* (New York: Maryknoll Publications, 1970), 33.

58. Ibid., 31.

59. Ibid.

60. Ibid., 37. Through the years, church groups have distributed material aid that has come from church, government, and nonprofit sources. Such aid has literally saved many lives and contributed to genuine development. Cámara's critique points out, however, that such aid does not resolve underlying problems of international injustice.

61. Ibid.

62. Ibid., 37-38.

63. Ibid., 38.

64. According to Jeffrey Klaiber, a professor at the Catholic University in Lima and a specialist in Peruvian history,

> Many of the missionaries were ignorant about the larger social and political situation in Latin America. Almost all of them came in the context of the Cold war. . . . Many . . . arrived . . . with the idea of preaching the Gospel and com-

bating communism at the same time. Convinced of the material superiority of Europe and the United States over against Latin America, and strengthened by the vigor of Catholicism in their own countries, some of the newcomers didn't bother to deepen their contact with the Peruvian reality. Instead they limited themselves to studying Spanish and assimilating a few facts found in tourist guidebooks.

See Jeffrey Klaiber, SJ, *La Iglesia En El Perú* (Lima: Pontifícia Universidad Católica del Perú, 1988), 370-71.

65. Those who left mission work should not be confused with those whose original commitment was made for a limited time; many fulfilled that commitment and were often replaced by others who took up where their predecessors had left off. Nevertheless, there was a general decline in the numbers serving in the missions after the surge of the 1960s. The number of U.S. personnel working in Latin America reached its peak in 1968 with a total of 4,589. In 1970, that number had dropped by 704 for a total of 3,885. It must also be remembered that this was a time of great loss of priests and religious in the United States as well. Between 1967 and 1970, the number of diocesan priests in the United States fell from 59,892 to 59,192; the number of religious women from 176,671 to 160,931, and the number of religious brothers from 12,539 to 11,623. (Statistics from the *Catholic Almanac*.) Many of those who had served in the missions returned to the United States as "reverse missionaries" with zeal to proclaim the gospel message in the United States enriched by the experience of ministry in the Latin American Church. Many of them continued to work on behalf of the Church in Latin America through organizations and activities at home.

66. *Pacem in Terris*, nos. 123, 125.

67. *Pacem in Terris*, nos. 151-52.

68. *Populorum Progressio*, nos. 1, 3.

69. *Mater et Magistra*, no. 236.

70. Included among the groups that used this basic methodology were not only Catholic Action organizations and the basic Christian communities, but also new groups such as ONIS (an informal organization of priests in Peru); CLAR, the Latin American Conference of Religious; and many congregations, dioceses, and parish organizations. One of the first official Latin American church events to use the methodology was the 1967 and 1968 Archdiocesan Synod in Santiago, Chile, under the leadership of Cardinal Raúl Silva. See Klaiber for additional information on ONIS and CLAR.

Medellín Heralds
a Renewed
Vision of Mission

August 24, 1968, Address of Pope Paul VI to the Latin American Bishops' Conference

When Pope Paul VI addressed the bishops assembled for the Medellín Conference, he carefully underscored the historic and theological import of the occasion. Looking toward a future that would demand heroic efforts on behalf of the gospel message, he called the Latin American Church to a thoroughly renewed pastoral activity capable of responding to the signs of the times.

> The first visit of the Pope in person on Latin American soil is cer-
> tainly not merely a simple and unusual fact of the news. It is a fact of
> history which becomes a part of the long evangelization of these im-
> mense territories. It recognizes, confirms and extols this evangeliza-
> tion while at the same time concluding its first centuries-old phase.
> Another period of ecclesiastical life is here today inaugurated by this

same visit. This hour seems to be, by Divine Providence, conclusive and decisive.

The labor already accomplished declares its own limitations, makes evident new necessities, demands something new and something great. The future calls for effort, daring and sacrifice which introduce a deep anxiety into the Church. We are in a moment of total deliberation.

The world watches us today in a particular way with regard to poverty, to simplicity of life. The angels watch us in the transparent purity of our only love of Christ. And the Church watches us with regard to the communion which makes us a unity. Blessed be this our tormented and paradoxical time, which almost obliges us to the sanctity corresponding to our office.

Speak, speak, preach, write, take a position, as is said, in harmony of plan and intention for the defense and elucidation of the truths of the faith, on the actuality of the Gospel, on the questions which interest the life of the faithful and the defense of Christian morality, on the drama, now great and beautiful, now sad and dangerous, of contemporary civilization.

We are not technicians, but we are shepherds, who must foster the well-being of their faithful and encourage the efforts for renewal taking place in the countries where our respective mission is being accomplished.

We will promote the profound and far-sighted transformation of which society has need. We will promote it by loving more earnestly and teaching others to love with energy, wisdom, perseverance, practical activity, trust in men and reliance on the fatherly aid of God and the innate power of good. The poor will welcome gladly the good tidings.

Faithful to the pope's vision and exhortation, the pastoral priorities set at Medellín would courageously address the signs of the times. Through a particular emphasis on the evangelization and integral well-being of the poor, the Church of Latin America began a process that would not only contribute to the transformation of Latin American Church and society, but that would reverberate throughout the Christian world.

Sharing Faith Across the Hemisphere

"This Hour Seems to Be, by Divine Providence, Conclusive and Decisive"

—Pope Paul VI

From Medellín to Puebla: A New Era in the Latin American Church

On August 24, 1968, Pope Paul VI declared that the first, centuries-long phase of the evangelization of Latin America had come to an end and that the second was just then being inaugurated.[1] Among the people in his audience, there were some to whom that declaration probably seemed to be fantastically and even fearfully exaggerated. There were others who heard it as a long-awaited recognition of the new "realities" being born in Latin America. Listeners of both persuasions heard his announcement and during the next few decades would play their respective parts to create the history of the Latin American Church according to their own readings of the "signs of the times."

Throughout the world, 1968 represented the most turbulent year of the agitated 1960s. It was the year of the "Prague Spring," France's student riots, and the massacre of Mexican students in the Plaza of the Three Cultures; it was the year when the United States witnessed the assassinations of Martin Luther King and Robert Kennedy, the demonstrations at the National Democratic Convention, and growing protest against the Vietnam War; it was the year when the world beheld massive starvation in Biafra and when Presidents Fernando Belaunde Terry of Peru and Arnulfo Arias of Panama were ousted by military coups. Without a doubt, 1968 was a landmark year.

In 1968, Latin America had 268 million inhabitants. Military dictatorships controlled 60 percent of its territory. Eight years after the declaration of the 1960s as the "decade of development," overall Latin American economic growth was estimated to average only $6 per year, compared with an annual growth rate of $60 in Europe and $150 in the United States. More than one-half of the Latin American population was illiterate and 17 percent had no access to health care.[2] In the words of Phillip Berryman, "When Latin Americans turned to look at the ' world,' they saw not so much the world of ' human progress' affirmed by Vatican II, as a world of poverty and even misery."[3] The unique impact of the Latin American bishops' conference at Medellín would come from the fact that the bishops began their reflections with a realistic assessment of the stark realities that characterized their continent.

Although it may have appeared to sprout like an unexpected green shoot from a dry trunk, Medellín was hardly an accidental or serendipitous occurrence. Its roots stretched back to the 1955 Latin American bishops' meeting in Río de Janiero and had been abundantly nourished during the Vatican Council, when six hundred Latin American bishops came into more prolonged and intense contact with one another than had been possible in the previous four hundred and fifty years of the Church's presence in the hemisphere.[4] After Vatican II, CELAM, under the direction of Bishop Manuel Larraín of Talca, Chile, sponsored theological study sessions and workshops for bishops, clergy, and lay people alike, thereby involving a wide spectrum of people in the reflections that would be synthesized in the conference documents. In addition to Latin American efforts at organization, in 1967, Pope Paul VI had published the encyclical *Populorum Progressio,* which further developed the social teachings of Vatican II and John XXIII. With the background of all of that preparation, Medellín appeared as both the firstfruits and the promising seed of the new Latin American Church.

"Speak, Speak, Write, Take a Position"

—Pope Paul VI

The Message of Medellín

No matter how well the ground had been prepared, the Medellín documents still astounded many because of the force and the clarity with which they outlined the Church's approach to twentieth-century Latin America. Echoing Paul VI's announcement that Latin America was embarking on a new stage of evangelization, the bishops declared that the new historical epoch made explicit demands on the Church: "This era requires clarity in order to see, lucidity in order to diagnose, and solidarity in order to act."[5] That pattern of describing the real circumstances of their people, reflecting on them in light of church teaching, and prioritizing pastoral activities in response to the specific needs of their world would be the hallmark and the unique strength of Medellín and the activities that would flow from it.

The bishops made their priorities explicit from the start: the first section of the Medellín document focused on the question of justice, refer-

Panel discussion at Medellín, 1968. Archbishop Marcos McGrath, CSC, presiding. Photo: CELAM Archives.

ring for the most part to economic justice and, therefore, to the questions raised by the massive poverty of their people and the Christian virtue of spiritual poverty. The bishops made it clear that their message came from the heart of faith, that it was religious and not limited to social reform. In that regard they said,

> Thus, for our authentic liberation, all of us need a profound conversion so that "the kingdom of justice, love and peace" might come to us. . . . The uniqueness of the Christian message does not so much consist in the affirmation of the necessity for structural change, as it does in the insistence on the conversion of men which will in turn bring about this change. . . . We do not confuse temporal progress and the Kingdom of Christ; nevertheless, the former "to the extent that it can contribute to the better ordering of human society, is of vital concern to the Kingdom of God."[6]

Acknowledging the many studies that had already described the misery besetting large masses of the population in all Latin American countries, and echoing recent papal teachings, they said that "misery, as a collective fact, expresses itself as injustice which cries to the heavens."[7] Then, adding concrete details that focused contemporary Catholic social teaching on Latin American realities, they added,

What perhaps has not been sufficiently said is that in general the efforts which have been made have not been capable of assuring that justice be honored and realized. . . . Often families do not find concrete possibilities for the education of their children. The young demand the right to enter universities . . . women, their right to a legitimate equality with men; the peasants, better conditions of life; . . . workers . . . security in buying and selling. . . . We cannot ignore the phenomenon of this almost universal frustration of legitimate aspirations which creates the climate of collective anguish in which we are already living. . . .

To all of this must be added the lack of solidarity which, on the individual and social levels, leads to the committing of serious sins, evident in the unjust structures which characterize the Latin American situation.[8]

In that latter statement, the bishops emphasized two basic points that characterize Medellín's teaching and therefore mark the future of the Latin American Church.

First, examining the Latin American economic situation, they declared that previous efforts at "development," the numerous and diverse campaigns that had been undertaken to help the poor, had been unsuccessful. Secondly, making a stronger theological judgment that had been made in previous church documents, they condemned the misery of their people as a situation that both resulted from and could be the cause of serious sin. When they combined those two ideas—and in the Medellín documents that cannot be separated—the bishops set the agenda for their Church. To effectively resolve the problem of poverty and its sinful causes, they called for a re-examination of history and current events—a process that could lead to a thorough renewal of the Church's pastoral activity.

The Need for Integral Development

The opening paragraph of Medellín's section on peace states, "If development is the new name for peace, Latin American under-development. . . is an unjust situation which promotes tensions that conspire against peace."[9] The bishops then described the three major forces that they saw as unjust situations producing "a positive menace to peace." Beginning with a critique of injustice among Latin Americans themselves, the bishops criticized the extreme and systematically maintained inequalities between

Latin American rich and poor, a situation they labeled as "internal colonialism." According to the bishops, this situation, which they described as bordering on slavery, would only grow worse in the future as the poor became more aware of the injustice of their plight.[10] Making a clear allusion to incipient communist movements in Latin America, the bishops warned that if the poor were frustrated in legitimate attempts to remedy their situation, there were already at hand "movements of all types interested in taking advantage of and irritating these tensions."[11]

The second force that the bishops cited as a threat to Latin American peace was "external neocolonialism." In this, they referred to unrestrained international capitalism and the ways in which their nations had become dependent on the foreign economic powers that controlled commercial exchange and made "the value of raw materials. . . increasingly less in relation to the cost of manufactured products." This neocolonialism maintained the poverty of the poor nations while the industrialized nations enriched themselves. Such injustice, they said, "nullifies the eventual positive effect of external aid and constitutes a permanent menace against peace, because our countries sense that one hand takes away what the other hand gives."[12]

The third force condemned by the bishops as militating against peace was the tension among various countries within Latin America. Affirming the necessity of Latin American integration, the bishops called their countries to abandon the scandal of the arms race and to renounce their exacerbated nationalistic attitudes so that union among them could help to overcome the weakness of national economies. The combination of the three forces of internal colonialism, foreign neocolonialism, and Latin American ultra-nationalism added up to what the bishops called a sinful "lack of solidarity," which trapped the majority of the population in poverty. This was the widespread reality to which they said the Latin American Church was obliged to respond.

"The World Watches Us with Regard to Poverty"

—Pope Paul VI

Theological Analysis: Three Types of Poverty
Of all of Medellín's contributions to the Church's theological reflection, its discussion of poverty is one of the most significant. While references to poverty and to the poor can be found throughout the document, the most

comprehensive treatment of this theme comes in chapter 14, entitled "Poverty of the Church." There the bishops make a clear distinction among three experiences of poverty and their religious significance.

Poverty as Institutionalized Violence

The first poverty the bishops analyzed is the lack of goods necessary to live decently as human beings. Relying on the testimony of the prophets, the bishops made a theological judgment declaring that such a lack "is itself evil . . . and most of the time the fruit of the injustice and sin of men." They used the term "institutionalized violence" to describe the poverty of their people and its sinful causes:

> Latin America finds itself faced with a situation of injustice that can be called institutionalized violence, when, because of a structural deficiency of industry and agriculture, of national and international economy, of cultural and political life, "whole towns lack necessities, live in such dependence as hinders all initiative and responsibility as well as every possibility for cultural promotion and participation in social and political life," thus violating fundamental rights.[13]

"Institutionalized violence" is a preventable lack of material and cultural necessities. It is "violent" because it implies a lack of the goods necessary for life; it is "institutionalized" because it is a result of the very structure of societies and international commerce. While poverty, and even the widespread misery of Latin America, might previously have been accepted as inevitable, at Medellín, the bishops boldly judged it as "sinful" and called the Christian community to action against it: "This situation demands all-embracing, courageous, urgent and profoundly renovating transformations."[14]

Then, lest their call contain the slightest hint of ambiguity, they directly named the individuals and groups who had the greatest responsibility to respond to the situation. First, they addressed the rich, "those who have a greater share of wealth, culture and power," warning that "if they jealously retain their privileges, and defend them through violence, they are responsible to history for provoking explosive revolutions of despair."[15] Refusing to allow the total burden to fall on only one class, the bishops added,

Sharing Faith Across the Hemisphere

Also responsible for injustice are those who remain passive for fear of the sacrifice and personal risk implied by any courageous and effective action. Justice, and therefore peace, conquer by means of a dynamic action of awakening (concientización) and organization of the popular sectors, which are capable of pressing public officials who are often impotent in their social projects without popular support.[16]

No group could consider itself exempt from the call to justice. The bishops warned the people with power that they had a grave responsibility in regard to the revolutionary urge that was growing in Latin America:

We should not be surprised . . . that the "temptation to violence" is surfacing in Latin America. One should not abuse the patience of a people that for years has borne a situation that would not be acceptable to anyone with any degree of awareness of human rights.[17]

At the same time, for those who might turn to violence, they had a different but equally strong message:

We address ourselves finally to those who, in the face of injustice and illegitimate resistance to change, put their hopes in violence. With Paul VI we realize that their attitude "frequently finds its ultimate motivation in noble impulses of justice and solidarity. Let us not speak here of empty words which do not imply personal responsibility. . . .

If it is true that revolutionary insurrection can be legitimate in the case of evident and prolonged tyranny that seriously works against the fundamental rights of man . . . it is also certain that violence . . . generally generates new injustices, introduces new imbalances and causes new disasters. . . . We earnestly desire that the dynamism of the awakened and organized community be put to the service of justice and peace.[18]

In summary, when the bishops dealt with the abject poverty that characterized the majority of their people, a poverty more aptly termed "misery," they did not hesitate to condemn it as a violent product of sinful actions and attitudes. In addition, they warned that the sinfully destitute conditions in which their people lived could too easily be the cause of harmful counter-violence.

Poverty of Spirit and Poverty as Commitment

The second type of poverty described in the Medellín documents is "spiritual poverty," the "attitude of opening up to God, the ready disposition of one who hopes for everything from the Lord."[19] Unlike the misery of the masses, the entire Church is called to live in spiritual poverty. According to the bishops, this "evangelical poverty" leads the Church to denounce the unjust lack of this world's goods and the sin that begets it; to preach spiritual poverty; and to bind itself to material poverty in accord with the particular demands of each person's vocation and charisms.

According to Medellín, a third type of poverty is the "commitment through which one assumes voluntarily and lovingly the conditions of the needy of this world in order to bear witness to the evil which it represents and to spiritual liberty in the face of material goods."[20] This latter experience of poverty is marked by two essential characteristics: it is voluntary, and it is assumed as a prophetic sign of protest. Medellín strives to be extremely clear about the fact that while all Christians are called to live the evangelical poverty that maintains their freedom, material poverty *per se* is an evil that the Church is called to denounce and overcome. The poverty assumed in solidarity with the poor is an act of love and of protest.

Overall, the questions of justice and peace, the first questions addressed in the Medellín document, led the bishops to make an honest assessment of the material conditions in which their people were living. That assessment of reality led them to diagnose the sinful causes of the misery of so many of their people. The combination of the assessment and the diagnosis led them to call themselves and all of their people to awaken their consciences, and to organize the activities that would be capable of transforming situations of sin into a just social order. On a very concrete level, the bishops were calling the whole Church to "utilize its moral strength to collaborate with competent professionals and institutions" and to "lend its support to the down-trodden of every social class so that they might come to know their rights and how to make use of them."[21] All of the recommendations produced by Medellín attempted to respond to that general call.

"New Necessities Demand
Something New and Something Great"

—Pope Paul VI

According to Pope Paul VI, divine providence had chosen 1968 as a conclusive and decisive hour for Latin America. The bishops assembled at Medellín produced a powerful reflection on that hour and made concrete suggestions about how the whole Church should respond to it. The real test, of course, was how that reading of the signs of the times and those lofty goals would be carried out in practice. The Church of Latin America, the laity and the pastoral workers, together with the bishops, did not ignore their new, grace-filled opportunity.

When the bishops reflected on the theme of economic and political "dependency," their words necessarily implied a critique of the Church as well as of social institutions and structures.[22] In their reflection on the religious vocation, the bishops had said, "One characteristic of true charity is the flexibility of spirit by means of which one is able to adapt to changing circumstances . . . even when such adaptation necessitates . . . the suppression of works. . . ."[23] In the years surrounding Medellín, commitment to the poor would move the Church to an adaptation that included the surrender of some particular ministries and the creation, not only of new ministries, but, underlying them, a thoroughly renewed theological reflection on its mission.

The Fundamental Option for the Poor

The "option for the poor," far from being born at Medellín, is one of the core characteristics of the Judeo-Christian tradition. What Latin America has brought to that tradition in the twentieth century is a new critical awareness of how that option must be lived in order to be authentic in contemporary historical circumstances. In that regard, the Medellín document teaches:

We ought to sharpen the awareness of our duty of solidarity with the poor. . . . This solidarity means that we make ours their problems and their struggles. . . . This has to be concretized in criticism of injustice and oppression, in the struggle against the intolerable situation which a poor person often has to tolerate, in the willingness to dialogue with the groups responsible for that situation in order to make them understand their obligations.[24]

The impact of that teaching, which was quickly and broadly put into practice, had, as Archbishop Marcos McGrath has said, "far broader and deeper consequences than what had been expected."[25]

As Medellín called for solidarity with the poor, the "theology of liberation" came into prominence as both a method and a growing body of written works through which to reflect on the implications of that call. The term "liberation" came into use as a biblical concept capable of responding to a wide variety of the "signs of the times." First of all, liberation, God's historical action to free people from slavery to sin and the material slaveries of history, is a key biblical theme. Secondly, when the Church was beginning to reflect on the economic and political realities of dependence and institutionalized violence, "integral liberation" proved to be a concept uniquely adequate to describe the reversal of everything that trapped people in inhuman conditions.[26] Finally, although the bishops had seemed to use the terms "development" and "liberation" almost synonymously, the failure of the 1960s as "the decade of development" and the inadequacy of development theories regarding economic and social progress made "liberation" a much more persuasive term to describe the goal and the hope of the Church in Latin America.[27] As an intellectual current, "liberation theology" was born in the same circumstances that gave birth to Medellín; some of its major thinkers helped write the Medellín documents, and it would quickly become known as Latin America's distinctive contribution to theology.[28]

"Solidarity with the Poor"—New Pastoral Priorities

The changes promoted by Medellín did not happen overnight. Medellín itself had avoided prescribing particular objectives—rather, through its assessment of overall conditions, its doctrinal reflection, and its pastoral recommendations, Medellín offered the Church general directives and a method for applying them to particular contexts. Specific applications would necessarily depend on national, diocesan, and even parish or community pastoral councils.

Guided by the methodology of Medellín and Vatican II, the Conference of Latin American Religious, CLAR, quickly began a study designed to paint a realistic picture of the numbers, preparation, location, and apostolates of Latin American religious men and women. What they learned was that in 1971, there were 131,000 religious women and 40,000 religious men serving in Latin America. Although the numbers, particularly of women, might have seemed impressive, the study reported that "the work that religious women do is unevenly and often unjustly distributed; most of the sisters . . . are in cities or towns . . . and 65 percent of their residences are in middle or upper-class areas in a continent where 58 percent of the people are rural."[29] The study went on to point out that 31 percent of the sisters had never finished elementary school; only 24 percent had college educations, and of those, only 4 percent had specialized in theological studies. Twenty-five percent of the religious women in Latin America were foreigners, as were three-quarters of their religious superiors.

The agenda that followed from reflection on those facts mirrored the plans of many other sectors of the Church. Leaders and pastoral workers alike heard the call to become more aware of the world around them, to be committed to personal and societal liberation, and to cherish work with the poor, giving special attention to basic education and the building up of basic communities.

CLAR's careful choice of vocabulary regarding work with the poor ("working for the poor is one of the most cherished of contemporary forms of commitment") reflected two very important realities. First, the Church had traditionally worked among the poor; second, as would be emphasized throughout the next two decades, the Church's renewed commitment to the poor had implications for the whole life of the Church, but it did not imply the abandonment of every other ministry.

In the 1960s and 1970s, foreign missionaries were well represented among those who were already working with the poor. Maryknoll priests, brothers, and sisters, who began their Latin American apostolate in 1942, had significant experience on which to build. They were pioneers in developing lay ministries among the poor and in developing self-help projects, such as parish-based credit unions and the innovative use of radio technology through which they promoted both educational and cultural development for large populations living in dispersed areas.[30] Another U.S. group, the St. James Society, had been founded to work in areas where there was a large population of Catholics and few priests. Once in Latin America, they were assigned by local bishops and were most often found among the poor whose means were insufficient to support a local priest. Many diocesan groups, like the Cleveland mission team in El Salvador, had also offered their services to work in the neediest areas of the country—a classification that often implied areas marked by poverty as well as by a shortage of church personnel.

At the same time, some other missionary groups reflected the general pattern noted by CLAR: they were working in populated areas which, even though they did not enjoy the numbers of religious personnel common in the United States and Europe, were still far more amply served than were the people in marginal urban and rural areas. The signs of the times and the reflections of Medellín spoke to both groups, inviting the former to a renewed and deeper commitment and calling on the latter to re-evaluate their ministerial priorities. As a result, the post-Medellín decade became one of deep and widespread change in the Church's pastoral activity.

In Peru, the reception of the Medellín documents coincided with political events and a natural catastrophe in a unique combination that called the Church into new ministries. Historian Jeffrey Klaiber, SJ, describes the political dimension:

> The reformist military government of Juan Velasco which took power in 1968 reinforced the progressive tendencies of the Church. In their desire to legitimize the revolutionary process, the military invited the Church to participate directly in the formulation and the implementation of many of the reforms. Never before in the history of the Republic had the Church been so involved in socioeconomic questions and their national and international repercussions.[31]

Sr. Teresa Avalos, CSJ, a native of Los Angeles who ministered in Peru from 1963 to 1995, fills out Klaiber's description with examples from her own experience. When asked about the military government's educational reform that restricted the presence of foreigners in school administration, she said,

> When we opened our schools in the early sixties, we had begun by talking about the fact that we were going to let go of them at some point and put them in the hands of the laity. It happened before we thought it

would, but it was our long range goal. After eight or nine years [the time that the sisters had directed the schools], there were teachers who were ready to step into those roles.

Sr. Teresa explained that the devastating earthquake of May 31, 1970, also had a dramatic effect on changing the pastoral activity of the Church.

After the earthquake, CLAR in Lima got teams together to help. They went mostly up to the mountains, to Juaraz and Yunguay, etc. That experience opened the eyes of the religious . . . even the Peruvians, to see a new reality. Documents of the Conference of Religious say that the time of the earthquake was the time when things began to break open. We were opened to a reality that we hadn' t been looking at.

In Peru, the combination of Medellín, the military coup, and the earthquake led to new priorities, and pastoral workers began to assume new ministries.

The factors that brought other Latin American pastoral workers—clergy and laity, native and missionary—into new service of the poor were as unique as each group and locale; the Spirit of God seemed to be working a similar effect through the combination of every possible variety of events. Sr. Veronica Wall, a nurse from Downers' Grove, N.Y., talked about her move from Lima to Abancay in the Southern Andes:

We staffed the nursing school at a military hospital. A priest had come to speak to the nurses about the lack of health care in the mountain and jungle regions. He mentioned the number of beds, nurses and doctors in Lima and he compared that with the numbers in the mountains and jungle. That sort of got into our mind. We didn' t say, "All right, let's do it!" but we talked about it, and we said that what we had heard was quite shocking.

Then a couple of weeks later, Fr. Al Stankard, a priest from Boston, came and knocked at the door. He said that he heard that there were North American nurses here and that he was looking for nurses to go to this place called Ocobamba in the sierra and to work with a Canadian nurse, Sr. Joan Marie Littlejohn. It was going to be for three months.

A few of us wanted to go, but I was the only one free. The minute I saw Ocobamba, I knew that it was where we belonged. Two months later some of our sisters from the hospital came up to visit me. They said that the sisters were discerning about leaving the hospital. I jumped at that and said, "We have to come here."

We began with two nurses and lived in the little clinic with Sebastian, the *sanitario* [health worker], his wife and their five kids. They had a bedroom and we had one. When more sisters came, we moved, and four of us shared a house—one bedroom and a kitchen, with a bathroom outside. Eventually, Fr. Jerry Pashby, a St. James priest, had a house built for us in the town of Ocobamba. We were there ten years.[32]

The Sisters of the Incarnate Word from San Antonio, Tex., reported an experience that directly paralleled that described by Sr. Veronica. After the earthquake, the sisters left a police hospital in Chimbote, Peru, and opened clinics for the poor in both the city and the mountainous regions beyond it.

At about the same time, the missioners from Jefferson City, Mo., who were working in southern Peru, changed not the locale, but the thrust of their mission. According to Alice Wolters, director of the Mission Office:

We had gone with the idea to save Latin America from the communists, but changes and transitions happened over the years. We were very naive and tried to transport all our American ways. It took a while, and we stumbled. We realized that we had been aligned with the wealthy. The sixties and seventies were a difficult period, it was one of those watershed times, and we were learning.

The Church of Peru was arriving at saying that we have to make a very definite statement and be a sign that we are a Church of the poor. We switched options, and personnel. We realized we're not "Big Daddy" down here, we're here as guests, not to lead, but to learn from them, to accompany them. We're here to respect the culture and to learn from it; to let the people be their own voice, be the authors and masters of their own destiny.

The specifics recounted by Sisters Teresa and Veronica and Ms. Wolters echo the experience of multiple U.S. mission groups. The period of the 1970s, between Medellín and Puebla, was one in which a great number of groups moved into closer contact with the poorest of their Latin American brothers and sisters. Although the moves were highly rewarding, they were rarely easy. They required tremendous adjustments on every imaginable level.

First, the move to service of the most marginated people often required new language studies. Although the inhabitants of the major cities were generally Spanish speaking, pastoral workers who moved to some rural areas in countries like Peru, Bolivia, Argentina, Guatemala, Nicaragua, and even Mexico found that indigenous languages were the primary and sometimes the only language of the people. In some cases, there were not even formal opportunities to study those languages, so the missioners had to find their own way to learn them.[33] There was also a new dimension of cultural adjustment as missionaries began to share more of the lifestyle of the poor; that adjustment not only implied becoming accustomed to having fewer material comforts and less privacy, but also brought them into more direct contact with suffering and death. A description of missionary life in Guatemala gives the following details:

> One could not live at Santiago Atitlán without frequent encounters with death. In 1969 [Fr. Stanley Rother] wrote, "It appears that we are at the brink of another measles epidemic. Two years ago 400 to 500 died from measles." He reported in February 1976 that the village had been spared deaths in the earthquake of that year which wrecked much of Guatemala, but added "Our cross came on Jan. 18th when 10 men died and 60 injured in a truck wreck." Earlier, in 1972, he had been waylaid by infectious hepatitis. Disease, injury and death were never far away.[34]

Another effect of taking on more direct ministry to the poor was that religious groups lost the income they had been earning in previous ministries. As they fulfilled their dreams of being able to hand over more of their work to the local laity, their hopes for becoming financially independent from sponsoring communities and groups often had to be postponed.[35] The tremendous adjustments required by more direct pastoral work among the poor had their effects on personnel. The changes brought new life to some. Others, particularly those most accustomed to working in institutions, decided that it would be best for them to return home.[36]

Those who stayed most often reported that, in spite of hardships, the changes had led to joyful and grace-filled experiences. Describing the experience of sharing the religious life of Peru's mountain people, Sr. Veronica Wall said,

> It was so alive. The difference between religion in the mountains and the cities . . . you just had to see it to understand it. The deep faith of the people . . . their prayer. People would come to Mass and be there for twenty or thirty minutes before it started, people were busy talking to one another . . . they had CHURCH—it was a place where people met and shared and prayed together. They would sing their hearts out, and also be able to kneel before a candle for hours, keeping it from flickering, and praying all the while. There was such faith and participation.
>
> What they had was gift, pure gift, something lacking in my life. And Holy Week! We were participating in traditions that had gone on among the people for hundreds of years. The whole meaning of the Pascal mystery became real to me there. It was there that Easter really hit me; it became real, I knew that it really happened.

Sr. Veronica's comments represent what is probably the most frequently given response to the question of what the Church in the United States can learn from its contact with Latin America. In one way or another, almost every respondent to the NCCB survey commented on the deep faith of the people and how much that faith has touched those who have had the opportunity to witness it.

At the same time, one of the most serious problems recognized by the Latin American Church at Medellín was that the deep faith of the common people needed a more firm grounding in order to successfully face the challenges of the modern world. The Medellín document explained that the "popular religiosity" of the masses was a "religion of vows and promises, processions and pilgrimages, and numberless devotions . . . based on the reception of the sacraments of Baptism and Eucharist."[37] As described in Medellín, the religiosity of the people favored "a cosmic approach in which God is the answer to every mystery and need."[38] It was therefore a faith that could "easily suffer a crisis—and indeed already has—faced with the scientific knowledge of the world about us."[39] Rather

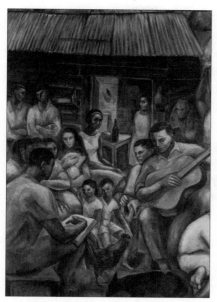

A mural from Cristo Redentor parish in San Miguelito showing the beginning of *comunidades eclesiases de base* in 1963. Mural by Lilian Brulc; photo by John Enright. Courtesy of the Archdiocese of Chicago.

than reject that faith, Medellín called on pastoral workers to evaluate it, not in terms of western culture, but rather through understanding its meaning in "the context of the rural and marginal urban groups" who lived it.[40] In order to better share and develop that faith, Medellín also called for the formation of small ecclesial communities as a specific means through which the masses of the people could arrive at a more profound participation in the communal and sacramental life of the Church and receive more adequate religious education.[41]

Basic Ecclesial Communities

Brazilian Bishop Agnelo Rossi is credited as being the instigator of the movement to form the Latin American basic ecclesial communities (BECs). According to Fr. José Marins, the movement to form such communities was born in 1956 as a response to the needs of people who lacked priestly ministry:

> It all began when an old lady told Dom Agnelo, during his annual pastoral visit to her area: "On Christmas day, the Protestant churches were all lit up and jammed with people. We could hear their hymns. But our Catholic church was shut, with its lights out, because we had not found a priest to say Mass for us." This challenge raised fundamental questions, like: If there are no priests, must everything stop? Can nobody do anything for the life of the Church community?[42]

In 1956, Dom Agnelo began to experiment with the formation of small communities in his diocese. They worked, and the idea spread like wildfire throughout Latin America.

One of the earliest and best known experiences of developing BECs was that carried out in Chicago's mission in the parish of San Miguelito in Panama. There, under the leadership of Fr. Leo Mahon, the groups developed so well that San Miguelito became a model to be visited by missioners working throughout Central and even South America.[43]

The very name of the groups, basic ecclesial communities, explains who and what they are. They are basic groups, implying that they are small, usually formed by natural relationships based on neighborhood or work associations. They are communities: that is, as small groups who know one another, they strive for the full and personal participation of each of the members in the reflection, prayer, and activities of the group. They are ecclesial: they see themselves as a vital expression of what it means to be Church and as "basic" units of larger expressions of Church from the level of the parish to the universal Church.[44]

The growth of basic ecclesial communities has more than once been described as the most significant ecclesiological development in Latin America.[45] Without a doubt, the BECs have had an unparalleled, two-pronged effect on the life of the Church. First of all, in the words of the Puebla document,

> The CEB brings together families, adults and young people in an intimate interpersonal relationship grounded in the faith. . . . It is a community of faith, hope and charity. It celebrates the Word of God and takes its nourishment from the Eucharist. . . .
>
> United in a CEB and nurturing their adherence to Christ, Christians strive for a more evangelical way of life amid people, work together to challenge the egotistical and consumeristic roots of society, and make explicit their vocation to communion with God and their fellow humans. Thus they offer a valid and worthwhile point of departure for building up a new society, "the civilization of love."[46]

What that means in very practical terms is, first, that people whose public religious celebrations often had been centered on the ceremonies surrounding major feasts, baptisms, weddings, and funerals, have begun to meet regularly. In the communities they pray together, read Scripture, discuss its implications for daily life, and organize activities that include visiting the sick, forming small banking or productive

Sharing Faith Across the Hemisphere

cooperatives, or even planning and executing land invasions.[47] Through participation in the communities, people have the opportunity to learn more about their faith and live it in ways that become more responsive to the problems and needs of their daily life. Second, because each person is encouraged to participate actively in group discussions and activities, the communities provide an environment of truly unprecedented personal development for individuals and a veritable training ground for new, grassroots leadership.[48] As community members develop their participative skills and their capacity for leadership, they are "conscientized" into new levels of faith-based awareness and commitment. Thus, as Puebla stated, they become more fully prepared to play a vital role in building up a new society.

The second prong of the BECs' effect on the life of the Church is the new relationship they facilitate between the people and pastoral workers. Whether the communities are parish based or spring from occupational associations, they are generally related to similar groups and larger expressions of Church through pastoral workers, teachers, or theologians, who contribute to their ongoing formation in faith and community organization. As the pastoral workers promote the development of critical consciousness and leadership among the members, they in turn receive a new kind of formation. Pastoral workers whose origins may not be in the social group with whom they are working learn from the community members just as the community learns from them. This close contact allows them to understand the problems and the possibilities of their people in a new way. Hearing the Scriptures interpreted from the vantage point of the poor, pastoral ministers and theologians have come to a new appreciation of the meaning of the Gospel.[49]

It is important to understand that there is no monolithic pattern that characterizes the BECs. They are as different as their particular circumstances and the formation they have received. Some may appear to be extremely traditional, while others would take pride in calling themselves radical.[50] The communities that have grown up in the marginal areas of large cities are often characterized by greater occupational and economic diversity among their members than are those that function in rural areas. The community may be formed on the basis of a "family catechesis" program, a mother's club, a student organization, or an explicitly self-aware cell of a total parish organization. More than any structure of membership pattern, what characterizes the BECs is the fact that they come together to form a community based on faith, related to the Church, and willing to work together to express their faith through concrete contributions to the world around them. When the BECs live out their potential, they are, as Pope Paul VI said, "a place of evangelization for the benefit of the bigger communities . . . and . . . a hope for the universal Church."[51]

The Poor Will Welcome Gladly the Good Tidings

Puebla: Affirmation and Advance

In 1979, eleven years after Medellín, the Latin American bishops met in Puebla, Mexico, for their third general conference, entitled "Evangelization in Latin America's Present and Future." With nearly two full years of broad consultations dedicated to its preparation, Puebla produced a much longer and more integrated document than the sixteen separate documents produced by Medellín.[52] Following the three-step methodology of *Gaudium et Spes* and consciously building on "the dynamic thrust of the Medellín Conference," the Puebla document began with an overview of the state of the Church in Latin America at the end of the decade of the 1970s.[53] In what may be the most poignantly poetic section of a modern church document, the bishops decried the destitution that characterized so many of their people:

> This situation of pervasive extreme poverty takes on very concrete faces in real life. In these faces we ought to recognize the suffering features of Christ the Lord, who questions and challenges us. They include:
>
> - the faces of young children, struck down by poverty before they are born, their chance of self-development blocked by irreparable mental and physical deficiencies; and of the vagrant children in our cities who are so often exploited, products of poverty and the moral disorganization of the family;
> - the faces of young people, who are disoriented because they cannot find their place in society, and who are frustrated, particularly in marginal rural and urban areas, by the lack of opportunity to obtain training and work;

- the faces of the indigenous peoples, and frequently of the Afro-Americans as well; living marginalized lives in inhuman situations, they can be considered the poorest of the poor;
- the faces of peasants; as a social group, they live in exile almost everywhere on our continent . . . ;
- the faces of laborers, who frequently are ill-paid and who have difficulty in organizing themselves and defending their rights;
- the faces of the underemployed and the unemployed, who are dismissed because of the harsh exigencies of economic crisis, and often because of development-models that subject workers and their families to cold economic calculations;
- the faces of marginalized and overcrowded urban dwellers, whose lack of material goods is matched by the ostentatious display of wealth by other segments of society;
- the faces of old people, who are growing more numerous every day, and who are frequently marginalized in a progress-oriented society that totally disregards people not engaged in production.[54]

More concretely than they had at the time of Medellín, the bishops went on to describe the root causes of their nations' dire situation. Explaining that they spoke of the causes so that the Church could offer help and cooperation in bringing about a change, they pointed first to "economic systems that do not regard the human being as the center of society." They then went on to signal lack of integration among Latin American nations; economic, technological, political, and cultural dependence; the arms race; lack of structural reforms in agriculture; and corruption, greed, and the absence of any social sense of practical justice and solidarity as expressions of the sinful realities that marked the continent.[55]

In reviewing their recent history, the bishops said,

The Church has felt itself summoned by a people who ask for the bread of God's Word and demand justice. The Church has turned its ear to this people, who are profoundly religious and who, for that very reason, place all their confidence in God. So in the past ten years the Church has put much effort into offering them an adequate pastoral response.[56]

When the bishops said that "the Church has felt itself summoned" by the people, they were speaking first for Latin America, but in a very real sense, for the whole Church. In addition to their own sense of vocation, they were reflecting on the way that the universal Church had been called by Latin America's pastoral pronouncements and also on the experience of the thousands of missionaries who had shared the life of their people over the years.

Latin America in the Universal Church

If in 1960, the Church of Latin America was characterized by "fundamental weaknesses of structure," by 1970, it had taken its place as a leader in the formulation of Catholic social doctrine and a model for pastoral action. The most obvious way in which Latin America contributed to the Church's social teaching was through its contribution to the 1971 Synod on Ministerial Priesthood and Justice.[57] Basic teachings of Medellín, and particularly the mandate that Christians not remain passive in the face of injustice, were applied to the whole Church when the Synod proclaimed:

> Action on behalf of justice and participation in the transformation of the world fully appear to us as a constitutive dimension of the preaching of the gospel, or in other words, of the church's mission for the redemption of the human race and its liberation from every oppressive situation.[58]

Along with the call to action, *Justice in the World* affirmed the key Latin American theme of liberation as an authentic expression of the Church's mission. It also seemed to reaffirm the community-building and educational processes of the BECs by emphasizing the importance of building solidarity among persons and nations, and calling for an education that would "awaken a critical sense" and lead to a reflection on society and its values that will "make men ready to renounce these values when they cease to promote justice for all."[59] If Latin America did not directly author the synod document, that document ratified the teachings and the pastoral priorities that had been made by the Latin American episcopacy and directed them to the whole Church. As José Comblin says, "More and more, church people everywhere have become aware not only of the specific problems of Latin America, but of the universal significance of their repercussions for the meaning of mission and self-consciousness of the Church in the world."[60]

A Time of Conflict

Although the Medellín documents received unanimous approval before they were promulgated, they were not uniformly understood or applied. Each national episcopal conference, together with its subsidiary dioceses and parishes, had to take responsibility for the implementation of Medellín's teaching. Along with the rich experiences of new pastoral ministries and approaches, the decade between 1968 and 1979 was marked by a profusion of episcopal teachings and theological writings. While many of these encouraged specific applications of the teachings of Medellín, there was also significant criticism of the directions that the Church had taken after 1968. The crux of the conflict had to do with what some called the growing "politicization" of ecclesial commitments.

In many ways, some kind of politicization seemed to be the inevitable outcome of church teaching. After all, both the Latin American bishops and Rome had called on Christians to take an active part in the building of a new society. Already in 1967, Pope Paul VI had written:

> The development of peoples has the Church's close attention, particularly the development of those peoples who are striving to escape from hunger, misery, endemic diseases and ignorance; of those who are looking for a wider share in the benefits of civilization. . . . Following on the Second Vatican Ecumenical Council a renewed consciousness of the demands of the gospel makes it her duty to put herself at the service of all, . . . and to convince them that solidarity in action at this turning point in human history is a matter of urgency.[61]

Nevertheless, the Church seemed unprepared for the results of awakening the sleeping giant of the Latin American poor. Suddenly, the Church found itself in the midst of ideological, political, and even armed conflicts. To the critics, the concept of liberation and the activities of BECs seemed to have grown out of hand. By the time of Puebla, some sectors of the Church were fearful that the bishops would retreat from the positions they had taken in Medellín, while others were actively involved in the effort to make it so. In the end the bishops did not retreat. At the same time, based on the experience of a very turbulent decade, they carefully clarified some of the teachings and recommendations that had led to most of the controversy.

Option for the Poor, Liberation, and BECs in Puebla

Far from retrenching, Puebla's treatment of solidarity with the poor took the concept one step further by pronouncing the Church's "preferential option for the poor." In language that could hardly have been more clear, they said:

> With renewed hope in the vivifying power of the Spirit, we are going to take up once again the position of the Second general Conference of the Latin American episcopate in Medellín, which adopted a clear and prophetic option expressing preference for, and solidarity with, the poor. We do this despite the distortions and interpretations of some, who vitiate the spirit of Medellín, and despite the disregard and even hostility of others. We affirm the need for conversion on the part of the whole Church to a preferential option for the poor, an option aimed at their integral liberation.[62]

The last phrase, "integral liberation," called attention to another disputed issue within the Church in 1979: the variety of currents of official teaching and theological reflection that was grouped under the general rubric of "liberation theology."

From its inception, liberation theology and the very use of liberation as a reflection on God's saving action had been controversial. To the accusation that the Church had inappropriately become involved in politics, the bishops replied by distinguishing social teaching that is necessary to promote the common good from partisan political activities, which the official Church should avoid.

> We must distinguish between two notions of politics and political involvement. First, in the broad sense, politics seeks the common good on both the national and international plane. . . . In this broad sense politics is of interest to the Church, and hence to its pastors, who are ministers of unity. It is a way of paying worship to the one and only God by simultaneously desacralizing and consecrating the world to him.

Sharing Faith Across the Hemisphere

So the Church helps to foster the values that should inspire politics. . . .

Second, the concrete performance of this fundamental political task is normally carried out by groups of citizens. . . . Here, then, we can talk about "party politics." No matter how deeply inspired in church teaching, no political party can claim the right to represent all the faithful because its concrete program can never have absolute value for all.[63]

Thus, the bishops explained that the Church had not only the right, but a positive obligation to speak about the general welfare of its people. But it was not the Church's role to advocate a particular party.

With this background, the bishops' teaching on liberation becomes more clear. According to Puebla, the liberation preached by the Church is an "integral liberation of human beings in terms of both their earthly and their transcendent dimensions." The promotion of this liberation is the responsibility of the entire Christian community.[64] And, lest anyone feel justified in spiritualizing the concept or diminishing its concrete ramifications, Puebla also states:

> The gap between rich and poor, the menacing situation faced by the weakest, the injustices, and the humiliating disregard and subjection endured by them radically contradict the values of personal dignity and solidary [sic] brotherhood . . . the religiosity of the Latin American people often is turned into a cry for true liberation. It is an exigency that is still unmet. Motivated by their religiosity, however, the people create or utilize space for the practice of brotherhood in the more intimate areas of their lives together: e.g., the neighborhood, the village, their labor unions, and their recreational activities. They shrewdly wait for the right opportunities to move forward toward the liberation they so ardently desire.[65]

The Church of Puebla was committed to continue to promote the full liberation of its people.

The bishops' mention of the "practice of brotherhood in more intimate areas of their lives" served as a description, among other things, of the basic Christian communities that had been developing prodigiously over the decade between Medellín and Puebla.[66] These too had their ardent critics and zealous supporters. Many of the positive contributions of the BECs have already been described. However, the critics questioned their vital connection to the universal Church, their susceptibility to political manipulation, and the danger that they could be understood as a "parallel church" or a "parallel magisterium." The Puebla document is very positive in its treatment of these criticisms. In language far different from that which it uses to denounce such things as unjust economic systems, Puebla summarizes its descriptions of the vitality and weaknesses of the BECs saying, "integrated into the whole People of God, the BECs will undoubtedly avoid such dangers and will measure up to the hopes that the Latin American Church has placed in them."[67] The bishops did not ignore the critiques, but their evaluation of the BECs remained positive and affirming.

At Puebla the Latin American bishops did not abandon the commitments they had made at Medellín. Rather, in spite of much publicized radical rhetoric from both the right and left, Puebla maintained and even strengthened the options of Medellín, while carefully pointing out the dangers of misunderstanding aspects of its theology or pastoral options.

International Pastoral Workers from Medellín to Puebla

At the time of Puebla, there were 2,793 U.S. Catholic Church personnel serving long-term in Latin America.[68] They, like their Latin American coworkers, had undergone the influences of the profound ecclesial changes engendered by Medellín. In response to the NCCB survey, their sending communities described two major changes that took place in their ministries during the 1970s. First, they mentioned Medellín and Puebla as the underlying motivation for a change in ministerial style and location. Second, they acknowledge a great decline in numbers; the number of U.S. personnel serving in Latin American had been reduced by approximately 30 percent over the decade. That decline was most often attributed to either the fulfillment of an originally limited-time commitment or to the lack of religious personnel in the sending community. Not one community said it withdrew from Latin America due to changes in the Latin American Church.[69]

Aside from the overall decline in personnel sent from the United States, the most frequently mentioned type of change by every category of respondent was that their work had shifted from a traditional institutional focus toward the training and preparation of local lay people to take on more pastoral responsibility. Additionally, the next most significant change mentioned by religious communities was a growth in the numbers of Latin Americans joining their congregations.[70]

Given that evidence, along with the narratives presented above, there is every reason to believe that the U.S. "missioners" in Latin America were undergoing a change of mentality. As participants in the growing process of the Latin American Church, they were hearing the call of the bishops as addressed to themselves as well as to their Latin American brothers and sisters. Working together in joint pastoral efforts with the leaders and members of the national Churches, they were responding to the signs of the times and following the lead of the Spirit of God, becoming more involved with the poor, listening to them, and learning together with them.[71] Seeing themselves less as foreigners than as co-members of the People of God, they were growing in the depth with which they lived the spirit of solidarity to which Pope Paul VI had called all humanity when he said:

> Person must meet person, nation meet nation, as brothers and sisters, as children of God. In this mutual understanding and friendship, in this sacred communion, we must also begin to work together to build the common future of the human race.[72]

That solidarity, particularly as it was expressed in the preferential option for the poor, was leading U.S. pastoral workers to fully participate in the joys and pains, the ecclesial and political conflicts, the very life, and even the prophetic shedding of blood of the Latin American Church.

DISCUSSION QUESTIONS

1. In his opening address at Medellín, Pope Paul VI declared that a new era was beginning in the evangelization of the territories of America. More than a quarter of a century has passed since he made that remark. What has characterized this time as a new phase of evangelization?

2. The Medellín documents give special emphasis to the traditional teaching that the whole Church is called to an authentic poverty of spirit, which includes concrete expressions of Jesus' option for the poor. In that regard, the bishops taught: "We ought to sharpen the awareness of our duty of solidarity with the poor . . ." (*Medellín*, Poverty, no. 10). How has the Church accomplished this goal over the past thirty years?

3. At Puebla, the bishops said: "The Church has felt itself summoned by a people who ask for the bread of God's word and demand justice . . ." (*Puebla*, no. 93). Through whose voice do we still hear that summons? How are we responding?

4. At Puebla, the bishops described the impoverishment of their people as a result of economic systems that do not regard the human being as the center of society. How can the Church offer concrete alternatives to such systems?

5. Since 1968, church documents have emphasized the importance of the evangelizing role of the poor. What have the wealthy nations learned from the poor?

Notes

1. The text in the chapter introduction is excerpted from Pope Paul VI's opening address to the Medellín Conference. See Second General Conference of Latin American Bishops, *The Church in the Present-Day Transformation of Latin America in the Light of the Council* (Washington, D.C.: United States Catholic Conference, 1973), nos. 7-21 (hereafter referred to as *Medellín*).

2. These figures come from World Bank data as cited by Miguel Angel Keller in "El proceso evangelizador de la iglesia en América Latina: De Río a Santo Domingo" in *Medellín, Teología y pastoral para América Latina* (Medellín: Marzo, 1995), no. 18.

3. Phillip Berryman, *The Religious Roots of Rebellion* (New York: Orbis, 1985), 27.

4. Just before the close of Vatican II, on November 24, 1965, Pope Paul VI met in Rome with the bishops of twenty Latin American nations to talk about the apostolic task that awaited them in their homelands. Among other things, the pope emphasized the necessity of beginning their work with serious study of the complex Latin American reality. See Marcos McGrath, "Vaticano II, Iglesia de los Pobres y Teología de Liberación" in *Medellín*, XXI:379-80.

5. "Message to the People of Latin America" in *Medellín*, no. 25.

6. *Medellín*, "Justice," nos. 3 and 5, quoting *Gaudium et Spes*, no. 39.

7. *Medellín*, "Justice," no. 1.

8. *Medellín*, "Justice," nos. 1-2.

9. *Medellín*, "Peace," no. 1.

10. *Medellín*, "Justice," no. 11.

11. *Medellín*, "Justice," no. 7.

12. *Medellín*, "Peace," no. 9, a.

13. *Medellín*, "Justice," no. 16, quoting *Populorum Progressio*, no. 30.

14. *Medellín*, "Justice," no. 16.

15. *Medellín*, "Peace," no. 17. The last phrase quotes Paul VI's homily in Bogatá on August 23, 1968.

16. *Medellín*, "Peace," no. 18.

17. *Medellín*, "Justice," no. 16.

18. *Medellín*, "Justice," no. 19.

19. See *Medellín*, "Poverty of the Church," no. 14, b.

20. *Medellín*, "Poverty," no. 14, c.

21. *Medellín* "Justice," no. 20.

22. See *Medellín*, "Justice," no. 2, and "Joint Pastoral Planning," among others.

23. *Medellín*, "Religious," no. 8.

24. *Medellín*, "Poverty," no. 10.

25. Archbishop Marcos McGrath, CSC, "The Second Vatican Council and the Origin of Liberation Theology in the Church of Latin America," paper presented at Notre Dame University, fall 1995.

26. Pope Paul VI described "integral development," saying that it "has to promote the good of every man and of the whole man" and went on to describe the vocation of each person and nation to be "the principal agent of his own success or failure" (*Populorum Progressio*, nos. 14, 16).

27. Only by the light of Christ is the mystery of man made clear. In the economy of salvation the divine work is an action of integral human development and liberation which has love for its sole motive" (*Medellín*, "Justice," no. 4).

28. A great deal of controversy has surrounded the various currents of thought that identify themselves with the "theology of liberation." The 1984 Vatican *Instruction on Certain Aspects of the Theology of Liberation* points out,

> Liberation Theology was born, first in the countries of Latin America . . . and then in other countries of the third world, as well as in certain circles in the industrialized countries. The "Theology of Liberation" refers first of all to a special concern for the poor and the victims of oppression, which in turn begets a commitment to justice.

The document then goes on to distinguish among and evaluate the diverse theological positions popularly identified with liberation theology in order to draw attention to the deviations and risks of deviations in certain forms of liberation theology. The dangers to which the document referred were described as a "novel interpretation of both the content of faith and of Christian existence which seriously departs from the faith of the church, and, in fact, actually constitutes a practical negation." The document summarizes its critique of the novel interpretation with the following description:

> Concepts uncritically borrowed from Marxist ideology and recourse to theses of a biblical hermeneutic marked by rationalism are at the basis of the new interpretation which is corrupting whatever was authentic in the general initial commitment on behalf of the poor.

The 1984 instruction was followed two years later by the *Instruction on Christian Freedom and Liberation* to highlight the main elements of Christian doctrine on freedom and liberation. The second document, affirming that the theme of liberation "is at the heart of the gospel message," was offered to "assist the testimony and action of all Christ's disciples, called to respond to the great challenges of our times." See the 1984 *Instruction*, Introduction, III:2-3, VI:9-10 and the 1986 *Instruction*, 2.

29. See "Priests and Sisters for Latin America," *The LADOC Keyhole Series*, no. 4 (Washington, D.C.: United States Catholic Conference) and "The Religious Woman in Latin America" (excerpts from the document issued late in 1971 by CLAR), 29-38.

30. According to their survey responses, in the 1960s Maryknoll began to put greater emphasis on lay leadership formation, indigenous apostolates, inculturation, and social communications. Msgr. Salcedo of Colombia began the radio school apostolate, which Maryknollers then developed in Bolivia and Peru, where Fr. Bob Kearns founded "*Radio Onda Azul*," a radio station that provided not only education and religious formation, but, over the years, a consistent source for news from a nongovernmental and noncommercial perspective. Maryknoll Frs. Dan McLellan and Bob Kearns were the pioneers in developing local credit unions in Puno, Peru.

31. Klaiber, *La Iglesia*, 378.

32. Sr. Veronica Wall, CSJ, currently lives in Albany, N.Y. Fr. Stankard, to whom she referred, became a member of the St. James Society. The sisters left Ocobamba in 1983, when Sendero Luminoso terrorists made it impossible for them to continue their work and threatened their lives.

33. The Maryknoll language school in Cochabamba, Bolivia, specialized in teaching not only Spanish, but also Quechua and Aymara, the major indigenous languages of the Andes. On a more local scale, there were ministers like Fr. Ramon Carlin, one of the original Oklahoma missioners sent to Santiago Atitlán, who produced the first written form of the Maya-derivative dialect, Tzutuhil, spoken by the people in that area of Guatemala.

34. See David Monahan, ed. *The Shepherd Cannot Run, Letters of Stanley Rother, Missionary and Martyr* (Oklahoma City: Archdiocese of Oklahoma City, 1984), 7. Hereafter referred to as *Rother*.

35. The Medical Mission Sisters reflected the experience of many communities when they responded to the NCCB survey saying that the turnover of institutional responsibilities led to the need for financial support for new, evolving, grassroots projects.

36. By 1975, the number of U.S. missionaries in Latin America had dropped to 3,101, a decline of approximately 30 percent from its 1968 peak of 4,589. The rate of decline would slow to approximately 10 percent between 1975 and 1980, when 2,803 U.S. missioners continued to serve in Latin America.

37. The description goes on to say: "First Communion is a ceremony having greater social significance than influence in the exercise of the authentic Christian life. Even though their conduct leaves much to be desired, the Latin American masses manifest an enormous reserve of authentic Christian virtues, particularly in the order of charity." See *Medellín*, "Pastoral Care of the Masses," no. 2.

38. Ibid.

39. Ibid.

40. Ibid., no. 4.

41. *Medellín*, "Pastoral Care of the Masses," nos. 10-15.

42. José Marins, "Basic Christian Communities (BCC's) in Latin America," in *LADOC Keyhole Series*, no. 14 (Washington D.C.: United States Catholic Conference, 1976).

43. The lay missioners who worked in San Miguelito were trained in BEC methods before they began their work in Panama. Largely as a result of Fr. Mahon's work, the BEC movement has also grown strong in Chicago. For more on San Miguelito, see Costello, 155.

44. There is abundant literature on the BECs. Their beginnings and basic theology are very well outlined in Marins. For an interesting Protestant evaluation of the BECs, see William Cook Jr., "The Ecclesial Communities: A Study of Reevangelization and Growth in the Brazilian Catholic Church" in *Occasional Bulletin: Quarterly of the Overseas Ministries Center* 4, 3 (July, 1980): 113-16.

45. See Antonio Bentue, "Panorama de la Teología en América Latina Desde el Vaticano II a Santo Domingo" in *Teología y Vida* XXXVI (1995): 159-91.

46. *Evangelization in Latin America's Present and Future: Final Document of the Third General Conference of the Latin American Episcopate*, 641-42. Citations here are from *Puebla and Beyond*, eds. John Eagleson and Philip Scharper (New York: Orbis, 1979). Hereafter the document will be cited as *Puebla*.
    Throughout the text these communities are referred to as BECs. Latin American documents use the abbreviation CEB, based on the original Spanish name, *comunidad eclesial de base*.

47. The term "land invasion" (*invasión* or *toma de tierra*) describes the activity of a group of homeless or displaced people who take over lands belonging to the government or to absentee owners in order to begin building a community for themselves. Many of the shanty towns around major Latin American cities originated as "land invasions."

48. For a recent analysis of the types of basic ecclesial communities and their impact in Latin America, see Daniel H. Levine, *Popular Voices in Latin American Catholicism* (Princeton, N.J.: Princeton University Press, 1992), 30-53. For an assessment of the communities and their impact in the United States, see Robert S. Pelton, CSC, *From Power to Communion: Toward a New Way of Being Church Based on the Latin American Experience* (Notre Dame, Ind.: University of Notre Dame Press, 1994).

49. Perhaps the best known instance of this sort of exchange is chronicled in Ernesto Cárdenal's various publications on *The Gospel in Solentiname*.

50. *Evangelii Nuntiandi* presents a careful analysis of the BECs, emphasizing that those that are truly ecclesial develop within the Church and are places of evangelization and a hope for the universal Church through their seeking of nourishment in the word of God, their avoidance of hypercritical attitudes, their attachment to and solidarity with the pastors of the Church, and their missionary zeal (*Evangelii Nuntiandi*, no. 58).

51. Ibid.

52. See Archbishop Marcos McGrath's introduction to the Puebla document in Eagleson and Scharper.

53. *Puebla*, no. 26.

54. *Puebla*, nos. 31-39.

55. *Puebla*, nos. 63-70.

56. *Puebla*, no. 93.

57. This was the second ordinary session of the general synod of bishops, held in Rome in 1971. The synod document will be referred to as *Justice*. Because it was not published with numbered paragraphs, references will cite the appropriate section of the document and include page numbers for its pamphlet publication under the title *The Synodal Document on the Justice in the World* (St. Paul Editions).

58. *Justice*, introduction, p. 4. This statement is a positive presentation of Medellín's statement that passivity in the face of injustice was a negation of the Christian responsibility to build peace ("Peace," 18).

59. *Justice*, Part III, "Education to Justice," p. 17.

60. José Comblin, *The Church and the National Security State* (New York: Orbis, 1979), 162.

61. *Populorum Progressio*, no. 1.

62. *Puebla*, no. 1134.

63. *Puebla*, nos. 521-22.

64. *Puebla*, nos. 474-75.

65. *Puebla*, no. 425.

66. In Brazil alone, there were 80,000 BECs in 1979, double the number there had been in 1976. (See Penny Lernoux, "The Long Path to Puebla" in *Puebla and Beyond*, 19.)

67. Puebla, no. 262. The critiques are outlined in nos. 98 and 261-63. An example of the strong language used regarding economic systems can be found in nos. 311-15.

68. The figure is taken from the statistics published in the *Catholic Almanac*. The description "long-term" is used to distinguish people with an ongoing pastoral commitment from the many who were beginning to get involved in short-term volunteer projects and twinning or sister relationships between U.S. and Latin American parishes and/or dioceses. Those relationships will be described and analyzed in later chapters.

69. One community of religious women did say that their ministry had been adversely affected by "difficulty in working with diocesan clergy," but there was no indication that the sisters were negatively affected by the results of Medellín or Puebla. In fact, they reported that their work had changed toward a "gradual phaseout of [more formal] ministries" toward "the building of small communities in very poor barrios and working with two diocesan missions."

70. Of the eighty-two religious communities that included narratives about their Latin American work in the 1970s, fourteen mentioned that they had begun or continued to receive Latin American vocations during the period. This figure is best understood as a low estimate because not all religious communities responded to the survey, and of those who responded, not all wrote narrative responses.

71. As a result of Medellín and Puebla, dioceses and parishes throughout Latin America entered into serious pastoral planning processes in which the whole community became involved in setting priorities and assuming the responsibility to see that objectives were carried out. One of the common terms often used to refer to this joint pastoral effort is *pastoral de conjunto.*

72. *Populorum Progressio*, no. 43.

CHAPTER SIX

Deepening the Bonds of Solidarity

The U.S. Catholic Church Speaks on Behalf of Central Americans

On November 19, 1981, the United States Catholic Conference issued a forceful statement intended to influence U.S. public opinion and policy regarding problems in Central America. The bishops spoke out not only because Central America had become a focus of concern in the United States, but also because of the strong and growing relationship between the Church in the United States and the Church in all of Latin America. In this statement, as in many that preceded and would follow it, the U.S. bishops added their widely respected voices to those of their Latin American counterparts and recent popes. Speaking as bishops and as citizens, they appealed for solutions that would genuinely benefit the suffering majority of the Central American population and thus promote the Gospel throughout the American continent.

The bishops' practice of writing such statements was the fruit of years of interrelationship between North and South American Catholics. The pronouncements were informed by official documents of the Latin American Church, by collaboration among the various episcopal conferences, and by reports from missionaries in the field. Through these statements, the bishops not only expressed the U.S. Church's solidarity with the suffering people of Latin America, but also made it clear that the faithful witness of that Church was further awakening the conscience of Christians in the United States. They said:

> In every country of Central America the Church plays a significant role. In word and deed, in the actions of bishops, priests, religious and lay people, the church daily influences the flow of events precisely because it is so intimately identified with the people in their pilgrimage of faith and their pursuit of justice.
>
> The killing of missionaries from the United States vividly reminds us of our relationship to the drama of Central America, but this is not our only bond. Those who go from the United States to serve in Central America, as well as local leadership of the church in these countries, have often described the multiple ways in which the United States daily influences the destiny of people in these neighboring nations. The bonds between the United States and Central America are complex and diverse; they are political, cultural, economic and religious.
>
> As bishops in the United States we feel a special tie to our brother bishops and to the church in Central America. The witness of the church there calls forth our own witness. . . .
>
> As bishops we are called to teach the full dimensions of the Gospel message, including, as Paul VI said in 1975, questions involving justice, liberation, development and world peace. As citizens of the most powerful nation in the Western hemisphere, we take seriously Pope John Paul II's injunction to us at Yankee Stadium, "to seek out the structural reasons which foster or cause the different forms of poverty in the world and in your own country, so you can apply the proper remedies."

The bishops' message was a call to work for justice—and a recognition that solidarity with Latin America offered a graced opportunity for the United States to become more faithful to its vocation as a world power.

The Church in the Midst of a Suffering People

When the bishops of Latin America met in Puebla, Mexico, for their Third General Conference, they described their pastoral role as one of accompanying a people who lived in circumstances of almost every imaginable kind of suffering:

> As pastors, we journey with the people of Latin America through our history. We are concerned about the anxieties of all those who make up the people, whatever their social condition may be. We are concerned about their loneliness, their family problems, and the lack of meaning in the lives of many of them. Today we wish in particular to share the anxieties that stem from their poverty.[1]

In stating the desire of the Church to stand with humanity in all its anxieties, the bishops mirrored the opening lines of *Gaudium et Spes*. They went on to identify the anxieties that particularly characterized Latin America by making specific reference to the political and economic spheres of life. By the time of the Puebla Conference in 1979, political violence, in the form of institutionalized violence, repression, and guerrilla activities, had become tragically present throughout vast segments of Latin America.

In 1964, Joao Goulart, president of Brazil, was overthrown by a military coup. In 1966, the same happened in Argentina, and by 1975, two years after the assassination of President Salvador Allende of Chile, three-fourths of Latin American governments were dictatorships. By that time the statements of national bishops' conferences had begun to be characterized by increasingly stronger statements denouncing repression and defending human dignity. In the latter part of the twentieth century, the Church that had arrived in America as the ally of government—and sometimes of *conquistadores*—had become the primary critic of both government and guerrilla abuses. In many cases the Church was the only voice capable of speaking out effectively on behalf of the victims of violence. That defense did not go unnoticed. While the perpetrators of the violence sought effective ways to silence the Church's voice, the world—and especially Catholics—began to listen, to learn more than they had ever known about their brothers and sisters in Latin America, and to become active in movements of solidarity with them.

When the bishops assembled at Puebla talked about the political "anxieties" of their people, they described them as

> anxieties that stem from abuses of power, which are typical of regimes based on force . . . on systematic or selective repression . . . accompanied by accusations, violations of privacy, improper pressures, tortures and exiles.[2]

Although it might sound like an excerpt from a political science text, that description, far from being theoretical, flowed directly from the experience of the Latin American people.

Brazil: A Model for Economic Growth and Political Violence

Brazil serves as an early example and prototype of what the bishops called "regimes based on force." In 1961, after only seven months in office, Brazilian President Janio Quadros unexpectedly resigned his position, leaving his populist vice-president, Joao Goulart, to pick up the pieces of an economy that could not satisfy the demands of its foreign creditors. Goulart began to distance himself from U.S. economic policies and enacted a law limiting the profit that foreign companies could invest outside of Brazil. At the same time, labor and even rural workers' organizations were growing in strength and gaining official support. Goulart's suggestion that the lower ranks of the military might also organize was the final straw for his opponents in the military and in the middle and upper classes. They were convinced that his policies were provoking class divisions that would spell the end of their power. On April 1, 1964, Goulart's government was deposed, and for the next twenty years a series of military dictatorships ruled the country.

The military dictators adhered to the demands of international creditors, and Brazil's economy turned around, at least in formal, statistical terms. National industries and foreign investment increased immensely; nevertheless, there was no progress in land reform, the conditions of labor, or the protection of indigenous peoples. From 1967 to 1974, the gross domestic product of the country grew at a rate of 10 percent per year. But the economic bonanza, often referred to as the "Brazilian miracle," took place at the expense of the poor. At the end of the first twelve years of military rule, the wealthiest 5 percent of the population was gaining 39 percent of the national income while the poorer 50 percent gained just under 12 percent. Due to the effects of growing inflation, the worth of the minimum salary decreased by 58 percent with the consequence that two-thirds of a minimum salary was required solely to buy basic food necessities.[3] That type of economic development produced a situation in which increased industrial production had to be exported because the majority of the population did not have the purchasing power to take advantage of it. As the rich grew richer, the poor grew more destitute and more discontent. The discontent of the poor, expressed in anti-government demonstrations and industrial strikes, was met with violent repression.

As early as 1968, some ecclesial leaders began to analyze the new political process inaugurated by the Brazilian military dictatorships.[4] According to their analysis, the radically rightist military governments were operating under the dictates of the doctrine of national security: "a politico-economic model which suppresses the broad based participation of the people in political decisions, justifies itself as the defender of the Christian civilization, and elaborates a repressive system which is in line with its concept of 'permanent war.'"[5] The states operating under the doctrine of national security tended to interpret every political movement and activity as a part of the world struggle (permanent war) between the East and West. Because winning that struggle took precedence over any other priority, the abandonment of democratic practices and institutions, flagrant disregard for basic human rights, and even unaccountability on the part of government agents were justified as regrettable but "temporarily" necessary steps on the way to the ultimate goal.

In Brazil, the dictatorship revealed its unequivocal commitment to the national security ideology in December 1968 with the declaration of Institutional Act V, which strengthened executive powers, eliminated the right of *habeas corpus*, and effectively declared war on "enemies of the state."[6] After the promulgation of Act V, government persecution of the people and the Church in Brazil began in earnest.

The Brazilian Church Talks Back

In 1973, responding to the evolution of political events, the bishops of northeastern Brazil produced one of the strongest ecclesial statements ever written about the conditions of their people and the Church's obligation to respond. The statement "I Have Heard the Cry of My People" described the situation of the majority of people in terms of their severe needs in income, employment, housing, nutrition, education, and health care. It described underdevelopment as a situation of oppression: a direct result of government policy. The bishops said that the development pursued by their government had become "defined, not in terms of the interests of Brazilian society, but in relation to the profit realizable by foreign corporations and their associates in our country." Because of that, they said, efforts to eliminate "regional disparities," the vast difference between the material conditions of the wealthy and the poor, "had to be sacrificed."[7] Noting that with the losses of freedom of the press, the right to form unions, and even the right to privacy, the people had been systematically deprived of all the usual methods of protest, they went on to say:

> When such conditions of oppression and injustice meet with resistance, the violation of human rights escalates in acts of still greater violence. Official terrorism establishes control through espionage and the secret police, in a growing state domination over the private life of the citizens, frequently resorting even to such extremes as torture and assassination.[8]

All of this added up to "signs of human degradation" to which the Church had to respond.

Asserting that the Church could not remain indifferent before such conditions, they made their own priorities clear, saying that by divine vocation we belong to the family of those who must commit themselves to those who are marginalized. They criticized the many people who transformed faith into a theory about our personal relations with God without interfering in social and political action. Those people, they explained, used religion as an ideological tool to defend groups and institutions opposed to God's design. Contrasting the "salvific thrust" of the common people's struggle with pseudo-religious efforts to maintain the status quo, they said:

> The "poor of Yahweh" are the privileged channel of God's revelation, the daily pulpit of God's Word, in the events of life, in the hope which is not illusive, in their longing for freedom, peace and brotherhood.
>
> The same cannot be said of oppressors, of those who at every moment give free rein to repression. The way they argue, God is a being

dragged at their side, is being used as a tool, is being put at the service of the "established order," because this is what is most convenient for them. Nevertheless . . . the Virgin Mary herself . . . turns this ideology upside down in her description of God's wisdom: "He has put down the mighty from their thrones and exalted the humble; he has filled the hungry with good things, and the rich he has sent away empty."[9]

In the light of their analysis and their reading of Scripture, the bishops went on to outline the task of the Church in their day. "We are convinced that this is the hour for an option for God and for the people." Clearly aware that "the price of such a choice has always been persecution from those who think that they are so offering a service to God," the bishops called their people to a profound love for the oppressed, to a change in socioeconomic structures built on oppression and injustice, and to an end to institutionalized violence and repression.[10]

As is obvious, this document was neither simple nor directed to the common people. It was, instead, the voice of the Church speaking to the educated "pharaohs" of society.[11] The document hit its mark so well that the government prohibited its publication in the country, thus inadvertently demonstrating that they understood all too well the bishops' message. The banning of the document also increased international interest in both the facts and the bishops' interpretation of the situation.[12] The news of its banning in Brazil was publicized in the foreign press, and translations were made available throughout the world. There can be no doubt that some of those publications made their way back to Brazil.

Repression Follows Protest

While economic statistics can paint a general picture of institutionalized violence, the extent of the repression exercised by the Brazilian government is impossible to document because so much was carried out in secret and during a period of severe censorship of the press. Nevertheless, Amnesty International estimates that by August 1976 there had been 1,801 documentable cases of torture and that 28,303 "suspicious" persons were arrested in the city of Sao Paulo during just the first two months of 1977. By November 1978, approximately three hundred political prisoners had died under torture.[13] The Church was in no way exempt from the repression. In fact, between 1968 and 1978 every Church statement denouncing abuses seemed to be followed by more repression.

Given its international character and relative independence, the Church was eventually able to publicize reasonably accurate records of its particular experience of government repression. In 1978, Cardinal Paulo Evaristo Arns, the archbishop of Sao Paulo, asked for a study of human rights in Latin America. The task was so vast that the researchers decided to limit their investigations to Brazil in the period from 1968 to 1978. The resulting study documented "aggressions" against the Church, which included defamatory attacks, invasions, imprisonment, torture, deaths, abductions, indictments, summons, expulsions, censorship, prohibitions, and falsifications.[14] Although the authors of the study admitted that their records were incomplete and that an exhaustive study of even one category would furnish material for a whole book, they published their findings as a symbolic sample of what had occurred in their recent history. They documented twenty-five defamatory attacks against bishops or priests, the arrest of 395 bishops, priests, or lay people, and the killing of seven priests or seminarians. Of the many incidents of such aggression, the story surrounding the murder of Jesuit Fr. Joao Bosco Penido Burnier seems to summarize their generally macabre character.

The chain of events began in October 1976 in the town of Ribeirao Bonito, in the Amazon prelature of Sao Félix de Araguaia, under the leadership of Dom Pedro Casaldáglia. The police chief of the town was murdered while the police were publicly torturing two brothers who had tried to organize the peasants of the area. A few days later, the brothers' family home was burned down. Then two women of the family, the wife of one of the men and their mother, were arrested, beaten, and tortured; the younger woman was also gang-raped by soldiers.

Six days after the latter events, Bishop Casaldáglia and Fr. Joao Bosco stopped in the town to question the police about the events. The police, unimpressed by the status of either the priest or the bishop, threatened to kill them if they registered a formal complaint. Then, as if to prove their power, one of the policemen hit Fr. Joao Bosco with a rifle and shot him in the head.

Even though, unlike Casaldáglia, Fr. Joao Bosco had not been the object of defamation campaigns and was also from a well-connected Brazilian family that included a bishop and two army generals, little was done to penalize the policemen responsible for the murder.[15] This incident had followed on the heels of the July murder of a missionary priest, Fr. Rodolfo Lunkenbein, and a September episode in which Bishop Adriano Hypólito of Nova Iguaçu had been kidnapped, maltreated, covered with red spray paint, and left, tied up and naked, on a street forty-five miles from where he had been picked up.[16]

Events such as these had their effect on the whole Brazilian Church, spurring the hierarchy to a deeper unity and calling forth two national pastoral letters that echoed the message of those written earlier by the bishops of particular regions: *A Pastoral Communication to the People of God* (1975), and *Christian Demands on a Political Order* (1977). Pastoral statements like these began to focus international attention on the practices of repressive governments. With the united voice of the local Church to back it, the Church in the United States had evidence with which to pressure its Congress to investigate the situation before continuing aid to a repressive government.[17] The Church was standing with the people and throwing the weight of its authority behind the demand that governments exercise moral responsibility.

Brazil: The Model Partner

Between 1966 and 1995, the pattern of political repression evident in Brazil was mirrored in numerous other Latin American countries. Although the types and degree of violence have differed from one country to the next, the practice of "disappearances" demonstrates how disregard for justice and human well-being could become commonplace in the course of a few years.

Human rights organizations have compiled a list of eighteen Latin American countries in which an estimated 88,761 people have been "disappeared" between 1957 and the present.[18] The tactic of "disappearing" people is perhaps the most cruel form of state terrorism. The person in question is seized, sometimes by official police forces, sometimes by unknown persons, but almost always by people associated with the government. If families or friends try to pursue legal channels to determine the person's whereabouts, the arrest may be denied or the interested parties may be told that the person escaped or was released. The feature marking all cases is that the victim taken into custody is never again seen. For

A Salvadoran refugee being kidnapped from La Virtud camp in Honduras. Photo: Rusty Davenport/Oxform America.

the victim's family in particular, disappearance is worse than assassination. They never attain certainty about the fate of the victim; they never know when—or if—the torture ended. Brazil, where there were an estimated 500 disappearances between 1966 and 1981, was the first South American country to apply the practice strategically, but Argentina, with approximately 20,000 victims between 1974 and 1982, tops the South American list. Nevertheless, no country can parallel Guatemala's record of an estimated 35,000 victims from a total population of less than ten million.[19]

Brazil was not just the first large Latin American nation to put the doctrine of national security and all of its accompanying procedures into practice. It also served as an international tutor and helper by aiding its neighbors to follow suit through example, and sometimes through training and economic aid.[20] By 1976, Argentina, Bolivia, Brazil, Chile, Ecuador, Paraguay, and Uruguay were under similar military dictatorships, sharing the same style of political and economic philosophies along with strong resistance to the "progressive" teachings of the Catholic Church.[21]

A particularly remarkable example of aggression against the Church took place in Riobamba, Ecuador, in August 1976. Bishop Leonidas

Sharing Faith Across the Hemisphere

Proaño was hosting an international pastoral meeting at a mountain retreat center when armed plainclothes police burst into the building and arrested all of the participants. The captives, including seventeen bishops, including a number from various Latin American countries and the United States, were crowded onto a bus for a three-hour ride to Quito. There, Proaño was questioned by the minister of the interior while the others were kept waiting without knowing what was happening to their host. By the next day, the government officials realized that they had made a colossal *faux pas* and began to deny that anyone had actually been arrested, saying that the interior ministry had only wanted to talk with the group and that they were all free to go to a hotel. Nevertheless, the international character of the incident had to do with more than the participants. One sign of international support for, if not actual collusion with, Ecuador came from Chile. When the Chilean bishop participants returned to their country, they were met at the airport by the "DINA" (the national security police) and a rock-throwing mob who had already read news reports of the "subversive" meeting they had been attending. In spite of protests by CELAM, the hierarchies of Ecuador and Chile, and the embassies of the United States, Venezuela, and Argentina, no formal apologies were offered to Proaño or his companions.[22]

Within a few weeks of the event, *America* magazine published an editorial on the incident and called it a sign of the "paranoid concern of the Latin American right with supposed communist influence in the church." The editorial also insisted that the episode "should be called what it is: religious persecution."[23] Such occurrences, particularly when they involved foreign religious leaders, ultimately promoted the defense of the Church and its position by focusing international attention on practices that might otherwise have been interpreted as local problems too convoluted for outsiders to understand.[24]

Puebla: Standing with the People in the Midst of Conflict

The bishops at Puebla did not specifically denounce the persecution of the Church in Latin America.[25] Nevertheless, the Puebla document did note two important developments that had occurred during the decade of the 1970s.

From the depths of the countries that make up Latin America a cry is rising to heaven, growing louder and more alarming all the time. It is the cry of a suffering people who demand justice, freedom, and respect for the basic rights of human beings and peoples. . .

The Medellín conference noted . . . "A muted cry wells up from millions of human beings.". . . The cry might well have seemed muted back then. Today it is loud and clear, increasing in volume and intensity, and at times full of menace. . . .

Our mission to bring God to human beings, and human beings to God, also entails the task of fashioning a more fraternal society here. And the unjust social situation has not failed to produce tensions within the Church itself. . . .[26]

First, in those and similar paragraphs, the bishops recognized that Latin America's "clamor for justice" had grown more intense since Medellín—so much so that in some cases the clamor had a menacing dimension, a description that could well allude to groups promoting violent reactions to repression. Second, such statements clearly admitted that the Church's response to the people's cries had produced some ecclesial discord as well as conflict with various governments.

It could hardly have been otherwise. The "signs of the times" were unquestionably difficult to interpret clearly, especially in the heat of the battle. Additionally, the Church could not remain immune to the ideological polarization that marked the world at large. Some Catholics, along with their bishops, believed that right-wing governments were necessary to ensure civil tranquility, even when that tranquility exacted a high cost in social welfare and even in human life.[27] The opposite extreme became more and more deeply committed to revolutionary ideologies and practices, to the extent that even some clergy took up arms in the attempt to overthrow the unjust structures that oppressed the people.

At Puebla, repeating the approach they had taken at Medellín, the bishops took an official position that criticized both extremes. Rather than condoning violence from either right or left, they called for an integral liberation from "all forms of bondage, from personal and social sin, and from everything that tears apart the human individual and society."[28] Reiterating and shedding new light on their teaching about the evangelical role of the poor, the bishops explained that the poor themselves are ultimately the best judges of true liberation: "Let us make no mistake about it; as if by some evangelical instinct, the humble and simple faithful spontaneously sense when the Gospel is being served in the Church and when it is being eviscerated and asphyxiated by other interests."[29] Recognizing that a commitment to a truly liberating evangelization would continue to exact a price, they said: "Those who hold to the vision of humanity offered by Christianity also take on the commitment not to measure the sacrifice it costs to ensure that all will enjoy the status of authentic children of God."[30] As they faced the 1980s, the bishops called the Church to maintain the commitments it had made and had begun to live out in the past two decades. The biggest difference was that they knew from experience how—in spite of their commitment to peaceful means of change—their passion for integral Christian liberation and their ardent desire to build up a just society would continue to place them in the middle of the bitter and often bloody conflicts that plagued their continent.

U.S. Solidarity—Shared Experience and Support

During the decades surrounding Medellín and Puebla, the United States experienced social crises of its own that demanded a church response. A simple reading of the topics on which the bishops issued official statements between 1964 and 1984 gives a historical overview of the major concerns confronting the nation and the Church in those years. In addition to issues of doctrine, internal discipline, political responsibility, family life, and abortion, the U.S. bishops issued no fewer than forty-seven statements on social issues such as race relations, peace, poverty, refugees, human rights, the economy, and U.S. relations with the Third World.[31] Throughout the 1960s and well into the 1970s, the three most pressing social problems in the United States were civil rights, the Vietnam War, and the scandalous proportions of poverty within the nation. With the Vietnam War as the centerpiece, the three issues combined to change the character of the nation, and in many ways, the stance of the Catholic Church in society.

Through the course of the war, various segments of society began to question their government to an unprecedented degree. Protesters not only raised doubts about the legitimacy of the war, but they also brought to light the fact that the poor and people of color—in both Southeast Asia and in the United States—were disproportionately represented among its victims. The three problems of racism, lack of effective concern for the poor, and unjust international relations came to be understood as interrelated. In addition, and most devastating of all for national unity, questions about the legitimacy or morality of the war began to erode public confidence in the government. Doubts, once begun, spilled over to other areas and were further exacerbated in the early 1970s by the Watergate scandal. In the midst of all of this, the United States, now self-assuredly the most powerful nation in the world, began to receive ever more urgent calls from its own Catholic Church to become more responsible and just as a nation and as a world leader.

In 1966, the Catholic Church in the United States, which had gained social respectability through patriotic participation in the two world wars, added its voice to those that were beginning to question U.S. military activity in Vietnam:

> We . . . consider it our duty to help magnify the moral voice of our nation. This voice, fortunately, is becoming louder and clearer because it is the voice of all faiths. . . . While we cannot resolve all the issues involved in the Vietnam conflict, it is clearly our duty to insist that they be kept under constant moral scrutiny. . . .
>
> There is grave danger that the circumstances of the present war in Vietnam may, in time, diminish our moral sensitivity to its evils. Every means at our disposal, therefore, must be used to create a climate of peace.[32]

Two years later, in 1968, the NCCB issued *Human Life in Our Day*, the first of a series of major statements that would spur national controversy within and outside the Catholic Church.[33] The document was designed to summarize Catholic doctrine on the defense of life. Although the section that treated the issue of birth control received the most public attention, the statement dealt with much more than sexual morality.[34] In fact, as the title and opening paragraph indicate, the statement was integrally pro-life; its theme was nothing less than the protection and promotion of human life in all dimensions:

> We honor God when we reverence human life. When human life is served, man is enriched and God is acknowledged. When human life is threatened, man is diminished and God is less manifest in our midst.[35]

Sharing Faith Across the Hemisphere

By focusing issues of family morality within the broad context of the national and international issues related to reverence or threats to human life, the bishops underlined the connections that link the major internal and international problems confronting U.S. society. According to the teaching of *Human Life in Our Day*, Christian family morality includes the responsibility to make positive contributions toward the implementation of social justice, particularly on behalf of the poor:

> The individual family is now challenged to new responsibilities toward the plurality of families which comprises the nation, the human community and the Church. And so, Christian families will want to share not only their spiritual heritage with families less privileged but also their material resources. They will seek by their own initiatives to supplement government action, being painfully aware that in our own country many families are victims of poverty, disease, and inadequate living standards. . . .
>
> The breakdown of the family has intrinsic causes, some of them moral, but these have been aggravated by the indifference or neglect of society and by the consequences of poverty and racist attitudes. The object of wise social policy is not only the physical well-being of persons but their emotional stability and moral growth, not as individuals, but whenever possible, within family units.[36]

Asserting that contemporary threats to life demand "urgent and difficult decisions concerning war and peace," the bishops called on the United States to recognize its moral responsibility as "a nation in many ways the most powerful in the world . . . whose arsenals contain the greatest nuclear potential for the harm we wish to impede or the help it is our obligation to encourage."

The statement called for an "entirely new attitude" toward war. While recognizing the legitimacy of wars of self-defense as a last resort, it urged all people of good will to dedicate their energies toward "forging the instruments of peace, to the end that war may at long last be outlawed."[37]

Saying that in their 1966 statement on Vietnam they had suggested that the U.S. presence there might be "useful and justified," the bishops admitted that two years later they had serious concerns about its morality. These concerns included the questions of whether the United States had passed beyond "the point where the principle of proportionality" justified the war and whether financing the war had not caused disproportionate cuts in the resources devoted to "education, poverty relief and positive works of social justice at home and abroad (including Southeast Asia)."[38]

Finally, going beyond the concerns of family and nation, the pastoral letter teaches that the Christian defense of life has international dimensions. In support of the United Nations and regional organizations that work "to extend the spirit and practice of cooperation," they warned against growing attitudes of exaggerated nationalism and isolationism:[39]

> We believe that the talents and resources of our land are so abundant that we may promote the common good of nations at no expense to the vitally necessary works of urban and rural reconstruction in our own country. The latter are the first order of domestic policy, just as the former should be the first order of foreign policy. Neither should be neglected, both being equally urgent; in the contemporary and developing world order, their fortunes are intertwined.[40]

Thus, during the same year that the Latin American bishops issued their Medellín document, the U.S. bishops made a major statement that called for a universal defense of life. Like Medellín for Latin America, *Human Life in Our Day* addressed the particular circumstances and problems of the United States: family life, poverty, war and peace, and international political responsibility. Also like Medellín, the document went beyond individualistic morality, teaching that defense of life necessarily included sharing with the poor, struggling to end war, and contributing to international peace through works of justice.

Promoting the International Mission of the Church

In addition to calling on the nation and its leaders to promote peace and international justice, the NCCB emphasized the Church's particular international obligations through a statement on the missions. Issued in December 1971, the statement recalled Vatican II's teaching that the Church is "missionary by its very nature" and then went to the heart of contemporary debates about the purpose—and therefore the methods to be used—in the missionary endeavor. The statement's succinct description of the debate summarized the major issues at stake and took a stand that mirrored the teachings of recent popes and Medellín.

> Salvation for some today means meeting people's needs in the temporal order. For others it cannot be found this side of eternity. The meeting of these two points of view constitutes the alleged conflict as to which is primary in the missionary effort, the development or the evangelization of people.
>
> Some who emphasize the development of people in the temporal order disagree as to the proper means to this end. There are those who feel violence must be done to existing social structures in order to free people from the tyranny of the past. Others would stop short of violence. Still others see liberation as a peaceful evolution under the guidance of the Gospel.
>
> For those who carefully follow the social teachings of Pope Paul and his beloved predecessor, Pope John, the resolution of these questions should be clear. . . . There can be little spiritual growth for people unless temporal needs are first satisfied. There can be no lasting spiritual growth for them unless sights are fixed firmly on God and an eventual union with Him. Missionaries generally were and are aware of these priorities. Unfortunately, modern man too often forgets this necessary balance.[41]

Like their Latin American brothers, the U.S. bishops took a stand for "integral liberation," a pastoral effort that would promote full human growth, neither omitting nor limiting the Church's efforts to promote material well-being. They asked for a new awareness of the missions throughout the whole country, called on every parish in the nation to become active in supporting the missions, and encouraged the dioceses to organize mission committees to coordinate their efforts. The bishops ended their statement by asking young people to consider the missionary vocation and saying that U.S. support of the missions "must continue so that together we can meet our collegial responsibility to the whole missionary Church."

Solidarity in Action

By 1974, worsening conditions in Latin America impelled the U.S. bishops to promulgate a *Statement of Solidarity on Human Rights* with specific reference to Chile and Brazil.[42] This statement served two purposes: raising a strong voice of international solidarity and simultaneously educating U.S. citizens about the issues at stake. In regard to the former, the bishops recalled what they had taught in 1973 about the responsibility of the United States to use its unique power to further the cause of human rights:

> The pervasive presence of American power creates a responsibility of using that power in the service of human rights. The link between our economic assistance and regimes which utilize torture, deny legal protection to citizens, and detain political prisoners without due process clearly is a question of conscience for our government and for each of us as citizens in a democracy.[43]

In the light of that U.S. responsibility, the bishops expressed their concern about the U.S. government's escalating financial aid to the government of Chile; they urged that all future aid be conditioned upon "the demonstration that human and civil rights have been restored in that country."

When they turned to the situation in Brazil, the essence of their political message remained the same: the U.S. government had the moral responsibility to be certain that aid sent to Brazil did not foster the repression of human rights. Quoting Pope Paul VI, they set the stage for a description of conditions in Brazil:

> Pope Paul said . . . as long as . . . those in power do not nobly respect the rights and legitimate freedoms of the citizens, tranquility and order . . . remain nothing but a deceptive and insecure sham, no longer worthy of a society of civilized beings.[44]

Then they explained how conditions in Brazil exemplified just such an insecure sham:

> We are compelled to focus attention on Brazil because of the level to which respect for human rights has deteriorated in that country and also because continuous efforts have been made there to eliminate sources of dissent in the public sector—in youth groups, political parties, labor unions, peasant associations.

One of the last remaining organized voices in Brazil's society with power to speak in opposition to repressive government tactics is the Church, and this obviously places it in a most vulnerable position.[45]

Through this statement, the bishops were not only registering an international denunciation of injustice, but were also making an effort to educate the U.S. Church. They quoted Robert McNamara, then president of the World Bank, whose general observations regarding developing nations were particularly relevant to Brazil. McNamara had said, "When the distribution of land, income, and opportunity becomes distorted to the point of desperation, what political leaders must often weigh is the risk of unpopular [among the rich] but necessary social reform—against the risk of social rebellion." The bishops then explained: "The Brazilian regime, rather than effecting necessary social reforms, seems to favor measures which suppress all sources of opposition and thereby hopes to eliminate 'the risk of social rebellion.' "[46] Twice mentioning the same phrases regarding lack of social reform and the resulting risk of social rebellion, the bishops were informing the U.S. public about underlying causes of Latin American unrest. Over and against those who would paint resistance movements as signs of communist influence, they were pointing out that nothing breeds rebellion as efficiently as repression and enforced poverty: the same "root causes" discussed by Medellín.

As a part of their expression of solidarity, the bishops also cited the manner in which Brazilian bishops had "chastised" their own government for unlawful arrests, kidnappings, torture, and murders. This statement marked the first time that U.S. bishops criticized right-wing governments in Latin America. It would not be the last.

In 1975 and 1976, the bishops would voice a message that touched a much more sensitive nerve in the conscience of the United States. It had to do with justice—or the lack thereof—in the relationship between Panama and the United States with regard to the Panama Canal. Control over the Canal Zone provided the United States with an impressive source of revenue and, more importantly, a strategically placed base of military operations. Panamanian opposition, not surprisingly, centered on those very two points; U.S. control over the canal deprived Panama of much-needed income and national sovereignty.

Even though the central issue at stake was control over the canal, the U.S. relationship with Panama also reflected many features of its relationship with other countries, especially in terms of U.S. involvement in the internal affairs of other American nations. While the government of Panama under the dictator General Omar Torrijos was far from exemplary, there was no question that the United States was maintaining an extremely unbalanced relationship with the country.[47] As the national debate about renegotiation of the Panama Canal treaty grew more heated, the U.S. bishops took a very clear stand. Based on consultations with Archbishop Marcos McGrath of Panama City, they discussed the core questions of international justice involved in the relationship. Decrying the shamefully one-sided scope of the situation, the bishops explained why they believed that renegotiation of the treaty was a moral imperative.

After briefly reviewing the history of the treaty, its "dubious validity," and the right of every nation to sovereignty, they reviewed the "main benefits that accrue to each side" from the treaty:

> The Canal Zone . . . is the heartland, the most valuable economic area of Panama. . . . Sixty-eight percent is designated for military use . . . with fourteen [U.S.] military bases. . . . The United States pays an annual $1.9 million, as contrasted, for example, to the $20 million paid annually for three bases in Spain.
>
> The goods that transit the Canal . . . have represented an annual saving to U.S. commerce of $700 million. In this way, Panama, a poor nation, is subsidizing the richest nation of the world and world commerce in general. . . .
>
> While these observations do not attempt to treat all questions relating to the Panama Canal issue, they do serve to place the question within an overall context of international social justice. For peace in the world, which can only come with justice, it is essential that we citizens of the United States, including our elected representatives, approach the Panama Canal issue with the same moral sensitivity we would apply to issues of justice within our own society.[48]

In 1977, General Torrijos and President Jimmy Carter signed treaties that allowed for the eventual return of the Canal Zone to Panamanian control.

Whether or not the bishops' statement had a significant effect on the president, it did attempt to educate and influence public opinion about an issue of international justice. At the same time, it openly acknowledged the U.S. bishops' dependence on consultation with their Latin American peers. Such interdependence and consultation would mark future decades as the U.S. bishops carried on extensible consultations with CELAM officials in the process of drafting official documents. According to Bishop William Weigand of Sacramento, the Inter-American bishops' meetings became a prime opportunity for such consultations and they were particularly important in the drafting of *Economic Justice for All*, the 1986 pastoral letter on the economy. The bishops, like the missionaries, were making it clear that dialogue on national and international levels was an essential component of reading the signs of the times. The U.S. Church's commitment to dialogue and solidarity with Latin America would continue to grow and be expressed not only in official statements, financial aids, and personnel support, but through the sacrifice of life itself.

The Repression Comes Home

Beginning with their 1974 statement, *Solidarity on Human Rights in Chile and Brazil*, the U.S. bishops published a series of statements of concern about justice and U.S. influence in Latin America.[49] In addition to official NCCB pronouncements and publications of the United States Catholic Conference, missionary organizations and certain segments of the U.S. Catholic press kept current events in Latin America in the limelight. The dioceses that sponsored missions often used local Catholic newspapers to keep their people informed about conditions in the area where they ministered. *The National Catholic Reporter*, especially while Penny Lernoux served as Latin American correspondent, averaged approximately one article per issue on some aspect of church or civil life in Latin America; *America* magazine followed close behind the *NCR* in terms of frequency of coverage.[50] In addition to the efforts of such publications, the missionaries themselves, through their personal correspondence, newsletters, and visits home, made a tremendous contribution toward informing ordinary U.S. Catholics about the people and places, the struggles and the joys, of the people and the Church in Latin America. Although the communications certainly didn't reach everyone, there was a multifaceted effort within the U.S. Church to educate its people about their brothers and sisters who lived south of their borders.[51]

As the political situation in Central America deteriorated, U.S. attention to the region grew proportionately and took on new emphases. Whereas communications about mission work in the 1960s and early 1970s frequently made great efforts to describe the poverty of the people, by the mid-1970s, major attention had turned toward explaining the causes of that poverty and related themes such as human rights violations, political unrest, and church-state conflicts.[52] A 1976 article from Cleveland's *Catholic Universe Bulletin* typified the new trend. Entitled "Church-State Clash Due in Latin America" it began by saying,

> Defense of human rights in Latin America will continue to place the Church in the midst of political controversies throughout 1976. Long range church-state flare-ups prove it. In Honduras, the murders of several priests are still clouded in mystery. . . .[53]

Then, after outlining the "bleak" human rights situations in Chile, Brazil, and Argentina, the article informed the readers:

> Besides these problems, Church sources . . . fear [that] the numerous anti-subversive campaigns mounted by governments are disguised attempts at eliminating all active and potential political opposition.
>
> This means going after people not opposed to the state, but who point their finger at specific injustices and inequalities. . . . These people include priests and socially active lay people.
>
> "The result is a critical-prophetic role for the Church," according to Archbishop Aloisio Lorscheider of Fortaleza, Brazil, the president of the Latin American Bishops Council.[54]

Although the article did not name the priest victims in Honduras, it was referring to Fr. Casimir (Michael) Cypher, a Conventual Franciscan from Wisconsin, and Fr. Ivan Betancur, a Columbian missionary, both of whom died as a result of an "anti-subversive campaign" that erupted into violence in late June 1975. Their brutal murders intensified U.S. Church awareness of the emerging issues in Central America and prompted the USCC to issue the first of a decade-long series of statements about Central America.

Rev. Casimir (Michael) Cypher, OFM Conv. Photo: Maryknoll Missioners.

Fr. Casimir, known for his simple and absent-minded manner, was anything but a "subversive." He carried out his priestly ministry in the prelature of Olancho, Honduras, under the episcopal leadership of Bishop Nicholas D'Antonio, a Franciscan from Rochester, N.Y. Outstanding among the many human development projects in Olancho were education programs for *campesinos* (poor rural farmers), many of which were carried out at the diocesan education center, El Centro Santa Clara. The diocese's work with *campesinos* so angered large landowners that they began to attack the bishop's credibility, labeling him a communist and a foreign agitator.[55] Fr. Casimir, who arrived in Honduras in 1973, did not teach in the Centro. His time was entirely taken up with ministry in rural villages and responding to an occasional medical emergency; the latter indirectly led to his death.

On June 24, 1975, Fr. Casimir drove a sick *campesino* to the departmental capital of Juticalpa, where he could receive medical attention. Because his truck had been damaged on the trip, Fr. Casimir decided to spend the night in the capital before returning home to his remote village parish. The next day, about a thousand *campesinos* from the entire region were organizing a hunger march in the city. On the morning of June 25, police officers attacked the building housing many of the *campesinos*. At about the same time, other officers spotted Fr. Casimir walking through a nearby park. For unknown reasons, they arrested him and brought him to the center where several *campesinos* and one government agent had already died. From there he and Fr. Betancur, who had also been arrested that morning, together with five *campesino* leaders and two women, were taken out to the countryside, where they were tortured, killed, and buried in a well that was then dynamited to erase all evidence. Government investigations eventually placed the blame for the murders on the two leaders of the local Landowners' Federation and two military officers. Although they were temporarily imprisoned, all four were freed under the terms of a general amnesty declared in September 1980.[56] There has never been an adequate explanation for Fr. Cypher's murder. Like many innocent *campesinos*, he simply seemed to have been in the wrong place at the wrong time or, others might say, he was associated with the wrong people.

Association with the "wrong people" was ultimately the most dangerous activity of church workers in Central America during the 1970s and 1980s. The "wrong people" were the poor. They were the people who knew that when it came to questions of their rights and fundamental needs, wealthy landowners gave "more importance to a cow than to a human being."[57] Although solidarity with those people brought accusations of capitulating to Marxism, the Church maintained its commitment to the preferential option for the poor.

In regard to the accusation that church workers were communists, Fr. Dennis St. Marie of Cleveland explained:

> I like to remind myself of Archbishop Romero's remark that "a communist is anyone who touches your pocketbook." So whatever we did that would touch a rich man's pocketbook, we always ended up being called Communists.
>
> While I was in El Salvador, the people on the political right called us leftists, and the leftists said we were on the right. To the army we were communists. We had people [from our communities] killed by all three sides.

When asked specifically about the political position of the Cleveland missioners in El Salvador, Fr. St. Marie said that the team had decided that both the U.S. and the Salvadoran members of their pastoral staff would avoid direct political involvement.

> We didn't take a political stand. We were guests in the country, I said that we don't want foreigners coming in the United States and telling us what we ought to do. We only trained [the people] in what we thought

Sharing Faith Across the Hemisphere

was the Gospel and the gospel principles. They had to make up their own mind about which political side they were going to choose.

I ran some of the national centers for the formation of catechists. It was my conviction that they could opt to go for whatever side they wanted to . . . it was their country, their lives and their families.

But I would not allow anyone to be a catechist and to take a side. They had to resign . . . not because I would stop them . . . [from getting involved in politics], I might even praise them. But if you were for the left or with the left, that would make you an enemy of the right. And our people were everybody.

We were committed to people and that was a wonderful thing.

As political conflict in El Salvador grew more intense, that "wonderful" commitment to the people became increasingly dangerous. In February 1979, *America* magazine published the report that four parish priests had been murdered in the past two years in the Archdiocese of San Salvador. Thirteen months later, that number had grown and included the name of Archbishop Oscar Romero. The addition of four U.S. missionaries to the list of victims of El Salvador's persecution of the Church came within eight months of Romero's assassination.

On December 4, 1980, *The Cleveland Plain Dealer* printed the headline "Two Clevelanders Missing in Chaos of El Salvador." The story that followed explained that on December 3, Jean Donovan and Sr. Dorothy Kazel, members of the Cleveland mission team in El Salvador, and two Maryknoll sisters, Maura Clarke and Ita Ford, had been reported missing. The two Cleveland women were known to have picked up the other two sisters at the airport the night before but had not been seen since. The women's bodies were eventually found in a shallow grave about ten miles from the airport, not far from the burned-out wreckage of the van in which they had been traveling. Among those who kept watch as the bodies were exhumed were members of the Cleveland mission team, Maryknoll sisters, and the U.S. ambassador to El Salvador, Robert White.[58]

In El Salvador, the deaths of the U.S. missionaries were one more brutal example of what was happening throughout the country. The U.S. women were killed on Tuesday, December 2, the same day that two thousand people had gathered for a memorial Mass honoring six political

Left to right: Jean Donovan and Sr. Dorothy Kazel, members of the Cleveland mission team; and two Maryknoll sisters, Maura Clarke and Ita Ford. Photos: Maryknoll Missioners.

leaders who had been ambushed and slain as they prepared to give a press conference at a Jesuit high school in San Salvador the week before. On Monday, December 1, there were news reports that a Salvadoran priest had been murdered, raising to nine the number of priests killed in the nation since the 1977 death of Fr. Rutilio Grande. On the same day, December 2, police reported finding nineteen bodies, including seven youths, throughout the country, adding to the total of 9,300 who had been killed since January 1, 1980.[59]

The murder of the four women missionaries caused a veritable scandal throughout the United States. Whether it was due to the fact that the victims were women, or because the U.S. government was arming the Salvadoran government, or simply because they were four U.S. victims of a conflict that the U.S. population preferred to think of as "far away," these deaths made an impact that the killing of thousands of *campesinos* and hundreds of Salvadoran pastoral workers had been unable to achieve.

In spite of the atmosphere of generalized violence in the country, it seemed that no one really expected U.S. missionaries to be killed. Fr. Dennis St. Marie commented: "Every single missionary who lived down there was threatened. We were all threatened . . . but that didn't make us leave." When the Kazel family first heard the news that Sr. Dorothy was missing, they assumed her car had broken down and that they would soon hear that all was well. When a friend had encouraged Jean Donovan not to return to El Salvador, she quipped, "They don't shoot blonde, blue-eyed North Americans down there." But then they did.

Reflection on the Experience

The murder of the four women sparked immediate reaction from all sides. Some spokespersons for the U.S. government tried to raise general doubts about the work of the Church in Central America and the activities of the four women in particular. Before two days had passed, Jean Kirkpatrick, the U.S. ambassador to the United Nations, said, "The nuns were clearly not just nuns. The nuns were also political activists. We ought to be a little more clear about this than we usually are." That statement caused such an uproar of protest that Secretary of State Alexander Haig was more careful in making suggestions as to the cause of the women's death. Testifying at House of Representatives hearings on the incident he said,

> I would like to suggest to you that some of the investigations would lead one to believe that perhaps the vehicle that the nuns were riding in may have tried to run a roadblock or may have accidentally been perceived to have been doing so, and there'd have been an exchange of fire and then perhaps those who inflicted the casualties sought to cover it up. And this could have been at a very low level of both competence and motivation in the context of the issue itself.[60]

But even among the U.S. government officials, there were some voices raised in defense of the work of the women and the Church. Speaking to a Senate committee, Ambassador White tried to explain the work of the Latin American Church in the following way:

> I think it's escaped . . . the attention of this administration that the poor tend to be more revolutionary than rich people. When you commit your life to the poor, in the simplistic minds of some people in El Salvador and certain people in the United States, this identifies the Church or church people with revolutionary activity—and this is not at all true. What they are doing is fulfilling the mission of the Church to work with the poor. . . . That commitment had been misunderstood and, I think, misinterpreted, whether deliberately or not, to try to find excuses for one of the most brutal forces in the world, namely, the security forces of El Salvador.[61]

Ambassador White's testimony reflected the general tone of U.S. church pronouncements on the issue.

On December 5, 1980, Archbishop John Roach, the president of the U.S. Catholic Conference, issued a statement that placed the death of the women in the broad context of the situation of El Salvador. Speaking on behalf of the Church in the United States, he demanded an immediate cessation of military assistance to the government of that country:

> The assassination of Archbishop Romero in March of this year has dramatized to Christians, as few other events could, the inherent risk faced today by those who would be faithful to the Gospel of Jesus Christ. The pastoral task of accompanying the people, especially the poor and oppressed, in their daily suffering and struggle has made the church of El Salvador a vibrant symbol to all the world.
>
> In these last days the price of such fidelity has brought death and destruction of unprecedented proportions to the Christian community of El Salvador. . . . This campaign of violence against the poor and those who side with the poor is an abomination that cries to heaven. . . .
>
> Let those who are responsible for the policy of the United States toward El Salvador, those now in office and those about to assume office, make unmistakably clear to all the revulsion of the American people at the sickening spiral of violence. . . .
>
> The United States is not a neutral or detached party in the crisis of El Salvador. The policies of the U.S. Government, in word and deed, have been and will continue to be the most important external force affecting developments in El Salvador. . . . The compelling need of the moment is to separate the U.S. Government in a clear and visible manner from the repression of the security forces and other military groups which seem to operate with impunity throughout the country.
>
> The suspension of all U.S. economic and military assistance to the government of El Salvador until an investigation of these murders takes place is a positive step which I endorse.[62]

The U.S. government did temporarily suspend its aid to El Salvador; nevertheless, aid was resumed in mid-January 1981. Although impunity in El Salvador continued, the people of the United States were being thrust into a new awareness of their government's complicity with

Sharing Faith Across the Hemisphere

right-wing regimes, and the Church was calling on all people of good will to apply moral pressure in every way possible to bring about a change in U.S. foreign policy. Although the U.S. government did not adopt the Church's position, that position did encourage and strengthen the work not only of missioners, but also of numerous Central American solidarity movements within the United States. Within the country, U.S. foreign policy toward Central America met with continual protest, some of which included not just symbolic but active civil disobedience in the form of harboring Central American refugees who were classified as illegal aliens.[63]

The four women who died in El Salvador were not the only U.S. missionaries who died during that turbulent period in Central America. Fr. Casimir Cypher's story has already been told.[64] Preceding the women, on November 20, 1976, Texas native Fr. William Woods, a Maryknoll priest who had helped develop cooperative farms among the indigenous people of Guatemala, died when the small plane he flew crashed for "unexplained" reasons. He had been warned several times that his life was in danger. On July 28, 1981, Fr. Stanley Rother, a diocesan priest from Oklahoma City, was murdered in his rectory in Santiago Atitlán, Guatemala. On February 13, 1982, a Wisconsin-born Christian Brother, Jim Miller, was shot and killed while he worked outside the building of the brothers' school for indigenous boys in Huehuetenango, Guatemala. Fr. James Carney, a native St. Louisan working in Honduras, "disappeared" and was presumed killed by the military in September 1983. And finally, in Nicaragua in January 1990, Sr. Maureen Courtney, a Sister of St. Agnes from Milwaukee, died together with a Nicaraguan sister when the jeep in which they and Bishop Pablo Schmitz were riding was apparently ambushed by "contra" guerrillas.[65] The only one of those ten who might have been involved in "political" activity was Fr. Carney.[66] The rest of them had committed only the offense of associating with the "wrong people."

The violent deaths of U.S. missionaries demanded not only the political action to which Archbishop Roach referred in his statement, but also a theological reflection on the part of the Church, especially among those who knew and loved the victims. Speaking about the life and death of the four women martyrs, Maryknoll Sr. Marcella Hoesl offered the following reflection:

This is an event of God's loving and mysterious plan. . . . We will not be the same because of it. . . .

We have been seized by the *mystery* of this event. . . . It has been the Christian experience that in every mystery there is part that is hidden . . . but also there is a light side, where something is revealed. . . .

The life and death of Maura and Ita, Dorothy and Jean . . . teaches us so much . . . [about] the *radicality of Christian witness*. Their witness did not begin at the point of death. It began long before, and it will continue on as we, in turn, are called to witness to the meaning of their death. . . .

To be credible in today's world, Christian witness must be radical, going to the core of human existence and the meaning of it. . . . Questions have been asked about us: Are you revolutionaries or missionaries?. . . What are you about? Why do you risk your lives? We have been called communists, Marxists, a variety of labels. Because of our radical commitment to continue in the mission of Jesus Christ let us hope that in who we are and in what we do we will be called Christians, above all by our love for one another.[67]

As has happened throughout Christian history, when the price of faithfulness has been persecution, the Church has felt itself called to a more radical love.

When the persecution hit home, the Church in the United States had to make hard decisions about how best to remain faithful.[68] In October 1980, Bishop Lawrence H. Welsh of Spokane was convinced that his whole diocese should be aware of the extent of the commitment being made by their missionaries in Guatemala. He therefore published a pastoral letter which included the following:

Because of its efforts to preach the good news of Jesus Christ in word and deed, the Catholic Church . . . is now paying the price in its own blood. It would be naive and irresponsible for any of us . . . to believe that this violence and the forces behind it cannot . . . touch our mission. . . . It is very important for you to know that our priests and sisters in Guatemala are now quite clearly risking their own blood by continuing to do their work there. I say this not to alarm you, but so that you may understand the depth of the love which binds them in Christ, to stand and suffer with the people of Guatemala.[69]

Bishop Welsh then went on to say that he supported the missionaries' decision to remain with their people and asked the entire diocese to renew their support of them, especially through prayer.

Bishop Welsh and Sr. Marcella spoke essentially the same message as they reflected on the possibility and the reality of offering one's life for the sake of others. For those who died and those who risked their lives, there was but one motivation: a Gospel-directed love for their brothers and sisters.

The missionaries, those who lost their lives, like their companions who continue to serve, live out a unique and privileged vocation in the Church. As they travel in some of the poorest, most hidden and forgotten areas of the world, they are there as people called and sent. By their presence, they become living links that forge and strengthen the bonds between the communities that send them and the communities that receive them. As the missionaries enter into the life of the people who receive them, they become bridges of international relations: not of the sort that are negotiated in the U.N. assembly or bartered in the meetings of the International Monetary Fund, but rather of the type that are built in living rooms, on park benches, and in parish halls. While they perform an inestimable amount of service, the greatest is ultimately the sharing of day-to-day relationships—and most especially, the common relationship they have together as human beings in community, as people of faith who stand as equals before God.

Ultimately, the work of the missionaries, like that of the whole Church, is subversive in the most radical sense. As they share the hopes and the anxieties of others, as they reflect together on the message of the Gospel, and as they serve as signs of the universal solidarity of humanity before God, the missionaries become counter-signs to every human power and ideology that would demean another or leave another to suffer alone. By the gift of their life—and if need be, through their death—missionaries incarnate the international dimension of the Church. Just as local churches throughout Latin America became the only voice that could be raised in protest against repression, the missionary Church, both through those who are sent and through their sending communities, has been and will continue to be a voice of solidarity, a sign of the love that binds us in Christ.

DISCUSSION QUESTIONS

1. In recent decades, the U.S. bishops have clearly recognized the United States as a world power and have called the nation to live up to its potential for good. How can members of the Church influence the nation to take better advantage of the graced opportunity such power offers?

2. In recent decades, thousands of people have been persecuted or put to death for living their faith, opposing injustice, and/or standing with the poor. At the same time, there have been cruel insurgent movements seemingly bent on little more than massive destruction. What criteria can be used to distinguish those who give their lives in imitation of Christ from those whose cause has little or nothing to do with the gospel message?

3. Sr. Marcella Hoesl interpreted the deaths of the four U.S. missionary women in El Salvador as a part of God's mysterious plan. What might be the revelatory message of such deaths?

4. Speaking in the name of the U.S. Catholic Church, the USCC has been extremely active in making public statements and giving official testimony on behalf of those suffering from repression and injustice in Latin America. Has the U.S. public been sufficiently informed of the Church's position in these areas of concern? If not, why, and what can be done to increase awareness of such activity in the future?

5. Beginning in 1968, the Church in Latin America has spoken prophetically and has significantly influenced the development of the Church's social teaching. Is the Church in the United States sufficiently aware of Latin America's contributions to Catholic social doctrine? How might we raise both our awareness of this theology and our response to it?

Notes

1. *Puebla and Beyond*, eds. John Eagleson and Philip Scharper (New York: Orbis, 1979), nos. 15, 27. Hereafter the document will be cited as *Puebla*.

2. *Puebla*, no. 42.

3. Figures from "Repression Against the Church in Brazil, 1968-1978," *LADOC Keyhole Series,* no. 18 (Washington, D.C.: United States Catholic Conference, 1980), 34.

4. Edward Cleary explains that in 1968, Bishop Cándido Padín presented the Brazilian bishops with an analysis of a pattern he described as the doctrine of national security. Although the bishops did not accept his analysis at the time, in 1979 they and others in Latin America had endured enough of the effects of national security states to describe and condemn them in at least four distinct parts of *Puebla*. See Cleary, *Crisis and Change, The Church in Latin America Today* (New York: Orbis, 1985), 157-58. See also José Comblin, *The Church and the National Security State* (New York: Orbis, 1979), and Penny Lernoux, *The Cry of the People* (New York: Doubleday, 1980), 47-48.

5. The description is excerpted from *Puebla*, no. 547. The bishops described national security as more of an *ideology* than a doctrine. By that they implied that like other *ideologies* promulgated through the continent, it was a "conception that offers a view of the various aspects of life from the standpoint of a specific group in society . . . manifests the aspirations of the group, summons its members to . . . combative struggle and grounds the legitimacy of these aspirations on specific values." They went on to warn that every ideology is partial and that they have such a tendency "to absolutize the interests they uphold" that they really become "lay religions" (*Puebla*, nos. 535, 536).

6. See Scott Mainwaring, *The Catholic Church and Politics in Brazil, 1916-1985* (Stanford, Calif.: Stanford University Press, 1986), 80.

7. *I Have Heard the Cry of My People*, Pastoral Statement of the Catholic Bishops of Northeastern Brazil, May 6, 1973. Translation published by *The Catholic Mind* 72 (November 1974): 53.

8. Ibid., 53-54.

9. Ibid., 61.

10. Ibid., 61-63.

11. At approximately the same time, the bishops of the Amazon region published a pastoral letter with a similar message but using language that was more directed at the common people. That document, "Marginalization of a People," denounced the widespread suffering of the people and called for broad-based reforms that went beyond the capitalist system: "What is really needed is to change the structure of rural production. . . . If we want a change, we must overcome private ownership of land and have socialized use of the land." See Mainwaring, 93.

12. For a U.S. assessment of the message, see Donnell L. Kerchner, CSSR, "Banned in Brasilia: Bishops' Pastoral," *America* 129 (Dec. 22, 1973): 479-81.

13. Amnesty International, known for the thoroughness of its investigations, will list only reasonably documentable cases in their statistics. Therefore, the numbers mentioned may be interpreted as conservative. See Lernoux, footnote, 170.

14. See "Repression Against the Church in Brazil," *LADOC Keyhole Series*, no. 18 (Washington, D.C.: United States Catholic Conference, 1980).

15. See Mainwaring, 155-56, and Lernoux, 314-17. Lernoux notes that the guilty policemen were temporarily arrested.

16. Mainwaring, 155.

17. The United States Catholic Conference has a history of calling Congress to foster international justice. Through the years, officials and staff of the USCC have not only supported Latin American bishops in their own struggles for justice but have also frequently appeared before U.S. congressional committees to offer testimonies based on their highly reliable sources of information.

18. See Patrick Rice, "The Disappeared: A New Challenge to Christian Faith in Latin America" in Keogh, *Church and Politics in Latin America* (New York: St. Martin's Press, 1990), 376. Rice charts the cases of disappearance in Argentina, Bolivia, Brazil, Chile, Columbia, the Dominican Republic, Ecuador, Guatemala, Haiti, Honduras, Mexico, Nicaragua, Panama, Paraguay, Peru, El Salvador, Uruguay, and Venezuela. According to his chart, the earliest documented cases are from Haiti in 1957. The practice was eradicated in seven countries between 1980 and 1986.

19. For the sake of comparison, the population of Brazil is approximately 155 million; Argentina, 32 million.

20. It can be argued that General Alfredo Stroessner, who took power in Paraguay in 1954 and maintained his dictatorship until 1989, pioneered the national security state. However, his dictatorship, like that of Haiti, which also maintained a strong record for repression, was typical of an older style.

21. In March 1976, a military coup ousted President Isabel Perón of Argentina and began "the dirty war," a vicious campaign against all "subversives." Having learned from Brazil that official arrests of enemies of the state could leave an embarrassing paper trail, between 15,000 and 20,000 people simply disappeared while the government admitted to holding 3,500 political prisoners. See Thomas E. Skidmore and Peter H. Smith, *Modern Latin America* (New York: Oxford University Press, 1989), 102. See also "Repression in Uruguay" in *America* 134 (March 20, 1976), which explains that Uruguay, with one-third the population of Chile, had imprisoned as many political prisoners as had Chile. The article also discusses repression in Uruguay.

22. The list of bishops involved in the incident included four from the United States: Archbishop Roberto Sánchez and Bishops Juan Arzube, Gilberto Chávez, and Patricio Flores. Also present were Mexican Bishop Sergio Méndez and the Belgian theologian, José Comblin, together with a number of members of the NCCB Of-

fice of Hispanic Affairs. See James R. Brockman, "A Chronicle of Persecution," *America* 135 (Sep. 25, 1976): 167-68 and Lernoux, 137-43.

23. *America* 134 (Sep. 4, 1976): 88.

24. One sign of such international attention is a report from DIAL, the French Bureau of Information on Latin America, which published documentation about more than 1,700 cases of persecution of Latin American clergy, religious, and pastoral workers that had occurred by 1978. See Lernoux, Appendix.

25. One possible reason for Puebla's reluctance to speak directly of persecution of the Church is that by denouncing human rights abuses in general without emphasizing persecution of the Church in particular, Puebla gave concrete witness to its identification with the people of Latin America; in effect, such an approach was another subtle but powerful statement that the Church stood in full solidarity with the people. In addition, different national episcopal conferences had taken significantly different positions regarding similar political situations in their own countries. For example, Brazil and Chile developed clear pastoral statements and established ecclesial organizations for the defense of their people, while Argentina's bishops were extremely reserved in their criticisms of the excesses of their government.

26. *Puebla*, nos. 87-90.

27. The Argentinean hierarchy avoided confrontation with the government through most of the "dirty war." In May 1977 they issued the pastoral statement *A Christian Reflection for the People of the Fatherland*, in which they acknowledged having received reports of widespread disappearances and stated that if such a thing were happening, it was incompatible with Christian doctrine. See Emilio Mignone, "The Catholic Church, Human Rights and the 'Dirty War' in Argentina," in Keogh, 352-69.

    In 1996, the bishops of Argentina published a pastoral letter in which they said that they deeply regretted "not having been able to further lighten the suffering produced by . . . [the] great tragedy" of those years. See *Origins* 26, 1 (May 23, 1996): 1-8.

28. *Puebla*, no. 482.

29. *Puebla*, no. 489.

30. *Puebla*, no. 490.

31. This figure is taken from the tables of contents of volumes III, IV, and V of *Pastoral Letters of the United States Catholic Bishops*.

32. *Peace and Vietnam*, a statement issued by the National Conference of Catholic Bishops, November 18, 1966, nos. 2, 3, 17 (*Pastoral Letters*, III:74-77).

33. While many statements made by the National Conference of Catholic Bishops have attracted broad attention and criticism, the three that prompted the greatest reaction have been *Human Life in Our Day* (1971), *The Challenge of Peace* (1983), and *Economic Justice for All* (1986).

34. Hugh Nolan notes that in the flurry of publicity surrounding the release of the statement, *America* magazine printed an editorial saying that it would be a shame if concentration on the issue of birth control obscured the document's teaching on family spirituality and its support of the United Nations (*Pastoral Letters*, III:63).

35. *Human Life in Our Day*, no. 1 (*Pastoral Letters*, III:165-94).

36. Ibid., nos. 72-73.

37. Ibid., nos. 93, 94, 97, 99.

38. Ibid., nos. 135, 137, 138. In addition, recognizing the positive contributions of public debate about moral issues, the letter underscores the diversity of opinion in the Catholic Church by saying that in the debate surrounding Vietnam, "one cannot accuse Catholics of being either partisans of any one point of view or of being unconcerned" (ibid., no. 136).

39. Ibid., nos. 120, 126, 130.

40. Ibid., no. 134.

41. *Statement on the Missions* (December 1971), nos. 4, 5, 6, 7 (*Pastoral Letters*, III:293-97).

42. This statement was issued by the United States Catholic Conference, the public policy arm of the bishops' organization; the official statements of the National Conference of Catholic Bishops relate to more specifically pastoral concerns.

43. *Statement of Solidarity on Human Rights: Chile and Brazil*, February 14, 1974, no. 1 (*Pastoral Letters*, III:453-55), quoting the 1973 *Resolution on the Twenty-Fifth Anniversary of the Universal Declaration of Human Rights* (ibid., 386-87).

44. *Statement of Solidarity on Human Rights*, no. 4.

45. Ibid., nos. 7-8.

46. Ibid., no. 10.

47. Torrijos had come to power through a coup in 1968. He remained as dictator until he died in an airplane crash in 1981. After a short interim of civil government, he was replaced by General Manuel Noriega. During Torrijos's rule, in 1971, Fr. Hector Gallego, a Colombian missionary, was disappeared, presumably on account of his work helping rural people in the Veraguas province to develop agricultural cooperatives. His case was an example of what could happen to anyone who defied the status quo. According to Archbishop Marcos McGrath, Gallego's murder was a "sad commentary on a society in which those with a little money and social ascendancy . . . prefer to hoard their small advantages rather than join the rest of the community for the betterment of all" (Lernoux, 124).

48. "Panama-U.S. Relations," a statement of the administrative board of the United States Catholic Conference, February 24, 1975 (*Pastoral Letters*, IV:44-46).

49. For the period from 1974 to 1987, the statements republished in the official series *Pastoral Letters* included the two statements on Panama (1975 and 1976), a

1980 statement on El Salvador, a 1986 statement on military aid to the Contras, and four statements on Central America (1981, two in 1983, 1987). In addition, a good number of the bishops' domestic statements had ramifications for Latin America; these include statements on immigrants and refugees (1977, 1980, 1985, 1986), on cultural pluralism (1980), on farm labor (1974, 1975), and on U.S. Hispanics (1983, 1987). Statements on topics such as peace, justice, and the economy also had clear ramifications for U.S.-Latin American relations. The pastoral statement on world mission, *To the Ends of the Earth* (1986), dealt specifically with the essentially missionary nature of the Church and relationships among the nations. Finally, even the many statements published in *Pastoral Letters* offer only a partial list; since 1975, the USCC has published more than forty statements on Central America.

50. *America*, in particular, seemingly made it a policy to publish occasional articles that not only covered current events, but put them in a historical context. For example, see James Brockman, "Geopolitics in the Southern Cone" 130 (Sept. 11, 1973): 392; "Challenge to Somoza" 132 (Jan. 18, 1975): 25; and "No Need For This Friend" [Somoza] 135 (July 24, 1976): 24. Other national Catholic publications that frequently published similar information were *The Register, Extension, Commonweal, Ave Maria, St. Anthony Messenger,* and *Sign.*

51. Most missionary congregations and dioceses have established plans through which their personnel return to the United States periodically and include some sort of mission education or reverse mission work as a part of their activity while in their home country. The annual bishops' collection for Latin America, which began in 1965, also includes a conscious effort to educate the Church in the United States about Latin American realities.

52. At least in part, that change was due to the fact that the poverty of the masses had grown worse from the 1960s through the 1970s. In 1961, 11 percent of the rural population of El Salvador was landless; by 1975, that number had grown to 40 percent. As in Brazil, while the overall growth rates of Central American nations rose, the living conditions of the masses of the people worsened. See Phillip Berryman, "El Salvador: From Evangelization to Insurrection" in Daniel H. Levine, ed., *Religion and Political Conflict in Latin America* (Chapel Hill: University of North Carolina Press, 1986), 63.

53. *Catholic Universe Bulletin* (Cleveland), April 6, 1976.

54. Ibid.

55. See Donna Whitson Brett and Edward T. Brett, *Murdered in Central America: The Stories of Eleven U.S. Missionaries* (New York: Orbis Books, 1988), 22.

56. Ibid., 17-37.

57. According to Bishop D'Antonio, this was the complaint of Honduran *campesinos* who were denied the right to land they had been promised through an agrarian reform law. Ibid., 23.

58. White apparently knew the women personally. According to Sr. Bartholomew, who was Superior General of the Ursuline sisters at the time, Sr. Dorothy had eaten at the White home before she left for the airport on December 2.

59. Information compiled from reports in *The Cleveland Plain Dealer*, December 4, 1980; *The Chicago Tribune*, December 4 and December 6, 1980; and *The New York Times*, December 5, 1980.

60. Alexander Haig, testifying in hearings before the House of Representatives, March 18, 1981.

61. Quoted from former Ambassador Robert White's April 9, 1981, testimony before Senate hearings.

62. Statement of Archbishop John R. Roach, December 5, 1980. For this and two subsequent statements see *The Catholic Mind* 79 (May 1981): 30.

63. The "Sanctuary" Movement, most active through the 1980s, is the major example of such "active civil disobedience." For bibliography, see Robin Lorentzen, *Women in the Sanctuary Movement* (Philadelphia: Temple University Press, 1991). In addition, groups such as sister-parishes which were not involved officially in Sanctuary sometimes also transported, took in, and supported political refugees.

64. The stories of many of the religious mentioned in the following paragraph can be found in *Murdered in Central America*.

65. Information based on an article from *The Kansas City Times*, January 3, 1990.

66. For more information about Carney, see his autobiography, *To Be a Revolutionary* (New York: Harper and Row, 1985).

67. Marcella Hoesl, MM, "Reflection on the Life and Death of Maura Clarke, Ita Ford, Dorothy Kazel and Jean Donovan," *Missiology: An International Review* IX, 4 (Oct. 1981): 389-92.

68. According to Fr. St. Marie, after the death of the four women, Bishop Pilla said that any member of the mission team who wanted to return to El Salvador should meet individually with him to explain their decision. He did that to be sure that they all felt free in their decision. They all remained.

69. "A Pastoral Letter on Guatemala by Bishop Lawrence H. Welsh," October 1980. Full text published in *Catholic Mind* 79 (June 1981): 5-7.

CHAPTER SEVEN

People to People: Building Lasting Relationships

From Nashville to Port Au Prince
To Say Church Is to Say Mission

It all started with one man who loved Haiti. Beginning in 1967, Harry Hosey used to visit Haiti every year. Each time he went, he was touched by the people and their needs, and so each year he tried to do a little more to help them. In 1978, a Haitian priest invited him to visit a parish where the people were suffering terribly from a drought. The extent of the deprivation convinced him that it was time to find others who would share his concern and join him in outreach to his new Haitian friends.

When he returned to Nashville he told his story to the people of St. Henry's Parish. He not only succeeded in convincing the parish to make a six-month financial commitment to that Haitian parish, but he found Theresa Patterson, the ally he needed to begin something that would really make a difference.

St. Henry's commitment planted a seed. The parish decided to make its financial commitment ongoing. The next year, Theresa Patterson accompanied Harry to Haiti. Then, as the two of them talked, the seed of a new idea began to grow: other parishes could get involved in similar projects. In 1996, after eighteen years of development, two hundred and ninety-two parishes have become involved in Harry Hosey's project, now known as the "Haiti Parish Twinning Program."

Reflecting on the growth of the program, Theresa Patterson says:

I'm not a person of great vision, but I do believe that the mission of the Church is to link us together. I think every parish in the United States should have a connection with another parish in the Third World. That's how we will grow as a Church. . . .

I feel that there's a great need in the Church for lay people to get involved in hands-on mission work. I've found that people have a real hunger and thirst to do that. When we do, it takes us out of our narrow focus on ourselves. . . .

We need to understand the people of the Church in other parts of the world. We share the same faith, but our lives are so different. We can share material things, but we learn so much more when we meet the people. When we are involved in twinning, we are involved as lay people with lay people, we make personal contact and that allows us to learn from their spirituality. . . .

Every day I thank God for the way this has grown. I've seen so many little miracles through the years. I feel sure that God has had a hand in it all. I think this is what we are meant to be as Church.

Toward the New Millennium

Pope John Paul II has invited the Church, and indeed all the world, to celebrate the year 2000 as a year of jubilee. In speaking of the jubilee, John Paul has offered the following guide for reflection:

In the Church's history every jubilee is prepared for by Divine Providence. . . . We look today with a sense of gratitude and yet with a sense of responsibility at all that has happened in human history since the Birth of Christ. . . . In a very particular way, we look with the eyes of faith to our own century, searching out whatever bears witness not only to man's history but also to God's intervention in human affairs.[1]

As the nations and Churches in America move toward the next millennium, it is a time for taking stock of where we are, where we have been, and where we are going. Five hundred years is a long time. For one quarter of its history, Christianity has been growing in America, adding the yeast of the Gospel to its cultures, and simultaneously developing new, diverse, and uniquely "American" expressions of that one, universal faith.

The intensified relationship between the Churches in North and South America began under the inspiration of Pope John XXIII and has had a very short history. By any count, it is hardly more than fifty years old: only 4 percent of Christian history. Could it be just a flash in the pan—one of those movements that, like the seed planted in rocky ground, springs up quickly, but takes no root, and so quickly withers in the first heat of the day?

Some might argue for that metaphor. Two years after Pope John XXIII's call in 1961, the number of U.S. missionaries in Latin American almost doubled, and by 1968, it had more than tripled. But then the decline began, and by 1992, there had been a 35 percent drop from the 1968 peak; the total number of U.S. pastoral workers in Latin American in 1992 was lower than it had been in 1962 (see Figure 1).[2] It might sound like the story of growth without roots. But statistics do not tell the whole story, and those are not the only statistics that apply to this story.

While U.S. Catholic religious communities and dioceses were sharing personnel with Latin America, the people at home were being informed and becoming involved in a broad outreach. There are no statistics available to compute the total U.S. financial contribution to the Latin American Church, but since 1965, the National Collection for the Church in Latin America has received and distributed more than $72.5 million in grants to aid specific projects in Latin America. Those grants have grown by more than 45 percent in just the last five years.[3]

Other statistics also bear out a general pattern of growth in U.S. church support for Latin America. All groups responding to the 1995 survey from the National Conference of Catholic Bishops (NCCB) said that their support for Latin America had grown over the decades; parishes and dioceses reported an 18 percent growth since the 1960s, Catholic institutions of higher education recorded an 8 percent growth, and religious communities a 5 percent growth (Figure 2).[4] At the same time, 100 percent of the colleges and universities, 95 percent of the parishes, 93 percent of the dioceses, and 78 percent of the religious congregations said they expect their

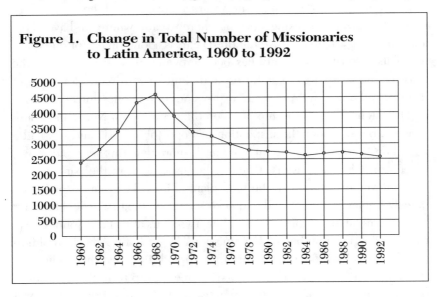

Figure 1. Change in Total Number of Missionaries to Latin America, 1960 to 1992

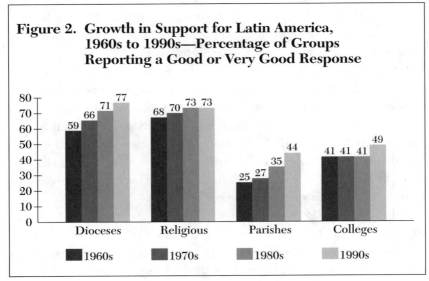

Figure 2. Growth in Support for Latin America, 1960s to 1990s—Percentage of Groups Reporting a Good or Very Good Response

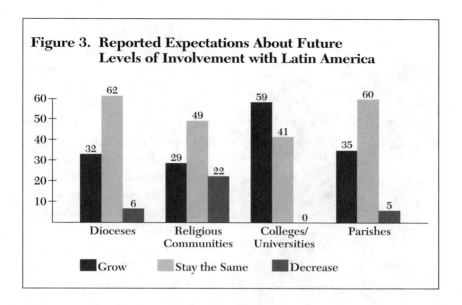

Figure 3. Reported Expectations About Future
Levels of Involvement with Latin America

Dioceses: Grow 32, Stay the Same 62, Decrease 6
Religious Communities: Grow 29, Stay the Same 49, Decrease 22
Colleges/Universities: Grow 59, Stay the Same 41, Decrease 0
Parishes: Grow 35, Stay the Same 60, Decrease 5

Grow | Stay the Same | Decrease

level of involvement with Latin American to increase or at least remain stable for the next five years (see Figure 3). In spite of the diminishing numbers of traditional missionaries, there is clearly more to the relationship than the sending of priests and sisters to work in Latin America.

Limited-Term International Mission

Although the movement toward a stronger relationship between the United States and Latin America began with a request for missionaries, many other dimensions of the relationship have grown along the way. First of all, the "sending" of personnel implies some level of activity on the part of a group "back home." Religious communities, dioceses, parishes, and small groups—in a word, representatives of every facet of the Church in the United States—have been involved in this movement, even if only minimally through hearing a mission talk or making a one-time monetary contribution. Nevertheless, research indicates that the involvement is anything but minimal; in response to the 1995 NCCB survey, 44 percent of U.S. parishes and 77 percent of dioceses ranked their support of Latin America as good or very good in the decade of the 1990s. Because it is clear that the number of traditional missionaries has decreased, it becomes obvious that something new is evolving. The evidence points to the conclusion that newly developing connections among the Churches in the

Missionaries in Guatemala. Photo: Mary-knoll Missioners.

hemisphere are frequently guided by a renewed mission theology, are characterized by a high degree of lay involvement, and may encompass either a shorter term of pastoral service or an altogether new type of relationship.

Renewal in mission theology has engendered a new appreciation for the universality of the Church. Just as the documents of Medellín and Puebla outlined a renewed pastoral theology for Latin America, the 1986 NCCB document *To the Ends of the Earth* sketched many of the important developments in missiology. One of the most basic of these is a new approach to the idea of mission. According to the document:

> The lands to which missionaries went used to be called "the missions." These countries were seen as mission-receiving. Other countries were thought of as mission-sending; they did not see themselves in need of receiving missionaries. A deeper understanding of the theology of mission leads us to recognize that these distinctions no longer apply. Every local church is both mission-sending and mission-receiving. . . . Together we are coming to see that any local church has no choice but to reach out to others with the gospel of Christ's love for all peoples. To say "Church" is to say "mission."[5]

In other words, every local church plays a role as a mission-sending church. In addition, the universality of that mission implies that local churches throughout the world are called into an ever deeper communion with one another.[6] Elaborating on that idea, the bishops cited the essential role of dialogue in the process of communicating the gospel message:

Sharing Faith Across the Hemisphere

Before all else, dialogue is a manner of acting, an attitude and a spirit which guides one's conduct. It implies concern, respect and hospitality towards the other. It leaves room for the other person's identity, his modes of expression, and his values. Dialogue is thus the norm and necessary manner of every form of Christian mission. . . . Any sense of mission not permeated by such a dialogical spirit would go against the demands of true humanity and against the teachings of the gospel.[7]

As summarized by the bishops, the renewed approach to mission is marked by dialogue that expresses a profound sense of mutuality and the realization that every local church and culture has unique and invaluable gifts to offer to the whole Church. Thus, every church is called to be in mission and to be evangelized by others. As that new understanding permeates the churches, new mission practices are beginning to emerge.

The traditional image of the missionary was of a person who left his or her homeland to serve another people by becoming a permanent part of their life and culture. It automatically included the stereotype that the missioner would be a priest or a religious. Both elements of that traditional description have undergone significant evolution in the past thirty-five years.

The development of groups like the St. James Society and the U.S. diocesan missions in Latin America introduced a new model for mission. In these groups, the general assumption has been that the people sent, unlike members of specialized mission societies, would serve for a limited time and then return, very often to be replaced by others who would do the same. Beginning with the decade of the 1960s, eighty-five dioceses reported sending 1,056 priests to serve in Latin America.[8] Of these, over three hundred have served through membership in the Society of St. James, some as Maryknoll associates, and numerous others as members of diocesan mission teams.[9] While a few of them, in diocesan missions in particular, have stayed in Latin America for many years, the majority have returned after their term to take up ministry at home, bringing with them new awareness of the breadth of the Church and its mission throughout the world.

The second part of the stereotype to change is the assumption that missionaries will be clergy or members of religious congregations. Although little known, the service of the laity in the missions is hardly new. Lay people accompanied and helped some of the earliest Spanish and Portuguese missioners who ministered in North and South America. In fact, an African slave, known only as Esteban, traveled with some of the first missionaries to explore and evangelize what is now U.S. territory.[10] In addition, lay "catechists" have traditionally offered invaluable aid to missionaries, often traveling with them, helping to translate the gospel message into the language and culture of peoples who had never before heard it. In more recent times, PAVLA, the Papal Volunteers to Latin America, and similar organizations have been founded precisely to prepare and support lay mission efforts. In addition, as U.S. dioceses began to sponsor mission projects, many of them included laity as a part of their mission team. One of the most interesting facts about the lay missionary movement is that while the numbers of priests and religious missionaries have decreased rather steadily since 1968, the involvement of lay persons in mission has followed a distinct trajectory: in 1960, there were an estimated 178 U.S. lay missioners; the number peaked in 1966 with 549 and has regularly fluctuated until 1992 when there were an estimated 406 (see Figure 4).[11]

Since Vatican II, various religious communities have sought ways of including the laity in their foreign mission efforts. One of the first and most

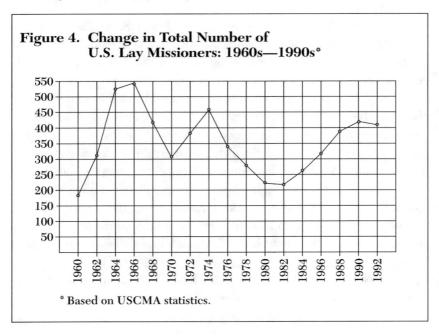

Figure 4. Change in Total Number of U.S. Lay Missioners: 1960s—1990s*

* Based on USCMA statistics.

Sharing Faith Across the Hemisphere

successful has been Maryknoll.[12] Maryknoll's efforts to incorporate lay people in active mission began almost immediately after Vatican II. In 1966, when the Maryknoll Society met in its Fifth General Chapter, one of the major topics of concern was how to cooperate with lay missionary organizations and help in the training of lay missioners. Maryknoll eventually developed its own lay missioner program and in August 1974, with the support of the Maryknoll sisters, the first lay missioners began work in Hong Kong and Peru.[13] By 1992, there were 153 lay missioners participating in Maryknoll's overseas and U.S. mission endeavors.

In July 1994, Maryknoll established the "Maryknoll Mission Association of the Faithful," an organization in the process of working toward canonical recognition as the third branch of Maryknoll.[14] Made up of lay people as well as priests and religious, members of the association enter into a renewable contract for an original three and one-half years of association with Maryknoll, a time that includes both their preparation and their actual mission assignment.[15]

Once it was established, one of the association's first official acts was to adopt a vision statement, a seven-paragraph self-description that articulates a simple theology of mission by applying church statements to their own lived experience. In 1975, Pope Paul VI wrote *Evangelii Nuntiandi*,

Missionaries in Bolivia. Photo: Maryknoll Missioners.

his encyclical on the missionary nature and task of the whole Church. In that, he said:

> Those who sincerely accept the Good News, through the power of this acceptance and of shared faith, therefore gather together in Jesus' name in order to seek together the kingdom, build it up and live it. They make up a community which is in its turn evangelizing.[16]

The Association of the Faithful's vision statement mirrors Pope Paul's statement and demonstrates how the members are living their faith through participation in the work of evangelization:

> We are a Catholic community called by the Holy Spirit to mission through our baptism and our ongoing journeys of faith. We seek the reign of God in our world, and commit our lives to witness to the Good News of Jesus Christ. . . .
> In evangelizing, we are inspired and called to conversion by the faith lives of those we serve. . . . Seeking to be a bridge between sending and receiving communities, we dedicate ourselves to weaving connections of mutual respect, understanding and solidarity among people worldwide.
> We are grateful to the communities who send us, to the people who receive us, and to those whose support makes our work possible. . . . The opportunity to dedicate ourselves to mission is a sacred challenge and a priceless gift from God.

Based on church teaching combined with their experience in mission, the Association's vision statement affirms that the laity are hearing and responding to the Church's call, underlines the mutuality of evangelization, and, most of all, articulates the excitement and gratitude that characterize Catholic laity as they become more and more involved in mission. That experience of mission rings true to many others whose particular commitments are very different from those of the long-term missioner.

Organizing Sister Parishes
In 1990, Pope John Paul II issued the encyclical *Mission of the Redeemer: On the Permanent Validity of the Church's Missionary Mandate*. Just as the title aptly summarizes the papal message, one paragraph of the

encyclical outlines the ways in which that mission mandate affects every level of the Church:

> Cooperating in missionary activity means not just giving but also receiving. All the particular churches, both young and old, are called to give and to receive in the context of the universal mission, and none should be closed to the needs of others. . . . I exhort all the churches, and the bishops, priests, religious and members of the laity to be open to the Church's universality, and to avoid every form of provincialism or exclusiveness, or feelings of self-sufficiency. Local churches, although rooted in their own people and their own culture, must always maintain an effective sense of the universality of the faith, giving and receiving spiritual gifts, experiences of pastoral work in evangelization and initial proclamation, as well as personnel for the apostolate and material resources.[17]

The story told by Theresa Patterson at the beginning of this chapter is one, albeit outstanding, example of how U.S. Catholics are accepting the Holy Spirit's call to mission and the mandate of Pope John Paul II. The responses to the NCCB survey indicate that 12.3 percent of U.S. parishes are involved in sister-parish relationships.[18] Only a few of them, however, are involved in efforts as broad-based and as organized as the Haiti Parish Twinning Program (HPTP). While the project is based in Nashville, the 292 parishes or groups involved in HPTP span the continental United States from New Jersey to Washington, from Wisconsin to Georgia—and HPTP hopes to increase its program to 400 linkages by the year 2000.

The HPTP maintained itself informally from 1978 until 1992, when it became officially incorporated as a nonprofit organization. Although each U.S. and Haitian parish sends financial reports to Nashville twice annually, 100 percent of every U.S. parish donation goes directly to the Haitian parish for which it has been collected. Money contributed directly to the HPTP helps defray the costs of communications: printing, mailings, phone, etc. What HPTP offers U.S. parishes or groups is a ready contact with a needy Haitian parish, support in organizing and publicizing the project, and assistance when parish representatives travel to visit Haiti. Three-quarters of the Catholic parishes in Haiti are currently twinned with at least one U.S. parish or group.

The one Haitian diocese with which HPTP does not work is Hinche, for the simple reason that since 1984, Hinche has been involved in a special relationship with the diocese of Richmond, Va. As a diocesan project, Richmond's "Haiti Outreach" is able to combine a number of features that would be more difficult to coordinate in a national project such as HPTP.[19] Richmond's special projects include a variety of short- or long-term volunteer opportunities as well as a program through which Virginia residents can make retreats to Haiti. Within the United States, the diocese works to further international solidarity with the Haitian poor through a focus on ministry with Haitian migrant workers, justice advocacy on behalf of Haiti with U.S. businesses and government groups, marketing of Haitian products in the United States, and provision of medical treatment in Virginia for Haitians with special needs. All of that is in addition to the "twinning" relationships that have been established between Haitian parishes and more than thirty Richmond parishes and institutions.

When Theresa Patterson described the twinning relationship, she explained its importance as a way for the laity to become involved in mission and emphasized that it implies far more than monetary contributions: "It's not just financial. It's personal. It's all about getting parishes and individual people connected through direct communication and prayerful support." In saying that, she is echoing Pope John Paul's teaching that local churches need to be involved with one another in a variety of ways in order to maintain an effective sense of the universality of the faith. When such involvement goes beyond the financial and even the long-term sharing of personnel, communities find that mission and the universality of the Church become integrated into their daily experience and expressions of faith. Such an integration is the goal of many sister-parish relationships.

The Sister Parish Experience

The HPTP is an example of how the movement to share faith across the American hemisphere has taken root and grown throughout the United States. What happens to the members and even the structures of an individual parish through involvement in such a relationship can only be understood through hearing them tell their story. While each sister-parish relationship is as unique as the individuals and groups involved, an in-depth look at one parish's growth in a sister relationship can illuminate the experience of many others throughout the nation.

Sharing Faith Across the Hemisphere

St. Peter's Parish in Kansas City, Mo., offers one typical example of how a sister-parish relationship affects a total faith community. In May 1996, one of St. Peter's small Christian communities devoted its regular meeting to a reflection on their experience of being a sister-parish to San Francisco de Asis parish in San Salvador. They asked themselves how the relationship began and how it has affected them and the rest of the parish. As Nancy Caccamo tells the story, St. Peter's sister-parish relationship began rather unexpectedly in 1986 through the parish peace and justice committee's concern about war refugees in El Salvador:

We were looking for ways that we as a church could do something to help the Salvadoran refugees who were returning to their country. It just seemed ridiculous for us to think that we could do anything—the problems were so huge. We studied it for a year or two and got to the point that the more we looked at it the more immobilized we became.

Then we heard that the SHARE Foundation was sponsoring a national delegation to El Salvador to help U.S. people learn about the situation there and find concrete ways to help. We decided that our pastor, Fr. Jerry Warris, should be a part of it. We asked him . . . no, we *told* him that he should go. When he came back he began to talk to people about what he had learned. He said a little in his homilies and did a lot more talking to individuals and small groups.

Later, in July 1989, with his encouragement, I went on a Kansas City delegation to El Salvador with three other parishioners from St. Peter's. We learned a lot, and one of the things that we learned was that even though the problems were huge, we could do *something*—we could be a sister parish.

When the delegates returned, they presented the sister-parish idea to the parish; the parishioners of St. Peter's voted overwhelmingly to support the sistering. The relationship began in October 1989. The parish started to send regular delegations to visit their sister-parish. As Nancy explains:

At that time, 1989, El Salvador was in a war and our sisters and brothers in San Francisco de Asis were asking for a relationship in which we would accompany them in their difficulties. The accompaniment took on different forms. Some of it was physical: to personally visit them and be with them. . . . When internationals were present, the military was more likely to leave them alone. It also took the form of education: the people of the parish educated us so that we could come back and educate people here. We were their voices and told people here what was really happening in El Salvador. The accompaniment was also financial: we supported projects in the parish with our money. Finally, there was faith accompaniment: we prayed with them while we were there and back home we prayed for them and for peace in El Salvador.

When the peace accords of 1992 ended the war, the relationship changed. El Salvador was no longer in the headlines, and some might have thought that accompaniment was no longer necessary. But the people of St. Peter's did not agree. They continued the delegations and found that in the absence of war, there was more time to deepen relationships—time to really become friends. As Jane Brummel explains:

For the past seven years we have called the people of San Francisco de Asis our friends. Our relationship has grown in that time from a formal

Missionaries in Chile. Photo: Maryknoll Missioners.

Sharing Faith Across the Hemisphere

level—an arranged marriage, so to speak—into one of a depth and respect never imagined in the beginning. To foster that growth, we as a community send visitors to the parish at least once and sometimes twice a year. They also send visitors to us each year.

The ongoing visits seem to be the key to the depth of the sister-parish relationship. Jim Caccamo, who made his first trip after his wife had already been to El Salvador, commented:

> The personal relationships bring an enhanced understanding of the social, economic, and political situation. Nancy went in 1989. I had been studying this stuff for a year . . . but Nancy made it come alive. She made it real for me. So then I went myself.

A sense of personal relationship extends beyond those who are actually able to travel. Each group that makes a trip is missioned by the parish in a blessing ceremony and then reports back to the parish during a Sunday liturgy. One parishioner who has never made a trip commented on how prayer for a delegation had made him a real participant in the communal commitment.

> While they were gone we kept a candle burning. It was a candle for the people of El Salvador and for our parish delegation. But we had seen pictures and heard names, so the candle had more meaning. It was Dick's candle, but it reminded us of children's faces. When we saw the candle we remembered pictures of tall Dick playing basketball with short kids. Those are the human connections that I failed to receive from any newspaper article.

The sense of total community involvement, of having a personal connection even without having gone oneself, brings the parish together in its ongoing commitment to the sister-parish relationship. According to Dick Brummel, there is no other parish commitment or activity that draws as much interest and support as the sister-parish projects:

> Every time we have asked the parish at large to involve itself in something for San Francisco de Asis we have gotten more response than we

could deal with. The fiesta for the sister-parish gets bigger and bigger every year. We draw more people to that than we do to any other activity we have as a parish. It's probably the biggest thing that happens in the parish except for Sunday Mass.

I had thought that only a few people were really interested. The biggest surprise came when the pastor from El Salvador visited here for the first time. We were going to meet with him in a small room, and hundreds of people came to hear him. . . .

We've brought someone up every year since we started. So at least once a year people hear somebody from El Salvador at Mass. If they're involved in any kind of small group they meet the visitor in that group too. The visitors also talk to all the kids in the parish school.

Special activities and the annual fiesta are a major source of funding for St. Peter's financial contribution to San Francisco de Asis. Although the projects funded from the United States are rarely the central topic of discussion, the whole parish is aware that they support a technical school that trains Salvadorans in a variety of sewing and tailoring skills. They are also proud to talk about a recently opened computer lab that offers courses to prepare young people for the increasingly technological job market of San Salvador.[20] Nonetheless, such projects are far from being the principal motivation for the relationship; the key, says Dick, "is just being there."

In fact, if St. Peter's feels that its relationship with San Francisco de Asis is unique, it is because it is not project oriented. The financial support that parishioners give is an established amount that fits into San Francisco's budget. When they support special projects like the computer lab, the people of San Francisco ensure that the project can become self-sustaining. Thus, now that the infrastructure has been provided, the reasonable tuition charged for computer classes will pay the instructors and the project's upkeep.

When Nancy Caccamo reported back to the parish from the June 1996 delegation, she described the purpose of the visits as being more like a family reunion than a volunteer activity:

I'm often asked why I go to El Salvador and what we *do* when we're there. Very simply, we go to visit our sisters and brothers there. We go to build our relationship. We spend time with them as family, get to know them as people, share their lives and their faith. Our relationship is based on our shared faith.[21]

That sharing of faith takes concrete shape in numerous ways. While they are in El Salvador, delegation visitors participate in liturgies, basic Christian community meetings, and prayer experiences with the people of San Francisco. Upon their return, they continue to reflect on their experience, on what they have learned from the faith of the Salvadoran people; they share that with the whole parish community in their reporting back, and, as one said, "hopefully we share it most through the very way we live." Every Sunday the people of San Francisco are remembered in St. Peter's eucharistic celebration and frequently the liturgical decor includes a cross, an altar cloth, or a wall hanging that visibly reminds the people of their Salvadoran friends.

Parish involvement with the sister-parish also seems to have helped develop a deeper level of communication among the parishioners themselves and between St. Peter's and other parishes in the diocese that have similar commitments. One parishioner commented that a wide variety of opinions can be expressed among the people of the parish, and that the Salvador connections has "caused some healthy discussions" about politics, war, and injustices both at home and in Central America. Another commented, "When the sister-parishes in Kansas City have gotten together, I have seen more interparish contact than we have had in anything except kids' sports." He then added that all of them could gain from more contact with one another. Commenting on how the sister-parish relationship eventually affects every other question of social justice, Jim Caccamo said:

> Every time a group has their sensitivity raised about one justice issue, it increases the possibility of having their sensitivity raised about other justice issues. When we talk about how it affects the parish as a whole, you have to know St. Peter's and know that it's different than it was before El Salvador. Some of it has to do with the transformation of the pastor, or the transformation of some of the parishioners . . . and the huge body is affected by that.

Such transformation can be both inviting and frightening. Reporting on her experience of the June 1996 trip to visit the sister-parish in El Salvador, Michele Chollet shared the following reflection during a Sunday liturgy:

> For at least the last three years, I have been thinking of going to El Salvador with one of our parish delegations. . . . People kept urging me to go, but I hesitated. My youngest child is just ten. . . . I worried about a lot of things . . . but they were not the real reasons I hesitated.
>
> Actually, I was more worried that if I went to El Salvador I would be so changed and even radicalized by the experience that I wouldn't be able to come home and quietly resume my normal life. I worried that my life would seem shallow and stupid compared to the obvious hardships of the people there. This may seem silly, but that really is what I worried about.
>
> However, by the time I left El Salvador, that worry was turned on its head. Now I worry that I will quietly resume my normal life, that I will forget the people there and will not allow the experience to affect me.

For the parishioners of St. Peter's, personal contact with their Salvadoran brothers and sisters is the key. Little by little, the "normal life" of St. Peter's is being transformed through the relationship with San Francisco de Asis. As they continue to build the sister-parish relationship, both parishes are responding to John Paul II's exhortation to be open to the Church's universality. When delegates from the United States and El Salvador visit one another's parishes, they break down boundaries of provincialism so that people once considered "foreigners" become "friends." As the people of both parishes share their faith and their gifts with one another they are effectively building up their awareness and their appreciation for the universality of the faith. As St. Peter's parishioners seek the reign of God together with their friends in El Salvador, they continually discover ways in which the faith of those to whom they reach out calls them to conversion. In the long run, as they have said, their effort to contribute to evangelization in El Salvador has been "turned on its head" and has evangelized their own Kansas City parish. Or, in the simpler and oft-repeated words of so many people who have been involved in every style of mission: "We receive much more than we give."

St. Peter's experience reflects that of many of the parishes that have become involved in sister-parishes or other types of mission outreach to Latin America. Pastors responding to the NCCB survey reported that personal requests for help were the single strongest motivating factor encouraging people to contribute time, effort, and money to Latin America. In regard to how people in their parishes have been changed by their involvement with Latin America, 60 percent of the pastors stated that they had noted an increased awareness of people of other cultures, and 56 percent said that their people had become more appreciative of their own blessings. In addition, 49 percent reported that their people expressed greater concern for the universal Church in their parish prayer and liturgy, and 44 percent agreed that involvement with Latin America had increased their people's sensitivity to social justice issues.

When pastors added narratives to their survey responses, it became clear that the effects of involvement don't fall easily into discrete categories. For example, one pastor commented that increased appreciation for cultural diversity creates greater awareness of social justice and an appreciation of the universal nature of the Church:

> When people come from Latin America, it's a great benefit to us. They challenge ethnic (racist) opinions; they jolt our people out of contentment and broaden our sense of Church.

While his commentary was unique in its blending three categories into one response, the majority of the pastors who made remarks about increased appreciation of cultural diversity connected it to racial and/or economic justice issues. Although a high number of pastors agreed that involvement with Latin America had made their people more aware of their own blessings, very few elaborated on that with narrative responses. The greatest number of narratives dealt with increased awareness of justice issues, appreciation for diversity, and an awareness of the universality of the Church and the Church's mission.[22]

In the mid-1990s, U.S. Catholics were contributing to multiple facets of the Church's missionary efforts.[23] On the parochial level, 10 percent of the parishes of the United States were committed to a twinning relationship, at least 13 percent were sponsoring mission personnel, and 90 percent were donating to mission collections.[24] Catholic colleges and universities reported that 56 percent had sent students and 48 percent had sent faculty or administrators to Latin America—all of this in addition to on-campus promotion of long- and short-term volunteer opportunities with other organizations.[25] Mission is clearly an important item on the agenda of the Church in the United States.

As is obvious from the reflections of individuals, the more intensely involved people and groups become, the more they grow to appreciate the mutuality implicit in the mission endeavor. With the growth of the short-term mission assignments and sister-parish relationships, the laity are finding and creating vastly increased opportunities for becoming active participants in the giving and receiving implied in mission. The more active they become, the more they seem to agree with the Maryknoll Associates in calling the opportunity to dedicate themselves to mission "a sacred challenge and a priceless gift from God."

Building International Solidarity

Beginning in the early 1960s, the United States responded to Pope John's call to aid the Church in Latin America in its time of crisis. The movement started with a large influx of missionaries who not only served the Latin American Church, but who in turn found themselves and their sending communities powerfully evangelized by that Church. In the 1970s, the Church in Latin America, while still short of ministers, became a prophetic voice in the world Church, calling all Christians to the preferential option for the poor and to the concrete commitments necessary to enflesh that option. The 1980s, bound together by "bookend" assassinations—in 1980, of Archbishop Romero and four U.S. missionaries, and in 1989, of six Jesuit professors and two women helpers—offered a dramatic exhibition of the bloody cost of taking that option seriously and putting it into practice. In the 1990s, U.S. lay Catholics are increasingly assuming the vital and active ecclesial role to which they have been called by Vatican II. As a result, they are making their own unique contribution to solidarity and mutual evangelization between the Churches in the United States and Latin America. As John Paul II has said, this is the history through which divine providence is preparing the Church for the third millennium. Thus the Church is called to contemplate this experience with eyes of faith, with a sense of gratitude and responsibility, always seeking to recognize God's intervention in human affairs.[26]

Sharing Faith Across the Hemisphere

In addition to meditation on developments in their particular histories, the pope is calling the Church in each nation to look with eyes of faith at recent events that have refashioned world history: to see in them the works of God and to hear through them the call of the Spirit. In his reflection on world events, Pope John Paul has emphasized two that not only have particular significance for world history, but also have unique implications when viewed from the vantage point of the American nations.

The first is the political developments of 1989. Referring to the fall of the Berlin Wall, symbolic of the independence of the nations of the former Soviet bloc, the pope said:

> It would be difficult not to recall that the Marian Year took place only shortly before the events of 1989. Those events remain surprising for their vastness and especially for the speed with which they occurred. The Eighties were years marked by a growing danger from the "Cold War." Nineteen hundred and eighty-nine ushered in a peaceful resolution which took the form, as it were, of an "organic" development. . . . In the unfolding of those events one could already discern the invisible hand of Providence at work with maternal care. . . .[27]

The second world development to which the pope calls attention is the twentieth century's return to an age of martyrdom. Of that, he says:

> The Church of the first millennium was born of the blood of the martyrs. . . . At the end of the second millennium, the Church has once again become a Church of martyrs. The persecutions of believers—priests, religious and laity—has caused a great sowing of martyrdom in different parts of the world. The witness to Christ borne even to the shedding of blood has become a common inheritance of Catholics, Orthodox, Anglicans and Protestants. . . .
>
> This witness must not be forgotten. . . . In our own century the martyrs have returned, many of them nameless, "unknown soldiers" as it were of God's great cause. As far as possible, their witness should not be lost to the Church. . . . The local churches should do everything possible to ensure that the memory of those who have suffered martyrdom should be safeguarded. . . .[28]

When the Churches in America look at those seemingly disparate developments with the eyes of faith, certain connections suggest themselves. First of all, there is a chronological association; in November 1989, one week after the fall of the Berlin Wall, six Jesuit educators, together with their housekeeper and her daughter, were murdered on the campus of their university in San Salvador. Noting that the Jesuits were killed because of their efforts to develop alternatives to the dominant socioeconomic system, Franz Hinkelammert, a Latin American economist, sees a philosophical connection between the two events. According to Hinkelammert, the Jesuits' murder was symbolic of a "new world order" in which there is no political or economic counterbalance to the all-powerful, unrestrained market economy poised to "devour" the Third World. In his view, the murders were a sign that the dominant economic system no longer needed to try to present itself as having a "human face."[29] Although Hinkelammert's thesis is extreme, his concern about safeguarding and creating alternatives to the reigning socioeconomic order echoes numerous contemporary church pronouncements.

In October 1992, the Latin American bishops met in Santo Domingo for their Fourth General Conference. The Church deliberately chose the date and the location of the meeting to emphasize a commemoration of five hundred years of evangelization in America. The Church in Latin America spent years preparing for the Santo Domingo conference, setting up consultation processes that involved every level of the Church from the basic ecclesial communities and parishes to the Vatican. While the central focus of the Santo Domingo conference was evangelization, the bishops, as they did at Medellín and Puebla, focused on the culture and the cultural realities of their people to address the gospel message to their particular circumstances.

When the bishops who gathered at Santo Domingo spoke of the pastoral challenges produced by impoverishment of their people, they strengthened what they had written thirteen years earlier in Puebla:

> Discovering the face of the Lord in the suffering faces of the poor challenges all Christians to a deep personal and ecclesial conversion. Through faith, we find faces emaciated by hunger as a result of inflation, foreign debt, and social injustice; faces disillusioned by politicians who make promises they do not keep . . . faces terrorized by daily and indiscriminate violence. . . .

The opening of CELAM's meeting in Santo Domingo, 1992. Photo: Robert Pelton, CSC.

The growing impoverishment in which millions of our brothers and sisters are plunged—to the point where it is reaching intolerable extremes of misery—is the cruelest and most crushing scourge that Latin America and the Caribbean are enduring. . . .

Statistics eloquently indicate that during the last decade situations of poverty have increased in both absolute and relative numbers. As pastors, we are torn apart by the continual sight of the throng of men and women, children, youth, and the aged who endure the unbearable weight of dire poverty, as well as the various forms of social, ethnic, and cultural exclusion. . . .

Policies of a neoliberal type now prevailing in Latin America and the Caribbean further deepen the negative impact of these mechanisms. The gaps in society have widened as the market has been deregulated in an indiscriminate way; major portions of labor legislation have been eliminated and workers have been fired; and the social spending that protected working-class families has been cut back.[30]

In those paragraphs, the bishops went even further than had Hinkelammert in his socioeconomic analysis. They cast a theological light on the new economic order, taking up one of the frequent themes promoted by Pope John Paul II.

When the pope visited Mexico in 1990, he spoke to business leaders about the moral dimensions of economic systems in the following terms:

> The science of economics makes it clear that material goods are scarce and hence ought to be administered rationally. . . . The Creator has destined the totality of the goods of creation for the benefit of all human beings. . . . Hence it is that the excessive cornering of goods by some deprives the majority of those goods, and thus is accumulated a wealth that produces poverty. This principle is likewise applicable to the international community.[31]

By describing their people as "impoverished," the bishops at Santo Domingo were referring to poverty as a dynamic and controllable process, not simply an economic status.[32] The process of "impoverishment" is the same that Pope John Paul had described as an "excessive cornering of goods by some," which "deprives the majority" of those goods. When they moved from economics to a theological reflection, the bishops at Santo Domingo shifted from social critique to moral imperatives. They made it clear that recognizing the face of Christ in impoverished, suffering people demands conversion and that conversion must be economic as well as religious.

Based on their reflection, the bishops committed the Church to a set of pastoral guidelines through which to respond to the impoverishment of their people. Those include:

- Assume with renewed decision the gospel-inspired and preferential option for the poor, following the example of and the words of the Lord Jesus. . . .
- Give priority to providing fraternal service to the poorest among the poor and helping institutions that take care of them. . . .
- Examine personal and community attitudes and behaviors, along with pastoral structures and methods, so that rather than alienating the poor they may facilitate closeness and sharing with them.
- Foster social involvement vis-a-vis the state by demanding laws to defend the rights of the poor.

- Make our parishes a space for solidarity.
- Support and encourage those organizations for economic solidarity with which our people are trying to respond to their desperate situations of poverty.
- Press governments to respond to the hardships that are being worsened by the neoliberal economic model whose primary impact is on the poor.[33]

Those pastoral guidelines illustrate the importance the Latin American bishops place on immediate and concrete action aimed at the creation of economic justice.

The New Evangelization: Comprehensive and Inculturated

The major theme of the Santo Domingo Conference was the "new evangelization": a theme tirelessly promoted by Pope John Paul II and applied specifically to the Latin American context in Santo Domingo. As described by Pope John Paul, the new evangelization is a call to conversion, a combination of activities and attitudes that will bring the Gospel into active dialogue with the cultures of modernity and post-modernity. The new evangelization aims at the creation of faith communities capable of generating a cultural alternative that is fully Christian. Its goal, in the words of John Paul II, is "to make the Church present at the cultural crossroads of our time, in order to imbue with Christian values the very roots of the 'coming' culture and of all existing cultures."[34]

According to the reflections of the bishops at Santo Domingo, "new evangelization" must be based on a faith so profound and informed that it will be capable of evangelizing social structures and human cultures. In order to plan for that, the Santo Domingo document begins with a reflection on the truth about Jesus Christ. It then elaborates on the concrete implications of that faith. Among those implications, one stands out as having particular relevance to the relationships among the nations of America: the Church in Latin America is called to be in mission to other nations.

The third section of the Santo Domingo document delineates the three "primary pastoral directions" assumed by the Conference:

1. A new evangelization of our peoples.
2. A comprehensive development of our Latin American and Caribbean peoples.
3. An inculturated evangelization.[35]

In the section that summarizes the new evangelization, the document states:

> This is the missionary moment in the Americas. We heartily and enthusiastically invite all to take part in evangelization, not only within our churches but beyond our borders. That will be our response to the example of missionaries who came to the Americas from other lands to communicate their faith to us. . . .[36]

The call to be a missionary Church is followed immediately by a short section describing how the Latin American Church is called to work for comprehensive human development:

> We make ours the cry of the poor. In continuity with Medellín and Puebla, we assume . . . this option which . . . will, in imitation of Jesus Christ, shed light on all our evangelization activity.
>
> With that light, we urge the development of a new economic, social, and political order in keeping with the dignity of each and every person, fostering justice and solidarity, and opening horizons of eternity for all of them.[37]

That combination of statements about the missionary task of Latin America and the place of comprehensive development in the work of evangelization makes it clear that Latin America is offering an evangelizing message to all of its brothers and sisters in the North. In so doing, the Latin American Church is following the lead of John Paul II and reinforcing what the U.S. bishops have said to their own people.

A Call to Deeper Conversion
When Pope John Paul II has spoken to the people of the United States, he has consistently called upon them to use all the power at their disposal on behalf of the needy of the world. While he has recognized and praised the

generosity of the people of the United States, he has also insisted that a response to the poor must go beyond charity.

In September 1987, speaking in Detroit, John Paul said:

Dear friends, America is a very powerful country. The amount and quality of your achievements are staggering. By virtue of your unique position as citizens of this nation, you are placed before a choice and you must choose. You may choose to close in on yourselves, to enjoy the fruits of your own form of progress and to try to forget about the rest of the world. Or, as you become more and more aware of your gifts and your capacity to serve, you may choose to live up to the responsibilities that your own history and accomplishments place on your shoulders. By choosing this latter course you acknowledge interdependence and opt for solidarity. This, dear friends, is truly a human vocation, a Christian vocation, and for you as Americans it is a worthy national vocation.[38]

In May 1988, Archbishop Rembert Weakland, speaking about the recently released encyclical, *Sollicitudo Rei Socialis*, explained how the pope's teaching applies to the United States in terms of both its economic policies and its ability to export its cultural values:

The encyclical calls for a new type of world vision, not one of conflict of ideologies . . . but one of mutual give and take. . . . The pope is concerned that the superpowers view poorer nations only in terms of their own national security and not in terms of the poorer nations' individuality and needs.

The pope has something to say to the communist bloc about freedom in markets and democratic structures and if we applaud those remarks it might also be helpful . . . to look at his criticism of the way capitalism is now functioning in order to create a more equitable world and a more just one.

[U.S. cultural dominance] places before us as Americans and before us as members of a church a tremendous challenge. We are that culture; we dominate that dominant culture. It is our responsibility; it is our product. *If* it is valueless . . . empty, full of superficiality . . . devoid of all transcendent vision, then we are to blame.

Weakland then went on in a whimsical tone and almost anticipated what the bishops at Santo Domingo would say about Latin America's missionary vocation:

> Sometimes, in my more creative moments, I ask myself if the church in the United States should not bring back all our missionaries from abroad to instill some new vision in our own society, some new sense of human and transcendent values. In this way we would be doing more for the poorer and missionary nations than by our direct evangelization there.

In a more serious vein he added:

> If our cultural export product would be full of the noblest of human and spiritual values, we would take our place in history as having brought about a much better world for all.[39]

In 1991, Bishop James Griffin of Columbus, Ohio, published his own "Reflections on Evangelization, Yesterday, Today and Tomorrow." In that document he explained the unavoidable connections between evangelization and economic realities in the U.S. culture. He said:

> Pope John Paul II has called for the decade of the 1990s to be a time of evangelization as we prepare to enter the third millennium. . . .
>
> The spirit of evangelization into which we are called today . . . involves the unshakable personal conviction of the truth, the relevance, and the surpassing value of the Gospel message . . . coupled with a desire to share this saving message with others. . . .
>
> The secularization of culture in the modern age has unfortunately eroded this spirit for far too many people. For too many, human life is lived without reference to the transcendent, to that which lies beyond what we can see, hear, taste, touch and smell. This creates a functional approach to life which cannot deal with questions of ultimate meaning. Possessions, power and pleasure all too easily become the dominant cultural values, and a competitive model of human relations becomes the way to acquire them. Our modern world is in need of a new age of evangelization.[40]

These are but two examples of how bishops in the United States, like their Latin American counterparts, are calling for a new evangelization. That new evangelization is one that must affect spiritual, social, and economic life. It must also be specifically applicable to particular cultural realities—in other words, it is both comprehensive and inculturated.

Time and again, Pope John Paul II and the U.S. and the Latin American bishops have called on the First World, and the United States in particular, to rise to the challenge of creating economic structures that are adequate to ensure global economic justice. That call is summarized in the USCC's 1996 booklet entitled *Political Responsibility*:

> It is essential that all aspects of international economic policy—trade, aid, finance, and investment—reflect basic moral principles and promote the global common good. The United States has a moral obligation to take the lead in helping to alleviate poverty through sustainable development, supporting programs that emphasize greater participation of the poor in grassroots development rather than large-scale government projects. . . . We must reform foreign assistance, not abandon it.[41]

U.S. Catholics involved in mission are playing a part among the many Catholic groups and institutions working for international economic justice. Returned missioners or delegation members are often among the strongest voices calling for new and more just economic policies. The Peru Peace Network, an organization founded by the Jefferson City mission office, uses its annual meetings and regular mailings to keep hundreds of people informed of both human rights and economic issues that affect Peru and the Andean region. The Richmond diocese has made advocacy for economic justice one of its major goals. Sister-parishes, like long-term missioners, are often involved in helping to develop small, sustainable economic enterprises in the areas in which they work.

In spite of all of those activities, the Latin American bishops still feel compelled to remind the world to recognize the face of Christ in the faces of the millions of our brothers and sisters who live in extreme misery. As long as Christians allow themselves to be torn apart by the continual sight of those throngs, they will be compelled to seek and find effective ways to respond to them. As the U.S. bishops so succinctly put it, "true charity leads to advocacy."[42]

The Church in America Transformed and Transforming the Third Millennium

In 1990, Pope John Paul wrote:

If we look at today's world, we are struck by many negative factors that can lead to pessimism. But this feeling is unjustified: we have faith in God our Father and Lord, in his goodness and mercy. As the third millennium of the redemption draws near, God is preparing a great springtime for Christianity, and we can already see its first signs. . . . People are gradually growing closer to gospel ideals and values. . . . There is a new consensus among people about these values: the rejection of violence and war; respect for the human person and for human rights; the desire for freedom, justice and brotherhood; the surmounting of different forms of racism and nationalism; the affirmation of the dignity and role of women.

Christian hope sustains us in committing ourselves fully to the new evangelization and to the worldwide mission, and leads us to pray as Jesus taught us: "Thy Kingdom come. Thy will be done, on earth as it is in heaven."[43]

As the Churches in America move toward the new millennium, there is much to look back on with gratitude, and much to look forward to with a sense of hope and responsibility. In his opening address at Santo Domingo, Pope John Paul II announced his plans to call a continent-wide Synod: a meeting of bishops from every part of America, to express their communion, and also to deal with issues of justice, solidarity, and international economic relations in view of the enormous gap between north and south among the nations of the Americas.[44]

The title of the synod, "Encounter with the Living Jesus Christ: The Way to Conversion, Communion, and Solidarity in America," well expresses John Paul II's hope and vision for the future of the Church in America. After more than thirty-five years of growth together, the Churches in America are again being offered the grace-filled opportunity to read the signs of the times made evident in the aspirations, the yearnings, and the often dramatic features of their world.[45] Trusting in the vivifying power of the Spirit, they will be called to "address the actual state of affairs affecting all the peoples and cultures on the American continent."[46] The Church in America is being called to respond to the unique circumstances which characterize America in the light of the Gospel and to remain true to their prophetic option expressing preference for and solidarity with the poor.[47] Keeping ever before them the faces of the suffering who represent Christ in this hemisphere, they will be challenged to continue their mission of mutual evangelization and to accept it as a priceless gift from God. To the degree that they cooperate with that grace, the members of the Church, and all of America, will be transformed. Trusting that Pope John's call for an increased and intensified sharing of faith across the hemisphere was one of God's interventions in human affairs, there is every reason to hope and to believe that the seeds of mutual evangelization already sown will continue to grow and bear the hundredfold.

DISCUSSION QUESTIONS

1. Pope John Paul II has called the Church to prepare for the millennium by reading history and the signs of our times with a sense of gratitude and responsibility. As we look at the growing relationship among Catholics in North and South America, for what do we have cause to be grateful? What are the unique responsibilities that follow from a faith-filled reading of our history and contemporary situation? How can we effectively include the experience and vision of Latin America in our reading of the signs of the times?

2. Since Vatican II, official teaching has emphasized that the whole Church is, by its very nature, missionary. How has the relationship between the Church in Latin America and in the United States furthered the evangelization and deepened the faith of both sides?

3. From the time evangelizers first set foot in America, there have been prophetic voices calling for a deeper practice of the Gospel. Who is speaking that message today?

4. The Church's long-standing critique of the dangers of communism has been far more widely publicized in the United States than has its critique of the dangerous dimensions of capitalism. Nevertheless, recent popes, Latin American and U.S. bishops, theologians, and the poor themselves have continually spoken out against the devastating effects of both the international debt and the imposition of neo-liberal economic policies. What needs to be done so that we hear and respond to those voices?

5. The appearance and message of Our Lady of Guadalupe symbolized a promise for a rich and unique expression of Christianity in America. In what ways has her promise become a reality? What hopes does her message symbolize now, five centuries after Christianity first came to America?

Notes

1. Pope John Paul II, *Tertio Millennio Adveniente* (*On the Coming of the Third Millennium*), no. 17. Hereafter the encyclical will be referred to as *Tertio Millennio*.

2. According to statistics in the 1995 *Catholic Almanac*, there were 1,505 U.S. Catholic missionaries in Latin America and the Caribbean in 1960. In 1962, the number had risen to 2,751; it peaked in 1968 with 3,885; and in 1992 there were 2,527 U.S. Catholics working in pastoral ministry in Latin America.

3. The uncalculated "total" contribution would include all that was contributed to and through religious congregations, diocesan and parish missions, and private organizations. Between 1965 and 1989, the grants distributed to Latin American projects totaled $49,286,197. The 1990 total was $2,538,490 and the 1995 total was $4,630,654. See *Sharing the Faith Across the Hemisphere*, 1995: Report of the 35th Year (Washington, D.C.: NCCB Secretariat for Latin America, 1996).

4. These figures are based on the responses to the first question on the survey, which asked for a ranking of support for the Church in Latin America by decades.

5. *To the Ends of the Earth*, 15-16.

6. Ibid., 36.

7. Ibid., 40.

8. These figures are based on responses to the NCCB diocesan survey in which eighty-five dioceses responded that they had sent priests and twenty-nine that they had not; twelve responses were missing. That represents a total of one hundred and thirty-six responses from the total of one hundred and seventy-five U.S. dioceses. The 1,056 total is calculated from the diocesan reported number of priests who served in Latin America during each of the decades from the 1960s through the 1990s.

9. Beginning in the early 1960s, the diocese of Jefferson City, Mo., has remained very close to the 10 percent contribution suggested by Msgr. Casaroli in 1961. The diocese has missioned a total of thirty of its priests to Peru. The greatest number to serve at any one time was thirteen, in 1968, when there were just one hundred and thirty-five active priests in the diocese itself. In 1996, Jefferson City has a total of one hundred and one diocesan priests, six of whom serve in Peru. Jefferson City, a missionary-receiving diocese itself, has twenty Irish-born priests in a diocese with a total Catholic population of 83,000.

10. See Cyprian Davis, *The History of Black Catholics in the United States* (New York: Crossroads, 1990), 28-29.

11. The statistics compiled by the U.S. Catholic Mission Association do not specify the numbers of lay missionaries serving in Latin America over the years. Nevertheless, the charts indicate something of a pattern for U.S. lay missionaries in general. Early growth, reaching a peak of 549 in 1966, was followed by a decrease to an absolute low of 217 in 1982, and since then the numbers have oscillated in a growing pattern, reaching a new high of 446 in 1990. It is important to note that the

USCMA figures include only those lay missionaries who spend one year or more in mission. The diocesan surveys reported a steady growth in the number of lay missioners: from 217 in the 1960s to 1,770 in the 1990s. The high figures reported by dioceses may be due to inclusion of short-term mission projects in their estimates.

12. Maryknoll is only one example of a religious congregation that has developed formal programs for lay volunteers in foreign mission. Other large-scale programs include those sponsored through the Jesuit Volunteer Corps and the Holy Cross Associates.

13. The first Maryknoll lay missioner assigned to Latin America was Ronald Bosse, a former Papal Volunteer originally from Pittsburgh.

14. Maryknoll priests and brothers officially belong to the "Catholic Foreign Mission Society of America." The sisters' official name is "The Maryknoll Sisters of St. Dominic." The "Maryknoll Association of the Faithful" has been formed to provide institutional stability and clear ecclesial definition for those who feel called to a temporary commitment to mission in the Maryknoll tradition.

15. The information on the Maryknoll Mission Association of the Faithful is summarized from "Maryknoll Lay Missioner Program: A Chronology of Significant Events," an unpublished report by Angela M. Donnelly, completed in 1992 and amended in 1993.

16. Pope Paul VI, *Evangelii Nuntiandi* (1975), no. 13.

17. *Mission of the Redeemer*, no. 85.

18. It is important to note that this number is based on a 10 percent sample. Although there is no independent source for comparison data, 48 percent of the dioceses reported that they were currently involoved in active sister-parish or sister-diocese relationships in Latin America. If those statistics provide a valid projection, the number of U.S. parishes with sister-relationships would be more than 1,700, indicating that the Haiti Parish Twinning Project organizes more than 15 percent of the twinning projects currently active between U.S. and Latin American parishes. Other U.S. groups that organize ecumenical sister-parish relationships include "SHARE," which sponsors a total of 46 twinning relationships between the United States and El Salvador, "Sister Parish," and the Christian Foundation for Children and the Aging. See Appendix A for an explanation of the survey and its validity.

19. The Haitian Ministry Commission is an official diocesan organization, created in July 1985. It has a formal pastoral plan and constitution that explain how it participates in the structure of the diocese. The commission publishes a regular newsletter from Richmond volunteers in Haiti, which frequently includes simple background information for those who are interested in doing advocacy work.

20. Those projects are partially funded by St. Peter's. Additional funding comes from St. Andrew by the Bay Parish in Fairfax, Va., which also has a sister-relationship with San Francisco de Asis.

21. St. Peter's emphasis on *being together*, rather than *doing for*, and of encouraging self-sustaining projects is similar to the volunteer philosophy of the Richmond dio-

cese. The Richmond volunteer guidelines specifically state that volunteers to Haiti "must clearly emerge from Haitian requests" and that "they will not replace Haitians or fill vacancies for which appropriately qualified Haitians are available." Their task is to "promote the development of Haitian skills . . . working themselves out of a job."

22. The reports here are culled from an overview of the fifty parish surveys that contained the greatest amount of narrative response.

23. One type of Latin American-U.S. Church contact that is growing but has not been thoroughly surveyed is the collaboration between parishes and dioceses along the U.S.-Mexico border. All along the Southwest border, the Church is involved in solidarity movements including not only the sharing of religious personnel but also advocacy on behalf of immigrants and help for refugees. One interesting example of this is the long-term relationship between the dioceses of Alta and Baja California.

24. These statistics come from the NCCB survey of parishes. The 13 percent figure is perhaps conservative because it reflects three different responses regarding personnel support. According to survey responses, 7 percent of the parishes said that they sponsored a priest in Latin America, 9 percent that they sponsored other religious, and 13 percent that they sponsored lay people to work or travel to Latin America—a description that would include sister-parish visits and other short-term volunteer or learning experiences.

25. The University of Notre Dame leads the country in its successful promotion of service projects. Approximately 10 percent of its graduates become involved in volunteer service in the year following their graduation, including such long-term projects as the Holy Cross Associates, the Maryknoll Association of the Faithful, and the Jesuit Volunteers.

26. See *Tertio Millennio*, no. 17, as quoted in the opening paragraph of this chapter.

27. *Tertio Millennio*, no. 27.

28. *Tertio Millennio*, no. 37.

29. See Franz Hinkelammert, "Changes in the Relationships Between Third World Countries and First World Countries," in *Mission Studies* (XII-2, 24, 1995), 133-45. In this same article Hinkelammert suggests that because the new economic system continues to need the raw materials of the Third World but no longer needs a large labor force for their production, that labor force, the mass of the population of the Third World, has become "redundant." Thus, that population will lose what little power it could previously yield as a result of its utility. His conclusion is that unless society as a whole creates a new basis of solidarity and respect for human dignity, there will be no human survival.

30. *Santo Domingo*, nos. 178-79.

31. See Pope John Paul II's address to Mexican business leaders, "Is Liberal Capitalism the Only Path?" *Origins* 20:17-21. In this, Pope John Paul was following the tradition of Catholic social teaching and restating Paul VI's statement that "both

for nations and for individual men, avarice is the most evident form of moral underdevelopment" (*Populorum Progressio*, no. 19).

32. It is important to note the bishops' careful use of vocabulary in this section of the document. When they speak of the economic suffering of their people, they refer to "impoverishment" (*empobrecimiento*), not simply "poverty." Impoverishment implies an actively worsening condition and one that is thrust upon the group by forces outside their own control. The very use of that word signifies an indictment of the economic order.

33. *Santo Domingo*, nos. 180-81.

34. Pope John Paul II, Opening Address at the Santo Domingo Conference, no. 22 and passim.

35. *Santo Domingo*, no. 292.

36. *Santo Domingo*, no. 295.

37. *Santo Domingo*, no. 296.

38. Pope John Paul II, Sept. 19, 1987 in Detroit. See *Origins* 17:548.

39. See *Origins* 18:71.

40. See *Origins* 21 (June 6, 1991).

41. See *Political Responsibility* (Washington, D.C.: United States Catholic Conference, 1995), 18-19. The section quoted ends with a bibliography of recent NCCB/USCC statements on international economic justice.

42. *Economic Justice for All, Pastoral Letter on Catholic Social Teaching and the U.S. Economy* (Washington, D.C.: United States Catholic Conference, 1986), 356.

43. *Mission of the Redeemer,* no. 86.

44. Pope John Paul II, *Santo Domingo*, "Opening Address," no. 17, and *Tertio Millennio*, no. 38.

45. Paraphrased from *Gaudium et Spes*, no. 4.

46. Preface to the Lineamenta of the Special Assembly of the Synod of Bishops for America.

47. Paraphrased from *Puebla*, no. 1134.

Overview
of the
1995 NCCB Survey

In 1995, the Secretariat for Latin America of the National Conference of Catholic Bishops, marking its thirty-fifth anniversary, commissioned a survey with the dual purpose of identifying the activities, projects, missions, and attitudes of the Church in the United States in relation to the Church in Latin America and the effect which the relationship between those Churches has had on the Church in the United States. This study was not set up to establish the statistical significance of various responses but instead to gather data and stories.

The data displayed in this report come from the national mail survey of all the dioceses, parishes, Catholic colleges and universities, and religious communities of men and women in the United States. The mailing list for the project was generated by Reed Reference Publishing, which produces the *Catholic Directory*.

The following summary is designed to present the methods of the survey and an overview of the data generated by the survey project.

Diocese Survey

The diocesan surveys were sent out in June 1995 to every diocese in the United States (N = 175). Ten days after the original survey was sent, a follow-up postcard was mailed as a reminder. After approximately one month, if the survey was not returned, researchers faxed a letter about the survey to the bishops (N = 80). One hundred twenty-eight surveys were returned, but only 126 had valid data, yielding a 72 percent valid return rate as of March 15, 1996. While not perfect, the 72 percent response rate does yield a very representative sample of the dioceses in the country. The data can be viewed as representative of the majority of dioceses in the United States.

An examination of the responses to questions shows a good deal of variance on all issues, which was consistent with our expectations. **Figure 1** shows the dioceses' current involvement with Latin America, with the majority of dioceses involved in some activity. As high as 89 percent of the dioceses participated in the NCCB Collection for Latin America. The most common reason dioceses reported for their support of the Church in Latin America was the belief that God had called them to mission work. Evangelization and the poverty of the area were also seen as important reasons to contribute (see **Figure 2**). This list was mirrored in the factors

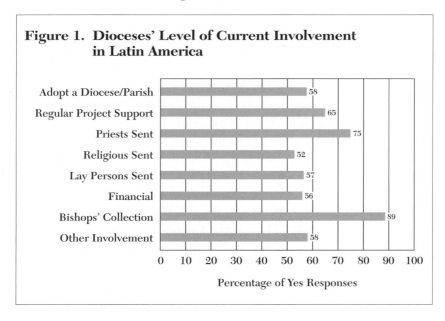

Figure 1. Dioceses' Level of Current Involvement in Latin America

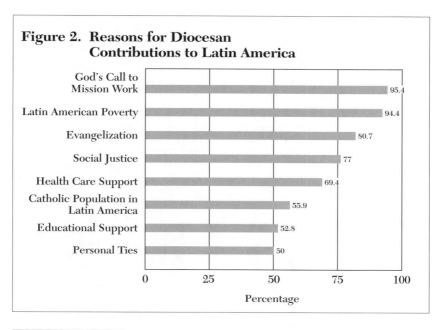

Figure 2. Reasons for Diocesan Contributions to Latin America

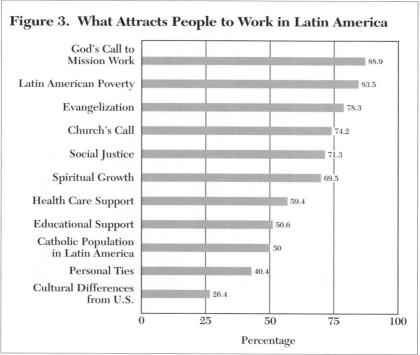

Figure 3. What Attracts People to Work in Latin America

that motivated individuals to work in Latin America (**Figure 3**). Involvement in Latin America has varied over the years, as shown in **Figure 4**. Despite the variance, the number of both people and parishes involved in Latin America has increased (see **Figures 5** and **6**).

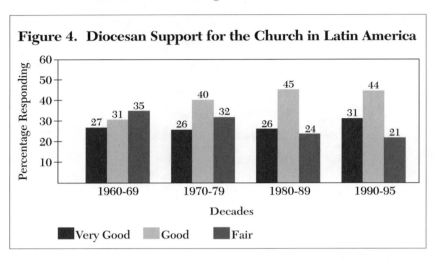

Figure 4. **Diocesan Support for the Church in Latin America**

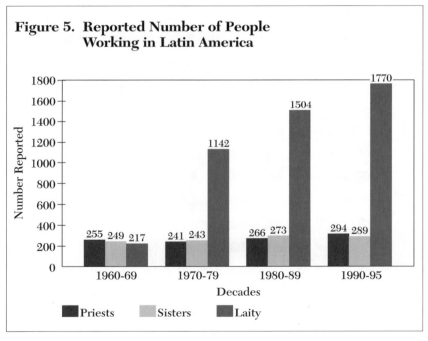

Figure 5. **Reported Number of People Working in Latin America**

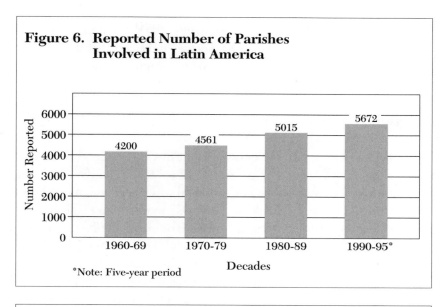

Figure 6. Reported Number of Parishes Involved in Latin America

°Note: Five-year period

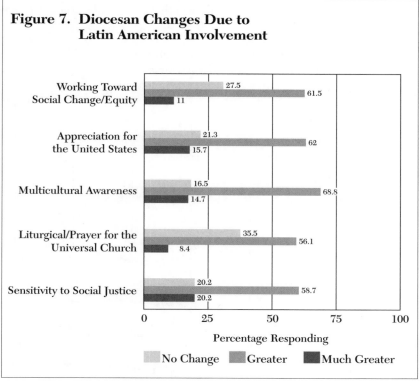

Figure 7. Diocesan Changes Due to Latin American Involvement

Involvement in Latin America has affected the Church in the United States. For example, 72.5 percent of dioceses indicated that their efforts toward working for social change were greater or much greater because of their involvement (see **Figure 7**).

Religious Community Survey

The religious community surveys were sent in October 1995 to all religious communities in the United States (N = 1,086). Ten days after the original survey was sent, a follow-up postcard was mailed as a reminder to fill out the survey, and a thank you note was sent to those who had responded. Of the 1,086 surveys sent, 348 were returned, for a return rate of 32 percent. Only 275 of the surveys had valid data. Some of the invalid data came from contemplative societies, which indicated that they had no information to report. This response rate was not as high as we would have liked, but we understood that many of the religious communities were very small and some did not have a charism that would cause them to have

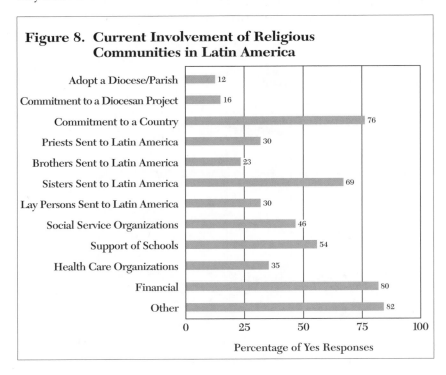

Figure 8. Current Involvement of Religious Communities in Latin America

any involvement with the Church in Latin America. While such communities could have been removed from the mailing list, the decision was made to risk receiving a lower response rate rather than eliminating any story that might have been told by a community.

While there may have been some amount of self-selection in the responses (with those with no involvement in Latin America not returning surveys), the data remain informative. **Figure 8** displays the types of involvement of the respondents. While human support has decreased, financial support has increased in most communities (**Figure 9**). The involvement of religious communities has had striking effects, as shown in **Figures 10** and **11**.

Catholic College and University Survey

The Catholic college and university surveys were sent in October 1995 to all Catholic colleges and universities in the United States (N = 481). Ninety-three surveys were returned, for a return rate of 19 percent. Only 71 of the surveys returned had valid data. Almost all of the invalid data came from institutions that reported that they had no dealings with Latin America.

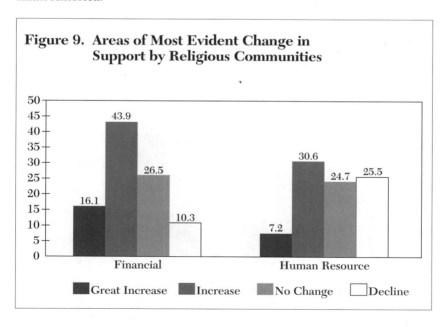

Figure 9. Areas of Most Evident Change in Support by Religious Communities

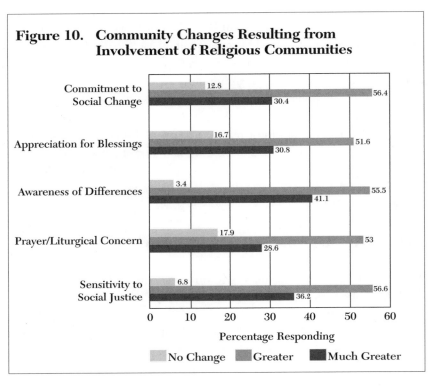

Figure 10. Community Changes Resulting from Involvement of Religious Communities

Commitment to Social Change
- No Change: 12.8
- Greater: 56.4
- Much Greater: 30.4

Appreciation for Blessings
- No Change: 16.7
- Greater: 51.6
- Much Greater: 30.8

Awareness of Differences
- No Change: 3.4
- Greater: 55.5
- Much Greater: 41.1

Prayer/Liturgical Concern
- No Change: 17.9
- Greater: 53
- Much Greater: 28.6

Sensitivity to Social Justice
- No Change: 6.8
- Greater: 56.6
- Much Greater: 36.2

Percentage Responding

No Change   Greater   Much Greater

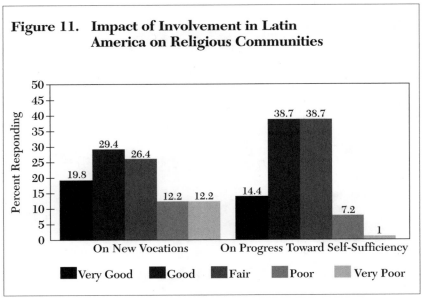

Figure 11. Impact of Involvement in Latin America on Religious Communities

Percent Responding

On New Vocations
- Very Good: 19.8
- Good: 29.4
- Fair: 26.4
- Poor: 12.2
- Very Poor: 12.2

On Progress Toward Self-Sufficiency
- Very Good: 14.4
- Good: 38.7
- Fair: 38.7
- Poor: 7.2
- Very Poor: 1

Very Good   Good   Fair   Poor   Very Poor

As with the previous sections, data are presented for current contributions to Latin America (**Figure 12**), motivating factors for involvement (**Figure 13**), and changes experienced because of involvement (**Figure 14**). Colleges' and universities' self-reported involvement has improved, both as a function of ranking their support as good or very good (**Figure 15**) and in terms of number of personnel who spent time in Latin America (**Figure 16**).

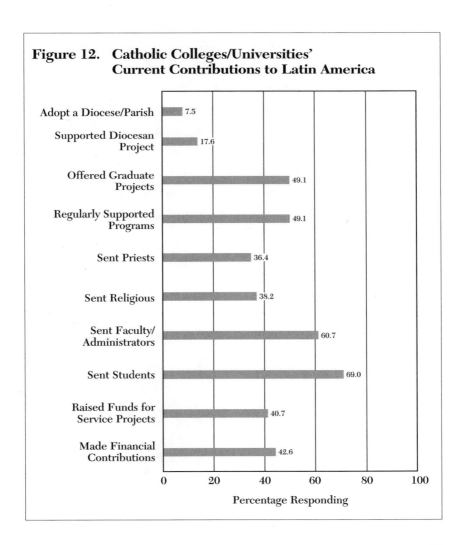

Figure 12. Catholic Colleges/Universities' Current Contributions to Latin America

Category	Percentage Responding
Adopt a Diocese/Parish	7.5
Supported Diocesan Project	17.6
Offered Graduate Projects	49.1
Regularly Supported Programs	49.1
Sent Priests	36.4
Sent Religious	38.2
Sent Faculty/Administrators	60.7
Sent Students	69.0
Raised Funds for Service Projects	40.7
Made Financial Contributions	42.6

Percentage Responding

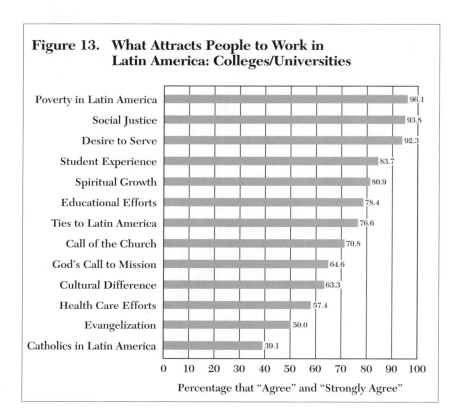

Figure 13. What Attracts People to Work in Latin America: Colleges/Universities

Poverty in Latin America	96.1
Social Justice	93.8
Desire to Serve	92.3
Student Experience	83.7
Spiritual Growth	80.9
Educational Efforts	78.4
Ties to Latin America	76.6
Call of the Church	70.8
God's Call to Mission	64.6
Cultural Difference	63.3
Health Care Efforts	57.4
Evangelization	50.0
Catholics in Latin America	39.1

Percentage that "Agree" and "Strongly Agree"

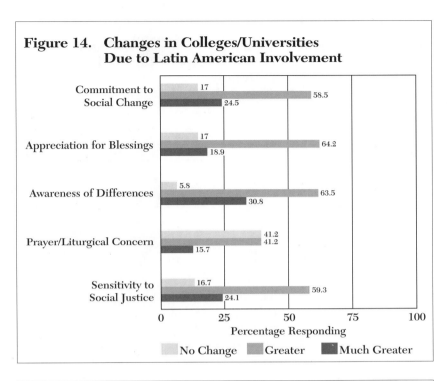

Figure 14. Changes in Colleges/Universities Due to Latin American Involvement

Commitment to Social Change: No Change 17, Greater 58.5, Much Greater 24.5

Appreciation for Blessings: No Change 17, Greater 64.2, Much Greater 18.9

Awareness of Differences: No Change 5.8, Greater 63.5, Much Greater 30.8

Prayer/Liturgical Concern: No Change 41.2, Greater 41.2, Much Greater 15.7

Sensitivity to Social Justice: No Change 16.7, Greater 59.3, Much Greater 24.1

Percentage Responding

No Change   Greater   Much Greater

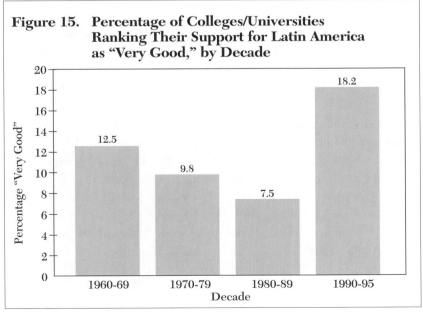

Figure 15. Percentage of Colleges/Universities Ranking Their Support for Latin America as "Very Good," by Decade

Percentage "Very Good"

1960-69: 12.5
1970-79: 9.8
1980-89: 7.5
1990-95: 18.2

Decade

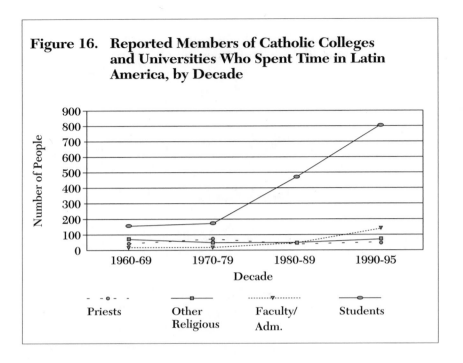

Figure 16. Reported Members of Catholic Colleges and Universities Who Spent Time in Latin America, by Decade

Parish Survey

The parish surveys were mailed in October 1995 to every parish in the United States (N = 17,428). A total of 1,717 were returned, for a return rate of 10 percent. Due to this low response rate, an attempt was made to determine how well the survey data represent the parishes in the United States.

The survey data were broken down by state and by diocese. The state breakdown indicated that every state was represented in the data. The smallest states in actual numbers of parishes were Wyoming, 37; Delaware, 40; and the District of Columbia, 40. The number of responses from these states were Wyoming, 4; Delaware, 2; and the District of Columbia, 6. Note that this represents 10 percent of the cases from these locales. The largest states in numbers of parishes were New York, 1,604; Pennsylvania, 1,276; and California, 1,075. The responses from these states were New York, 149; Pennsylvania, 90; and California, 87. This represents an 8.2 percent response rate from these states. In all, it appears that the sample was representative across both large and small states.

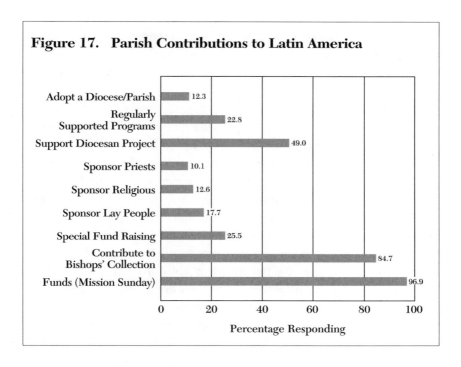

Figure 17. Parish Contributions to Latin America

Adopt a Diocese/Parish — 12.3
Regularly Supported Programs — 22.8
Support Diocesan Project — 49.0
Sponsor Priests — 10.1
Sponsor Religious — 12.6
Sponsor Lay People — 17.7
Special Fund Raising — 25.5
Contribute to Bishops' Collection — 84.7
Funds (Mission Sunday) — 96.9

Percentage Responding

Only one diocese was not represented (Baker, Ore.). The smallest dioceses in actual number of parishes (excluding the dioceses in Alaska) were Tyler, Tex., 27; Colorado Springs, 30; and Shreveport, La., 31. The responses from these dioceses were Tyler, 3; Colorado Springs, 1; and Shreveport, 4. This represents a 9.1 percent response rate. The largest dioceses in terms of numbers of parishes were New York, 413; Boston, 397; and Chicago, 380. The responses from these dioceses were New York, 32; Boston, 22; and Chicago, 38. This represents a 7.7 percent response rate from these dioceses. In all, it appears that the data were representative across both large and small dioceses.

A further examination of the parish data compared the percentage of Catholic schools (elementary and high school) in the United States and their responses to the survey question, "Does your parish have a school?" The national rate of schools per parish is 40 percent; the survey rate of responding parishes with schools was 41 percent. It would appear that the sample reflects the population positively on this measure.

Responding parishes, then, are similar to the national averages on all the variables we can use for comparison. Although a 10 percent sample is small and it is impossible to determine why certain parishes did not respond or whether their responses would significantly change the outcome, the above comparisons reflect positively on the representative character of the data.

The data from the parishes show that 49 percent support diocesan programs and almost all are involved in some type of fund raising (**Figure 17**). While most report no change in their overall support of Latin America in recent years, 14 percent indicate a great increase in the number of people involved, and more than 40 percent report some increase in financial and human support (**Figure 18**). National collection amounts from parishes increased through the 1980s but have subsequently decreased (**Figure 19**). The various reasons people contribute are explored in **Figure 20**; the most commonly chosen reasons were the personal request of a missionary (90 percent) and the poverty in Latin America (67.2 percent). The majority saw some improvement in their awareness of different cultures and appreciation of blessings in this country because of their involvement; however, unlike other groups of respondents, the majority of parishes did not report an improved commitment to social change (**Figure 21**). This comparison with other groups is shown in **Figure 22**.

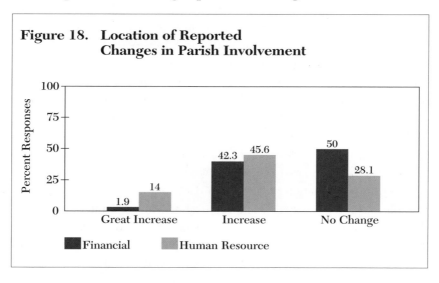

Figure 18. Location of Reported Changes in Parish Involvement

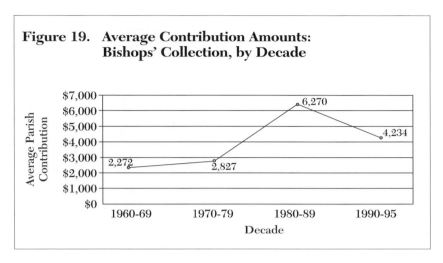

**Figure 19. Average Contribution Amounts:
Bishops' Collection, by Decade**

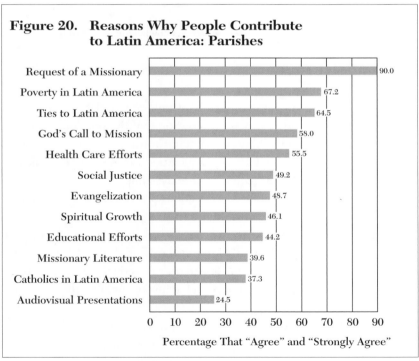

**Figure 20. Reasons Why People Contribute
to Latin America: Parishes**

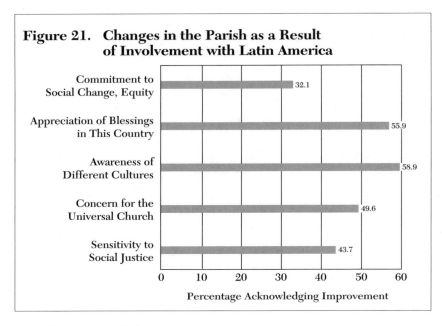

Figure 21. Changes in the Parish as a Result of Involvement with Latin America

Category	Percentage
Commitment to Social Change, Equity	32.1
Appreciation of Blessings in This Country	55.9
Awareness of Different Cultures	58.9
Concern for the Universal Church	49.6
Sensitivity to Social Justice	43.7

Percentage Acknowledging Improvement

Key Summary Issues

When data are collected from a variety of unique populations, it is often difficult to compare issues across groups. Some of the problems inherent in this process are the inability to maintain wording on questions across survey populations, the need to ask unique questions relevant to a particular population, and the difficulty in directly comparing data that come from different proportions of the populations due to non-response. Given these problems, it is still reasonable to search for areas of agreement and synthesize the data around the two key issues driving the research: to identify the ways in which the Church in the United States has been involved with the Church in Latin America over the course of the past three and one-half decades and the impact of that involvement on the Church in the United States.

Across all four surveys, three types of involvement in Latin America were consistently reported: (1) sending people to work in Latin America; (2) some type of regular commitment or support for the Church in a country or in Latin America in general; and (3) some type of financial support sent to Latin America, whether through the bishops' collection or some other avenue. In addition, across all four categories, approximately half of

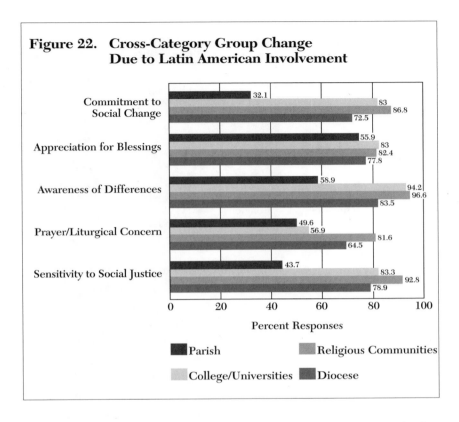

Figure 22. Cross-Category Group Change Due to Latin American Involvement

Commitment to Social Change
- 32.1
- 83
- 86.8
- 72.5

Appreciation for Blessings
- 55.9
- 83
- 82.4
- 77.8

Awareness of Differences
- 58.9
- 94.2
- 96.6
- 83.5

Prayer/Liturgical Concern
- 49.6
- 56.9
- 81.6
- 64.5

Sensitivity to Social Justice
- 43.7
- 83.3
- 92.8
- 78.9

Percent Responses: 0 20 40 60 80 100

■ Parish   ■ Religious Communities
  College/Universities ■ Diocese

the respondents reported increased support for Latin America in the last five years. This was generally in the form of increased financial contributions, with the exception of the college and university data, which indicated an increase in human resource contributions. Approximately one-half of the respondents reported that they thought they should be more involved in Latin America in the next five years, and about one-third actually expected their involvement to increase. Very few respondents thought that their involvement should decrease. An important point to note is that across the categories, a large percentage of respondents did not feel that they were well-enough informed of the impact of U.S. Church involvement on Latin America (**Figure 23**).

There seems to be a very strong positive relationship between the respondents' level of involvement and their desire for increased involvement with Latin America: the greater the current involvement, the greater the desire to do more. Across the categories of the survey, the three reasons

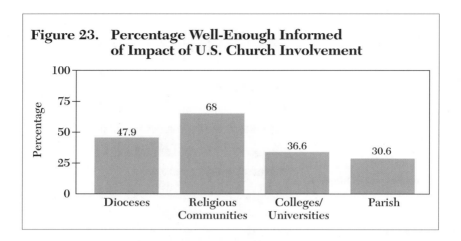

Figure 23. Percentage Well-Enough Informed of Impact of U.S. Church Involvement

most often reported for why people contribute time, effort, and money to Latin America are (1) poverty in Latin America, (2) a response to God's call to mission or evangelization, and (3) a personal tie to Latin America. The most often reported reasons why people are attracted to work in Latin America are (1) poverty in Latin America, (2) social justice, and (3) God's call to mission or evangelization.

Both the survey and the stories reported throughout this book demonstrate that the Church in the United States has been growing over the past thirty-five years in its involvement with and commitment to Latin America. The survey, in particular, demonstrates that while the mode of that involvement is changing, with fewer long-term missionaries leaving home to serve in another country, the U.S. Church's level of commitment to Latin America continues to grow. Additionally, the survey indicates that the Church in the United States increasingly recognizes its involvement with Latin America as a mutually beneficial relationship. As each side puts its unique gifts at the disposal of the other, both are enriched and motivated to strengthen and deepen the bonds of solidarity and communion that they have forged over the years.

The experience of the relationships among the Churches in Latin America and the United States is giving concrete expression to a renewed understanding of the essentially missionary character of the whole Church. The data that have been gathered give strong evidence that the Church in the United States desires to move into the coming millennium with renewed commitment to an ever-growing sharing of faith across the hemisphere.

List of Survey Respondents Involved in Latin America

A. Dioceses and Parishes

Key:

H/High level of involvement = Adopt a diocese/parish or support for a special project

M/Medium level of involvement = Sponsorship of priests, religious, or lay missionaries

L/Low level of involvement = Fund raising (e.g., Collection for Latin America or Mission Sunday collection)

X/No reported involvement (applicable only to dioceses that have some involved parishes; parishes with no involvement are not listed)

Note: From survey data as reported by dioceses and parishes.

Albany (X)

All Saints, Granville (L)
Holy Spirit, East Greenbush (M)
Immaculate Conception,
    Schenectady (L)
Immaculate Conception, Watervliet
    (L)
St. Adalbert, Schenectady (L)
St. Anthony of Padua, Troy (M)
St. John Francis Regis, Grafton (M)
St. John the Evangelist, Schenectady
    (M)
St. Mary, Crescent (H)
St. Mary of the Assumption,
    Waterford (M)
St. Pius X, Loudonville (L)

Alexandria (H)

Sacred Heart, Oakdale (H)
St. Anthony of Padua, Bunkie (L)
St. Peter, Bordelonville (M)

Allentown (H)

Annunciation B.V.M.–St. Mary's,
    Catasauqua (H)
Immaculate Conception, Tremont
    (H)
Our Lady of Good Counsel, Bangor
    (L)
Our Lady of Pompeii, Bethlehem (L)
St. John the Baptist, Allentown (M)
St. John the Baptist, Pottsville (L)
St. Kieran, Heckscherville (M)
St. Matthew's, East Stroudsburg (H)
St. Richard, Barnesville (M)

Altoona-Johnstown (L)

Christ the King, Houtzdale (L)
Holy Child Jesus, Windber (L)
Holy Trinity, Ramey (L)
St. Agnes, Morrisdale (L)
St. Francis of Assisi, Johnstown (H)
St. John Gualbert, Johnstown (M)
St. Joseph's, Coupon (L)
St. Leo the Great, Altoona (M)
St. Timothy, Curwensville (L)

Amarillo (X)

Sacred Heart, Plainview (H)
St. Anthony's, Hereford (L)
St. Laurence, Amarillo (M)

Anchorage (L)

Our Lady of Perpetual Help,
    Soldotna (L)
Our Lady of the Angels, Kenai (H)
St. John the Baptist, Homer (L)
St. Joseph, Cordova (L)

Arlington (X)

All Saints, Manassas (L)
Christ the Redeemer, Sterling (L)
Our Lady of the Valley, Luray (M)
Sacred Heart of Jesus, Winchester
    (H)
St. Ann, Arlington (M)
St. Anthony's, Falls Church (H)

Atlanta (X)

Christ Our Savior, Greensboro (L)
Immaculate Conception, Atlanta (H)
Our Lady of LaSalette, Canton (L)
Our Lady of Lourdes, Atlanta (L)
Our Lady of Perpetual Help,
    Carrollton (H)
St. Anna's, Monroe (M)
St. Clement's, Calhoun (L)
St. Gabriel, Fayetteville (M)
St. John Vianney, Lithia Springs (M)
St. Lawrence, Lawrenceville (L)
St. Michael's, Gainesville (M)
St. Peter's, LaGrange (L)
St. Thomas Aquinas, Alpharetta (M)

Austin (H)

Immaculate Heart of Mary, Abbott
    (L)
Lakeway Ecumenical, Austin (H)
Nativity of the B.V.M., Penelope (L)
Nuestra Senora de Dolores, Austin
    (L)
Our Mother of Sorrows, Burnet (M)
San Francisco, Austin (M)
San Jose, Austin (H)

St. Catherine of Siena, Austin (H)
St. Francis on the Brazos, Waco (M)
St. John Neumann, Austin (H)
St. Paul the Apostle, Smithville (M)

Baltimore (H)
Corpus Christi, Baltimore (H)
Good Shepherd, Perryville (L)
Holy Face, Great Mills (M)
Holy Family, Hillcrest Heights (M)
Holy Ghost, Issue (H)
Holy Spirit, Forestville (L)
Holy Trinity, Glen Burnie (H)
Mother Seton, Germantown (M)
Our Lady Help of Christians, Waldorf (L)
Our Lady of Mercy, Potomac (M)
Our Lady of Mt. Carmel, Thurmont (M)
Our Lady of the Fields, Millersville (L)
Our Lady's, Medley's Neck (L)
Resurrection, Ellicott City (H)
St. Ambrose, Cresaptown (L)
St. Andrew by the Bay, Annapolis (H)
St. Anthony, Emmitsburg (M)
St. Cecilia, St. Mary's City (M)
St. Clare, Baltimore (L)
St. Elizabeth Ann Seton, Crofton (L)
St. Francis de Sales, Abingdon (H)
St. Francis of Assisi Mission, Fulton (L)
St. John, Westminster (M)
St. John the Evangelist, Columbia (H)
St. Joseph, Cockeysville (M)
St. Joseph-on-Carrollton Manor, Buckeystown (M)
St. Patrick's, Havre de Grace (H)
St. Peter's, Hancock (L)
St. Rose of Lima, Gaithersburg (L)
St. Stephen, Bradshaw (M)
St. Veronica, Baltimore (M)

Baton Rouge (H)
Christ the King, Baton Rouge (H)
St. Clement of Rome, Plaquemine (H)
St. George, Baton Rouge (H)
St. Michael the Archangel, Convent (L)

Beaumont (X)
Our Mother of Mercy, Beaumont (L)
St. John, Port Arthur (L)
St. Theresa the Little Flower, Port Arthur (L)

Belleville (H)
Immaculate Conception, Pierron (L)
Our Lady of Mt. Carmel, Herrin (L)
SS. Peter and Paul, Alton (M)
St. Agatha, New Athens (H)
St. Ambrose, Godfrey (L)
St. Boniface, Germantown (H)
St. Clare, O'Fallon (H)
St. Damian, Damiansville (H)
St. Francis of Assisi, Teutopolis (H)
St. Jerome, Troy (L)
St. John the Baptist, Red Bud (H)
St. Joseph, Cobden (M)
St. Joseph, Marion (M)
St. Joseph, Olney (H)
St. Joseph, Prairie du Rocher (M)
St. Mary, Anna (L)
St. Mary, Marshall (L)
St. Mary, Mt. Carmel (H)
St. Nicholas, O'Fallon (H)
St. Patrick, Tipton (L)
St. Paul, Highland (M)
St. Stephen, Caseyville (M)

Biloxi (H)
St. John, Biloxi (H)
St. Matthew the Apostle, White Cypress (M)

Birmingham (L)
Holy Spirit, Winfield (L)
Our Lady Queen of the Universe,
Birmingham (L)
St. Francis of Assisi, Tuscaloosa (L)
St. Francis Xavier, Birmingham (H)
St. Mary, Eutaw (L)

Bismarck (H)
Holy Spirit, Bismarck (H)
St. Francis Xavier's, Anamoose (L)
St. Hildegard, Menoken (M)
St. Joseph, Dickinson (M)
St. Patrick, Dickinson (L)

Boise (H)
Risen Christ, Boise (M)
SS. Peter and Paul, Grangeville (H)
St. Anthony's, Pocatello (M)
St. Jerome's, Jerome (H)
St. John's, Pocatello (L)
St. Joseph's, Sandpoint (H)
St. Matthew, Eagle (M)

Boston (H)
Assumption, Bellingham (M)
Holy Cross, South Easton (M)
Holy Family, Boston (H)
Holy Family, Duxbury (L)
Holy Family, Rockland (H)
Immaculate Conception, Malden (H)
Our Lady of the Assumption,
Marshfield (H)
Sacred Heart, Boston (L)
Sacred Heart, Lowell (M)
St. Albert the Great, Weymouth (L)
St. Barnabas, Portsmouth (M)
St. Joachim, Rockport (L)
St. John the Evangelist, Wellesley (M)
St. Margaret Mary, Westwood (L)
St. Mary, Waltham (M)
St. Patrick, Lawrence (M)
St. Paul, Hingham (L)
St. Robert Bellarmine, Andover (M)
St. Thomas of Villanova, Wilmington
(L)
Star of the Sea, Salisbury (M)

Bridgeport (H)
St. Edward the Confessor,
New Fairfield (L)
St. Peter's, Bridgeport (L)
St. Thomas the Apostle, Norwalk (L)

Brooklyn (H)
Immaculate Conception, Queens (H)
Our Lady of Miracles, Brooklyn (M)
Sacred Heart, Brooklyn (M)
St. Agatha's, Brooklyn (M)
St. Andrew Avellino, Queens (L)
St. Ann's, Queens (H)
St. Benedict Joseph Labre, Queens
(M)
St. Bonaventure's, Queens (L)
St. Catherine of Genoa, Brooklyn (L)
St. Finbar's, Brooklyn (L)
St. Fortunata, Brooklyn (M)
St. Francis Xavier, Brooklyn (L)
St. Gerard Majella, Queens (M)
St. John Vianney, Queens (L)
St. Joseph, Brooklyn (M)
St. Margaret's, Queens (M)
St. Nicholas, Brooklyn (H)
St. Pascal Baylon, Queens (M)
St. Pius V, Queens (L)
St. Rita, Queens (L)
St. Teresa of Avila, Queens (L)
St. Thomas Apostle, Queens (M)

Brownsville (L)
Holy Spirit, McAllen (H)
Holy Spirit, Progreso (M)
Our Lady of Mercy, Mercedes (H)
Our Lady of Perpetual Help,
McAllen (L)
Our Lady Star of the Sea, Port Isabel
(M)
Our Lady, Queen of the Universe,
San Benito (L)
Sacred Heart, Edinburg (H)
Sacred Heart, Elsa (M)
St. Joseph the Worker, San Carlos
(M)
St. Mary, Santa Rosa (L)

Sharing Faith Across the Hemisphere

Buffalo (X)

Assumption, Buffalo (L)
Coronation of the B.V.M., Buffalo (L)
Good Shepherd, Pendleton (L)
Holy Angels, Buffalo (M)
Holy Name of Mary, Ellicottville (L)
Immaculate Conception, Ransomville
   (L)
Infant of Prague, Cheektowaga (H)
Nativity of the Blessed Virgin, Buffalo
   (L)
Our Lady of Peace, Clarence (H)
Our Lady of Victory, Frewsburg (L)
Sacred Heart, Lakewood (L)
St. Aloysius, Springville (L)
St. Aloysius Gonzaga, Cheektowaga
   (L)
St. Anthony of Padua, Buffalo (L)
St. Casimir, Buffalo (L)
St. George, West Falls (M)
St. Gregory the Great, Williamsville
   (L)
St. Hyacinth, Lackawanna (M)
St. Joan of Arc, Perrysburg (L)
St. John Gualbert, Cheektowaga (L)
St. Leo, Amherst (L)
St. Mary, Lockport (H)
St. Mary of the Angels, Olean (L)
St. Pacificus, Mission of St.
   Humphrey (L)
St. Patrick, Fillmore (L)
St. Paul, Kenmore (L)
St. Peter and Paul, Jamestown (M)
St. Pius X, Getzville (L)
St. Timothy, Tonawanda (M)
St. Vincent, North Evans (L)
Visitation of the B.V.M., Buffalo (L)

Burlington (M)

Holy Cross, Colchester (M)
St. Anthony, Bethel (L)
St. Anthony's, Burlington (L)
St. John the Baptist, Castleton (L)
St. John the Baptist, Enosburg Falls
   (L)

St. John the Evangelist, St. Johnsbury
   (M)
St. Luke, Fairfax (H)
St. Margaret Mary, Arlington (M)
St. Mary's, Brandon (H)
St. Pius X, Wauwatosa (L)
St. Stephen, Winooski (L)

Camden (H)

Christ the Redeemer, Mt. Holly (L)
Holy Eucharist, Tabernacle (H)
Resurrection, Marmora (M)
St. Mary's, Rosenhayn (M)
St. Michael's, Gibbstown (M)
St. Michael's, Minotola (L)
St. Teresa of the Infant Jesus,
   Runnemede (M)

Charleston (M)

Corpus Christi, Lexington (L)
Holy Spirit, Charleston (H)
Jesus Our Risen Savior, Spartanburg
   (M)
Sacred Heart, Abbeville (M)
St. Andrew's, Myrtle Beach (L)
St. Anthony of Padua, Greenville (L)
St. John the Baptist, Charleston (M)
St. Joseph, Columbia (M)
St. Mary of the Angels, Anderson (L)
St. Philip Benizi, Moncks Corner (M)

Charlotte (X)

Our Lady of Grace, Greensboro (M)
Our Lady of the Highways,
   Thomasville (H)
St. Andrew the Apostle, Mars Hill
   (H)
St. Ann, Charlotte (H)
St. Benedict, Greensboro (M)
St. Francis of Assisi, Franklin (L)
St. Joseph, Greenfield Center (M)
St. Michael, Gastonia (H)
St. Therese, Mooresville (L)
St. Thomas Aquinas, Charlotte (L)

Cheyenne (H)

St. Joseph's, Cheyenne (M)
St. Leo's, Lusk (L)
St. Matthew's, Gillette (L)
St. Paul's, Pine Bluffs (L)

Chicago (H)

Holy Apostles, McHenry (L)
Holy Innocents, Chicago (L)
Holy Name, Chicago (H)
Holy Trinity, Chicago (H)
Immaculate Conception, Chicago (H)
Immaculate Conception, Highland
  Park (L)
Our Lady of Hope, Rosemont-Des
  Plaines (H)
Our Lady of Humility, Zion-Beach
  Park (M)
Our Lady of Mercy, Chicago (M)
Our Lady of Tepeyac, Chicago (M)
Resurrection, Chicago (M)
Santa Teresita, Palatine (M)
St. Aloysius, Chicago (L)
St. Ann, Chicago (L)
St. Basil/Visitation, Chicago (L)
St. Camillus, Chicago (H)
St. Emily, Mt. Prospect (M)
St. Francis of Assisi, Luebbering (M)
St. John Berchmans, Chicago (L)
St. John Neumann, St. Charles (L)
St. John the Apostle, Villa Park (H)
St. Joseph, Addison (L)
St. Joseph, Wilmette (H)
St. Margaret of Scotland, Chicago (M)
St. Mark, Chicago (M)
St. Mary, Elgin (M)
St. Mary, Lake Forest (H)
St. Mary of Perpetual Help, Chicago
  (L)
St. Michael, Wheaton (L)
St. Peter, Geneva (M)
St. Simon the Apostle, Chicago (L)
St. Sylvester, Chicago (L)
St. Turibius, Chicago (M)
St. Walter, Roselle (H)
Transfiguration of Our Lord, Chicago
  (L)

Cincinnati (H)

All Saints, Cincinnati (L)
Ascension, Dayton (M)
Emmanuel, Dayton (L)
Guardian Angels, Cincinnati (H)
Holy Angels, Sidney (H)
Immaculate Conception, Bradford
  (L)
Mary Help of Christians, Fort
  Recovery (H)
Our Lady of Guadalupe, Montezuma
  (H)
Our Lady of Mercy, Dayton (H)
Our Lady of the Rosary, Dayton (L)
Our Mother of Sorrows, Cincinnati
  (L)
St. Aloysius, Shandon (L)
St. Anthony, Cincinnati (M)
St. Bernard, Cincinnati (M)
St. Catharine, Cincinnati (H)
St. Francis de Sales, Cincinnati (L)
St. Henry, St. Henry (H)
St. John the Baptist, Cincinnati (L)
St. John the Baptist, Maria Stein (H)
St. Joseph's, Hamilton (H)
St. Jude the Apostle, Cincinnati (L)
St. Mary's, Hillsboro (H)
St. Paul's, Englewood (H)
St. Robert Bellarmine, Cincinnati (H)
St. Teresa, Cincinnati (M)
St. Teresa, Covington (L)
St. Therese, the Little Flower,
  Cincinnati (L)
St. Thomas More, Withamsville (M)

Cleveland (H)

Annunciation, Cleveland (M)
Ascension, Cleveland (M)
Christ the King, Akron (M)
Conversion of St. Paul, Cleveland (M)
Gesu, University Heights (L)
Holy Family, Stow (L)
Holy Trinity, Barberton (M)
Immaculate Conception, Cleveland
  (M)
Nativity of the Lord Jesus, Akron (M)

Our Lady of Good Counsel,
Cleveland (H)
Sacred Heart, Barberton (M)
Sacred Heart, Rock Creek (L)
Sacred Heart, Wadsworth (M)
San Juan Bautista, Cleveland (M)
SS. Philip and James, Cleveland (M)
St. Anne, Rittman (L)
St. Anthony of Padua, Fairport
Harbor (M)
St. Anthony of Padua, Parma (M)
St. Barnabas, Northfield (M)
St. Bartholomew, Middleburg
Heights (H)
St. Bede the Venerable, Mentor (M)
St. Bernard, Akron (H)
St. Edward, Parkman (M)
St. Elizabeth Ann Seton, Columbia
Station (L)
St. Felicitas, Euclid (L)
St. Francis de Sales, Parma (M)
St. George, Cleveland (L)
St. Jerome, Cleveland (L)
St. John Vianney, Mentor (H)
St. Joseph's, Mantua (M)
St. Jude, Elyria (H)
St. Julie Billiart, North Ridgeville (M)
St. Justin Martyr, Eastlake (M)
St. Louis, Cleveland Heights (H)
St. Lucy, Middlefield (M)
St. Mark, Cleveland (H)
St. Mary, Bedford (M)
St. Mary, Vermilion (L)
St. Mary Magdalene, Willowick (M)
St. Matthew, Akron (L)
St. Patrick, Wellington (M)
St. Peter of the Fields, Rootstown
(M)
St. Pius X, Bedford (M)
St. Procop, Cleveland (M)
St. Stanislaus, Cleveland (M)

Colorado Springs (X)
St. Joseph's, Colorado Springs (M)

Columbus (H)
Holy Trinity, Jackson (H)
St. James the Less, Columbus (M)
St. Joan of Arc, Powell (M)
St. Joseph, Ironton (L)
St. Leo, Columbus (L)
St. Mary, Columbus (L)
St. Mary, Delaware (M)
St. Mary of the Woods, Russells Point
(L)
St. Mary, Queen of the Missions,
Waverly (L)
St. Matthias, Columbus (M)
St. Philip the Apostle, Columbus (L)

Corpus Christi (X)
Immaculate Conception, Skidmore (L)
Our Lady of Guadalupe,
Hebbronville (L)
SS. Cyril and Methodius, Corpus
Christi (M)
St. Anthony, Robstown (L)
St. Theresa of the Infant Jesus,
Premont (M)

Covington (H)
Mary, Queen of Heaven, Erlanger (L)
St. Agnes, Covington (L)
St. Henry, Erlanger (M)
St. Joseph, Warsaw (M)

Crookston (H)
SS. Peter and Paul, Warren (M)
St. Francis de Sales, Moorhead (M)
St. Joseph, Bagley (L)
St. Mary's, Warroad (M)
St. Michael's, Mahnomen (L)

Dallas (H)
All Saints, Dallas (L)
Cathedral-Santuario de Guadalupe,
Dallas (L)
Christ the King, Dallas (M)
Holy Cross, Dallas (H)
St. Jude, Gun Barrel City (M)
St. Martin, Forney (M)
St. Monica, Dallas (L)

Davenport (X)

St. Frances Xavier Cabrini, Richland (M)

St. John Vianney, Bettendorf (H)

St. John's, Houghton (M)

St. Joseph's, Fort Madison (M)

St. Mary Magdalen, Bloomfield (L)

St. Mary of the Assumption, Iowa City (H)

St. Mary's, Centerville (M)

St. Mary's, Davenport (M)

St. Mary's, Williamsburg (M)

St. Patrick, Brooklyn (L)

Denver (H)

All Souls, Englewood (M)

Christ the King, Denver (H)

Holy Family, Denver (L)

Holy Name, Steamboat Springs (L)

Our Lady of Peace, Greeley (M)

Risen Christ, Denver (H)

St. Dominic's, Denver (H)

St. Elizabeth Ann Seton, Fort Collins (M)

St. John the Baptist, Johnstown (M)

St. Louis, Louisville (M)

St. Patrick's, Minturn (H)

Des Moines (M)

Sacred Heart, Chariton (L)

SS. Peter and Paul, Atlantic (L)

St. Anthony's, Des Moines (H)

St. Boniface, Garwin (H)

St. Joseph's, State Center (L)

St. Mary, Anita (L)

St. Mary, Portsmouth (L)

St. Mary of Nazareth, Des Moines (L)

St. Patrick, Audubon (L)

St. Patrick, Massena (M)

St. Patrick's, Corning (L)

St. Theresa of the Child Jesus, Des Moines (L)

Detroit (H)

Blessed Sacrament, Burton (L)

Gesu, Detroit (L)

Good Shepherd, Montrose (H)

Holy Family, Novi (M)

Holy Redeemer, Detroit (H)

Immaculate Conception, Milan (M)

Immaculate Heart of Mary, Detroit (L)

Most Holy Trinity, Detroit (H)

Our Lady of Mt. Carmel, Emmett (M)

Our Lady of Mt. Carmel, Temperance (M)

Presentation-Our Lady of Victory, Detroit (M)

Sacred Heart, Roseville (M)

St. Albert the Great, Dearborn Heights (M)

St. Ambrose, Grosse Pointe Park (M)

St. Andrew, Saline (L)

St. Benedict, Waterford (L)

St. Blase, Sterling Heights (L)

St. Fabian, Farmington Hills (L)

St. Gabriel, Detroit (M)

St. Gregory, Detroit (M)

St. Irene, Dundee (H)

St. Isidore, Macomb (L)

St. John, Davison (L)

St. John Bosco, Redford (L)

St. Joseph, Argyle (M)

St. Joseph, Dexter (H)

St. Joseph, Lake Orion (L)

St. Joseph, Rapson (H)

St. Kenneth, Plymouth (L)

St. Kieran, Shelby Twp. (M)

St. Matthew, Detroit (L)

St. Matthias, Sterling Heights (H)

St. Michael, Port Austin (L)

St. Pius X, Flint (L)

St. Priscilla, Livonia (M)

St. Regis, Birmingham (M)

St. Rene Goupil, Sterling Heights (L)

St. Thomas the Apostle, Ann Arbor (L)

St. Vincent de Paul, Pontiac (M)

Dodge City (H)
> St. Nicholas, Kinsley (L)
> St. Teresa, Hutchinson (H)

Dubuque (M)
> Immaculate Conception, Riceville (M)
> Sacred Heart, Fillmore (M)
> Sacred Heart, Meyer (L)
> Sacred Heart, Waterloo (L)
> St. Ansgar, St. Ansgar (L)
> St. Anthony's, Dubuque (H)
> St. Columbkille's, Dubuque (H)
> St. Francis de Sales, Ossian (M)
> St. Francis Xavier, Belmond (M)
> St. John's, Waterloo (H)
> St. Joseph the Worker, Dubuque (H)
> St. Joseph's, Earlville (M)
> St. Joseph's, Marion (H)
> St. Margaret Queen of Scotland, Albany (L)
> St. Nicholas, Evansdale (M)
> St. Patrick's, Buffalo Center (L)
> St. Patrick's, Clear Lake (H)
> St. Raphael's, Dubuque (H)

Duluth (X)
> Holy Family, Cloquet (L)
> Holy Spirit, Virginia (L)
> Our Lady of the Rosary, Duluth (L)
> St. Leo's, Hibbing (L)
> St. Mathias, St. Mathias (L)
> St. Pius X, Babbitt (L)

El Paso (H)
> Our Lady of Guadalupe, El Paso (M)
> Our Lady of Mt. Carmel, El Paso (M)
> San Lorenzo, Clint (L)
> St. Pius X, El Paso (M)

Erie (H)
> Our Lady of Peace, Erie (M)
> St. Bernard, Falls Creek (L)
> St. Catherine, Du Bois (H)
> St. George, Erie (H)
> St. Mark the Evangelist, Erie (H)
> St. Stanislaus, Erie (L)
> St. Titus, Titusville (L)
> St. Tobias, Brockway (H)

Evansville (X)
> All Saints, Cannelburg (L)
> Christ the King, Evansville (L)
> Holy Cross, Fort Branch (H)
> Sacred Heart, Schnellville (L)
> SS. Peter and Paul, Haubstadt (L)
> St. Boniface, Fulda (L)
> St. Joseph, Dale (H)
> St. Mary, Evansville (H)

Fairbanks (X)
> Our Lady of Sorrows, Delta Junction (H)

Fall River (X)
> Holy Redeemer, Chatham (L)
> St. Ann, Raynham (L)
> St. Anne's, Fall River (M)
> St. Anthony's, Taunton (L)
> St. John the Baptist, Westport (H)
> St. Mary's, Fairhaven (M)
> St. Mary's, Our Lady of the Isle, Nantucket (L)

Fargo (M)
> Our Lady of Peace, Mayville (M)
> St. Anthony's, Mooreton (M)
> St. Bridget's, Cavalier (H)
> St. John the Evangelist's, Grafton (L)
> St. Mary's, Munich (M)
> St. Mary's, Park River (H)
> St. Michael's, Grand Forks (M)
> St. Patrick's, Enderlin (L)
> Transfiguration, Edgeley (H)

Fort Worth (M)
> Good Shepherd, Colleyville (M)
> Sacred Heart, Breckenridge (M)
> San Mateo, Fort Worth (M)
> St. George, Fort Worth (M)
> St. John the Apostle, Fort Worth (M)
> St. Mary of the Assumption, Fort Worth (M)

Fort Wayne/South Bend (L)
> Holy Cross, Hamlet (L)
> Our Lady of Good Hope, Fort Wayne (H)
> Our Lady of Guadalupe, Milford (M)
> Queen of Peace, Mishawaka (H)
> St. Anthony de Padua, South Bend (L)
> St. Bavo, Mishawaka (L)
> St. John the Baptist, Fort Wayne (M)
> St. John the Evangelist, Goshen (M)
> St. Therese, Fort Wayne (H)
> St. Vincent de Paul, Fort Wayne (H)

Fresno (H)
> Holy Spirit, Fresno (L)
> Our Lady of Victory, Fresno (L)
> Santa Rosa, Lone Pine (L)
> St. Frances Cabrini, Huron (L)
> St. John, Tipton (L)
> St. Patrick, Kerman (L)
> St. Thomas Aquinas, Ojai (L)

Gallup (X)
> Our Lady of Blessed Sacrament, Fort Defiance (L)
> St. Isabel Mission for Navajo Indians, Lukachukai (L)

Galveston-Houston (H)
> Christ the Redeemer, Houston (H)
> Holy Cross, East Bernard (L)
> Holy Name, Houston (L)
> Immaculate Conception, Sealy (L)
> Our Mother of Mercy, Ames (M)
> Sacred Heart, Conroe (L)
> Sacred Heart of Jesus, Manvel (M)
> Santa Teresa's, Bryan (M)

> St. Alphonsus, Houston (L)
> St. Anne, Houston (M)
> St. Francis de Sales, Houston (M)
> St. Francis of Assisi, Houston (L)
> St. Jerome, Houston (H)
> St. Leo the Great, Houston (M)
> St. Martin de Porres, Prairie View (L)
> St. Mary of the Immaculate Conception, Brenham (H)
> St. Mary's, College Station (H)
> St. Mary's, Hearne (M)
> St. Matthew the Evangelist, Houston (H)
> St. Stephen, Houston (M)

Gary (H)
> Holy Angels, Gary (M)
> Holy Trinity, East Chicago (L)
> Holy Trinity, Gary (L)
> Notre Dame, Michigan City (M)
> Our Lady of Guadalupe, East Chicago (L)
> Our Lady of Sorrows, Valparaiso (M)
> Sacred Heart, East Chicago (L)
> St. Catherine of Siena, Hammond (L)
> St. John Bosco, Hammond (H)
> St. Margaret Mary, Hammond (H)
> St. Mark, Gary (L)

Gaylord (L)
> Assumption of St. Mary, Burt Lake (M)
> St. Anne, Alpena (M)
> St. Bernard, Alpena (H)
> St. Mary, Alpena (M)
> St. Philip Neri, Empire (L)

Grand Island (H)
> Blessed Sacrament, Grand Island (H)
> Immaculate Conception, Elm Creek (L)
> Mother of Sorrows, Grant (M)
> Our Lady of Guadalupe, Scottsbluff (H)
> St. Agnes, Scottsbluff (H)
> St. Leo's, Gordon (H)
> St. Mary's, Aurora (H)
> St. Mary's, Mullen (L)

Grand Rapids (X)
Our Lady of Grace, Muskegon (L)
Sacred Heart, Muskegon Heights (M)
St. Anthony of Padua, Grand Rapids (H)
St. Catherine, Ravenna (L)
St. Francis de Sales, Holland (H)
St. Francis Xavier, Conklin (L)
St. Paul's, Big Rapids (H)

Great Falls (H)
Sacred Heart, Bridger (L)
St. Benedict's, Roundup (L)
St. Gabriel's, Chinook (M)
St. Leo's, Lewistown (L)
St. Pius X, Billings (H)
St. William, Dutton (M)

Green Bay (H)
Annunciation of the B.V.M., Green Bay (H)
Holy Martyrs of Gorcum, Green Bay (L)
Nativity of Our Lord, Green Bay (H)
Resurrection, Green Bay (M)
SS. Edward and Isidore, Flintville (H)
St. Benedict, Suamico (M)
St. Boniface, Manitowoc (M)
St. Francis, Hollandtown (L)
St. Francis Xavier, Green Bay (M)
St. Joseph, Norman (M)
St. Joseph, Sturgeon Bay (L)
St. Matthew, Green Bay (H)
St. Patrick, Stiles (M)
St. Rose, Clintonville (M)
St. Stanislaus, Berlin (L)
St. Stanislaus Kostka, Armstrong Creek (M)

Greensburg (H)
St. James the Greater, Apollo (L)

Harrisburg (X)
Our Lady of Refuge Mission, Doylesburg (L)
Sacred Heart of Jesus, Lewisburg (H)
Sacred Heart of Jesus, Williamstown (L)
St. Peter, Elizabethtown (L)
St. Richard, Manheim (L)
St. Theresa of the Infant Jesus, New Cumberland (M)

Hartford (H)
Holy Infant, Orange (M)
Incarnation, Wethersfield (M)
Nativity, Bethlehem (H)
Our Lady of Pompeii, East Haven (M)
Purification of the B.V.M., Ellwood City (M)
Sacred Heart, Vernon (M)
St. Andrew, Colchester (L)
St. Ann, Bristol (L)
St. Jerome's, New Britain (L)
St. Joseph, Chester (L)
St. Joseph, Rockville (L)
St. Mary's, East Hartford (M)

Helena (X)
Christ the King, Missoula (M)
Holy Family, Three Forks (H)
Immaculate Conception, Deer Lodge (L)
Sacred Heart, Ronan (M)
St. Catherine, Bigfork (M)

Honolulu (L)
Annunciation, Kamuela (L)
Our Lady of Lourdes, Honokaa (L)
Our Lady of Sorrows, Wahiawa (L)
St. John the Baptist, Honolulu (M)

Houma/Thibodaux (X)
Our Lady of Prompt Succor, Chackbay (L)
St. Philomena, Labadieville (L)

Indianapolis (H)
Holy Spirit, Indianapolis (L)
Holy Trinity, Indianapolis (L)
Our Lady of the Greenwood,
Greenwood (M)
St. Anthony of Padua, Clarksville (M)
St. John the Apostle, Bloomington
(H)
St. John the Baptist, Starlight (L)
St. John the Evangelist, Indianapolis
(M)
St. Joseph, Lebanon (H)
St. Joseph, St. Joseph Hill (M)
St. Joseph, Terre Haute (M)
St. Joseph's, St. Leon (L)
St. Lawrence, Indianapolis (M)
St. Louis de Montfort, Fishers (M)
St. Mary, New Albany (L)
St. Nicholas, St. Nicholas (L)
St. Philip Neri, Indianapolis (M)
St. Pius X, Indianapolis (H)
St. Simon, Indianapolis (L)
St. Vincent de Paul, Bedford (M)

Jackson (H)
Immaculate Conception, West Point
(H)
St. Francis of Assisi, Madison (H)
St. James, Tupelo (M)
St. John, Oxford (H)
St. Joseph, Greenville (H)
St. Joseph, Starkville (H)
St. Mary, Jackson (M)
St. Mary, Natchez (H)
St. Patrick, Meridian (M)
St. Teresa, Chatawa (M)

Jefferson City (H)
Columbia Newman Center, Univ. of
Columbia (M)
Holy Family, Hannibal (M)
Most Pure Heart of Mary, Chamois
(M)
St. Andrew, Holts Summit (M)
St. Boniface, Brunswick (M)
St. Cecilia, Meta (M)

St. Mary, Milan (M)
St. Peter, Fulton (H)
St. Peter, Jefferson City (M)
St. Peter, Marshall (M)

Joliet (H)
Immaculate Conception, Braidwood
(M)
Sacred Heart, Aurora (L)
Sacred Heart, Joliet (M)
SS. Mary and Joseph, Chebanse (L)
St. Andrew the Apostle, Romeoville
(H)
St. Anne, Oswego (M)
St. James, Sauk Village (M)
St. John the Baptist, Joliet (M)
St. Joseph, Downers Grove (M)
St. Leonard, Berwyn (L)
St. Liborius, Steger (H)
St. Margaret Mary, Herscher (L)
St. Mary of Celle, Berwyn (L)
St. Paul, Chicago Heights (L)
St. Peter's, Clifton (L)
St. Rita of Cascia, Aurora (L)
St. Therese of Jesus, Aurora (L)

Juneau (X)
St. Catherine of Siena, Petersburg (L)

Kalamazoo (X)
Our Lady of the Lake, Edwardsburg
(H)
St. Anthony, Buchanan (M)
St. Joseph, Kalamazoo (L)
St. Margaret, Otsego (M)
St. Martin, Vicksburg (M)
St. Mary, Paw Paw (M)
St. Philip, Battle Creek (M)

Kansas City (H)
Corpus Christi, Lawrence (H)
Holy Angels, Garnett (M)
Holy Spirit, Overland Park (M)
Immaculate Conception, St. Mary's
(H)
Most Pure Heart of Mary, Topeka (H)
Nativity, Leawood (H)

St. Aloysius, Meriden (M)
St. Joseph's, Nortonville (L)
St. Mary-St. Anthony, Kansas City (H)

Kansas City/St. Joseph (H)
Blessed Sacrament, Bethany (L)
Guardian Angels, Kansas City (M)
Holy Rosary, Clinton (L)
Immaculate Conception, Montrose (L)
St. Ann's, Plattsburg (M)
St. Francis Xavier, St. Joseph (H)
St. John Francis Regis, Kansas City (H)
St. Joseph the Worker, Independence (H)
St. Mary, Lamar (L)
St. Peter's, Kansas City (H)
St. Robert Bellarmine, Blue Springs (H)
St. Thomas More, Kansas City (H)

Knoxville (X)
Sacred Heart of Jesus, Knoxville (H)
SS. Peter and Paul, Chattanooga (H)
St. Francis of Assisi, Fairfield Glade (H)
St. Paul the Apostle, Tullahoma (L)
St. Peter the Apostle, Pascagoula (H)

La Crosse (H)
Immaculate Conception, Fountain City (M)
St. Elizabeth Ann Seton, Holmen (M)
St. John the Baptist, Plum City (H)
St. Pius X, La Crosse (H)

Lafayette, Ind. (H)
St. Bernard, Wabash (M)
St. Francis of Assisi, Muncie (M)
St. Francis Solano, Francesville (L)
St. Joan of Arc, Kokomo (H)
St. Mary, Union City (L)

Lafayette, La. (X)
Notre Dame de Perpetuel Secours, St. Martinville (L)
Sacred Heart of Jesus, New Iberia (L)
St. Anne, Cow Island (M)
St. Elizabeth, Coteau Holmes (M)
St. Thomas More, Eunice (H)

Lake Charles (L)
Our Lady of LaSalette, De Quincy (L)
Our Lady of LaSalette, Sulphur (L)
St. Peter Apostle, Hackberry (L)
St. Philip Neri, Kinder (L)

Lansing (X)
Immaculate Heart of Mary, Lansing (M)
Most Holy Trinity, Fowler (L)
St. Augustine, Deerfield (L)
St. Charles, Greenville (H)
St. Joseph's, Del Rio (L)
St. Joseph, Owosso (H)
St. Jude, De Witt (L)
St. Mary, Charlotte (L)
St. Mary, Westphalia (M)
St. Patrick's, Portland (L)
St. Thomas Aquinas, East Lansing (M)

Las Cruces (X)
Assumption of the B.V.M., Roswell (L)
Holy Cross, Las Cruces (L)
Our Lady of Guadalupe, Mesilla Park (M)
San Isidro, Garfield (L)
St. Eleanor, Ruidoso (M)
St. Francis de Paula, Tularosa (L)
St. Genevieve, Las Cruces (L)

Lexington (H)
SS. John and Elizabeth, Grayson (L)
St. Martha, Prestonsburg (L)

Lincoln (H)
All Saints, Holdrege (L)
North American Martyrs, Lincoln (L)
Sacred Heart, Crete (H)
St. James, Trenton (M)
St. Joseph's, Auburn (M)
St. Teresa's, Lincoln (L)
St. Vincent de Paul, Seward (M)

Little Rock (X)
Christ the King, Little Rock (M)
Mary, Mother of God, Harrison (L)
Our Lady of the Holy Souls, Little
Rock (L)
Perpetual Help, B.V.M., St. Vincent
(L)
Sacred Heart, Charleston (M)
Sacred Heart of Mary, Barling (H)
St. Anne, Little Rock (M)
St. Joan of Arc, Hershey (H)
St. Mary's, Siloam Springs (H)
St. Michael's, West Memphis (L)
St. Patrick's, Little Rock (M)

Los Angeles (X)
Holy Innocents, Long Beach (M)
Holy Name of Jesus, Los Angeles (L)
Holy Spirit, Los Angeles (L)
Our Lady of Mt. Carmel, Rancho
Cucamonga (L)
Our Lady of the Miraculous Medal,
Montebello (H)
Sacred Heart, Los Angeles (M)
San Buenaventura Mission, Ventura
(L)
San Francisco, Los Angeles (M)
St. Anne's, Seal Beach (H)
St. Barbara, Santa Barbara (M)
St. Cecilia, Los Angeles (M)
St. Francis of Assisi, Fillmore (M)
St. Hilary, Pico Rivera (H)
St. Jerome, Los Angeles (L)
St. Paschal Baylon, Thousand Oaks
(L)
St. Patrick, Los Angeles (L)
St. Polycarp, Stanton (M)

St. Teresa of Avila, Los Angeles (H)
St. Thomas the Apostle, Los Angeles
(L)
St. Vincent de Paul, Los Angeles (L)

Louisville (H)
Christ the King, Louisville (L)
Holy Rosary, Springfield (M)
Holy Spirit, Louisville (H)
St. Aloysius, Pewee Valley (M)
St. Benedict, Lebanon Junction (L)
St. Denis, Louisville (M)
St. Dominic, Springfield (M)
St. Gabriel the Archangel, Louisville
(H)
St. John Vianney, Louisville (L)
St. Joseph, Bardstown (H)
St. Michael, Fairfield (M)

Lubbock (X)
Immaculate Heart of Mary, Sweetwa-
ter (L)
Sacred Heart, Abilene (H)
St. John Neumann, Lubbock (H)

Madison (X)
Holy Mother of Consolation, Oregon
(H)
Holy Rosary, Darlington (M)
SS. Andrew-Thomas,
Tennyson-Potosi (L)
St. Aloysius, Sauk City (M)
St. Augustine, Platteville (L)
St. Catherine, Sharon (H)
St. James, Madison (L)
St. John Vianney, Janesville (M)
St. Joseph, Argyle (M)
St. Joseph, Dodgeville (L)
St. Martin, Martinsville (L)
St. Mary-St. Paul, Mineral Point (H)
St. Patrick, Doylestown (L)
St. Raphael, Madison (L)
St. Victor, Monroe (M)

Manchester (X)
Sacred Heart, Marlborough (M)
St. Anthony of Padua, Manchester (H)

St. Catherine of Siena, Portsmouth (L)
St. Joseph, Dover (L)
St. Mary, Claremont (M)
St. Patrick, Bennington (M)
St. Paul, Franklin (M)

Marquette (H)
Sacred Heart of Jesus, Munising (M)
St. Joseph, Ishpeming (L)
St. Thomas the Apostle, Escanaba (M)
St. Joseph, St. Joseph (H)

Memphis (H)
Immaculate Conception, Memphis (M)
Our Lady of Perpetual Help, Memphis (L)
St. Alphonsus, Covington (L)

Metuchen (H)
Blessed Kateri Tekakwitha, Sparta (H)
La Asuncion, Perth Amboy (M)
Our Lady of Lourdes, Whitehouse Station (M)
Our Lady of Mt. Carmel, Swartswood (M)
Our Lady of Mt. Virgin, Middlesex (L)
Our Lady Star of the Sea, Lake Hopatcong (M)
Sacred Heart of Jesus, Manville (L)
St. Bernard's, Mt. Hope (L)
St. Clement, Pope and Martyr, Rockaway Twp. (L)
St. Francis, Metuchen (L)
St. Matthew, Edison (L)
St. Paul the Apostle, Highland Park (L)

Miami (X)
Annunciation, Washington (L)
Christ the King, Miami (L)
Gesu, Miami (L)
Immaculate Conception, Hialeah (L)

Mother of Christ, Miami (H)
St. Gabriel, Pompano Beach (L)
St. John Neumann, Miami (L)
St. John the Baptist, Fort Lauderdale (M)
St. Martin de Porres, Leisure City (M)
St. Mary, Star of the Sea, Key West (M)
St. Maximilian Kolbe, Pembroke Pines (H)
St. Michael the Archangel, Miami (L)

Milwaukee (H)
Holy Trinity, Newburg (L)
St. Anthony of Padua, Milwaukee (M)
St. Bernard's, Wauwatosa (L)
St. Boniface, Germantown (L)
St. Catherine, Milwaukee (M)
St. Dominic, Brookfield (H)
St. Dominic, Sheboygan (M)
St. Francis Xavier, Brighton (M)
St. James, Mequon (H)
St. James, Mukwonago (L)
St. John, Milwaukee (H)
St. John Nepomuk, Racine (L)
St. Joseph's, Cudahy (M)
St. Lawrence, Milwaukee (L)
St. Martin's, Ashford (H)
St. Mary Magdalen, Milwaukee (L)
St. Mary's, Elm Grove (H)
St. Matthew's, Milwaukee (H)
St. Matthias, Milwaukee (M)
St. Peter of Alcantara, Port Washington (M)
St. Sebastian's, Milwaukee (H)
St. Thomas Aquinas, Kenosha (H)
St. Wendel, Cleveland (L)

Mobile (M)
St. Bede, Montgomery (L)
St. Columba, Dothan (M)
St. Dominic, Mobile (L)
St. Margaret, Foley (L)
St. Martin, Troy (M)
St. Maurice, Brewton (L)

Monterey (X)
St. Francis Xavier, Seaside (L)
St. John the Baptist, King City (L)

Nashville (H)
St. Ignatius of Antioch, Antioch (H)
St. Joseph's, Madison (L)
St. Matthew, Franklin (L)
St. Patrick, McEwen (L)
St. Rose of Lima, Murfreesboro (H)
St. Stephen, Old Hickory (H)

New Orleans (H)
Infant Jesus of Prague, Harvey (L)
Most Sacred Heart of Jesus,
    Gramercy (M)
Our Lady of Lourdes, New Orleans
    (L)
Our Lady of Pompeii, Tickfaw (L)
St. Clement of Rome, Metairie (M)
St. Francis de Sales, New Orleans (L)
St. Genevieve, Slidell (M)
St. Gerard, New Orleans (L)
St. Gertrude, Des Allemands (L)
St. James, St. James (L)
St. Jane de Chantal, Abita Springs (L)
St. Jerome, Kenner (H)
St. Joseph the Worker, Marrero (H)
St. Matthew the Apostle, River Ridge
    (L)
St. Matthias, New Orleans (L)
St. Monica, New Orleans (L)
St. Peter, Covington (L)
St. Peter, Reserve (H)
St. Raphael the Archangel,
    New Orleans (M)
St. Stephen, New Orleans (L)
St. Stephen Martyr, Maurepas (M)
St. Theresa of the Child Jesus,
    New Orleans (L)

New Ulm (H)
Assumption of the B.V.M., Morris (H)
Holy Redeemer, Marshall (H)

Holy Redeemer, Renville (M)
St. Aloysius, Olivia (M)
St. Edward, Minneota (M)
St. Malachy, Clontarf (H)
St. Mary's, Chokio (M)
Visitation, Danvers (H)

New York (H)
Corpus Christi, Port Chester (M)
Epiphany, New York (M)
Holy Name of Mary,
    Croton-on-Hudson (L)
Immaculate Conception, Tuckahoe
    (L)
Immaculate Conception,
    Woodbourne (L)
Most Holy Trinity, West Point (M)
Most Precious Blood, New York (M)
Most Precious Blood, Walden (L)
Our Lady of Lourdes, New York (L)
Our Lady of Mt. Carmel-St.
    Benedicta, Staten Island (M)
Our Lady of Sorrows, New York (L)
Sacred Heart, Bronx (L)
St. Ann, Bronx (L)
St. Bridget, Copake Falls (H)
St. Catherine of Siena, New York (L)
St. Dominic, Bronx (L)
St. Francis de Sales, New York (L)
St. Joan of Arc, Bronx (L)
St. John the Evangelist, Centerville
    (M)
St. Joseph, Croton Falls (H)
St. Joseph, Middletown (M)
St. Mary, Bronx (L)
St. Mary, Poughkeepsie (L)
St. Mary, Washingtonville (L)
St. Matthew, Hastings-on-Hudson (L)
St. Nicholas of Tolentine, Bronx (M)
St. Patrick, Newburgh (M)
St. Paul the Apostle, New York (L)
St. Pius V, Bronx (L)
St. Stephen of Hungary, New York
    (L)
St. Thomas Aquinas, Forestburgh (L)

Newark (H)

Holy Name of Jesus, East Orange (L)
Immaculate Heart of Mary, Newark (L)
Our Lady of Grace, Hoboken (M)
Sacred Heart, Jersey City (L)
St. Anthony of Padua, Passaic (M)
St. Anthony of Padua, Union City (H)
St. Boniface's, Jersey City (L)
St. Cecilia's, Kearny (H)
St. John the Baptist, Fairview (L)
St. Joseph's, Demarest (M)
St. Leo's, Irvington (M)
St. Nicholas, Passaic (L)
St. Paul, Clifton (H)
St. Paul's, Jersey City (H)

Norwich (X)

Sagrado Corazon de Jesus, Windham (M)
St. Mary, Star of the Sea, New London (H)
St. Matthias, East Lyme (M)
St. Paul, Waterford (M)

Oakland (H)

Holy Rosary, Antioch (H)
Holy Spirit, Berkeley (H)
St. Augustine, Pleasanton (M)
St. Bernard's, Oakland (L)
St. Clement, Hayward (L)
St. Cyril, Oakland (M)
St. Edward's, Newark (L)
St. Joan of Arc, San Ramon (H)
St. Lawrence O'Toole, Oakland (M)
St. Leo's, Oakland (M)
St. Mary Magdalen, Berkeley (H)

Ogdensburg (X)

Our Lady of the Sacred Heart, Watertown (L)
St. Alexander, Morrisonville (H)
St. Andrew, Sackets Harbor (M)
St. Brendan, Keene (M)
St. Edmund, Ellenburg (M)
St. Joseph, West Chazy (M)
St. Lawrence, Louisville (M)

St. Mary, Brushton (H)
St. Mary of the Lake, Plattsburgh (M)
St. Michael, Antwerp (M)
St. Paul, Black River (M)
St. Paul, Bloomingdale (H)

Oklahoma City (H)

Our Lady of Victory, Purcell (M)
Sacred Heart, Alva (M)
St. Benedict, Shawnee (M)
St. Eugene's, Weatherford (M)
St. Monica, Edmond (H)

Omaha (H)

Assumption, Omaha (L)
Assumption, West Point (M)
Holy Family, Omaha (L)
Our Lady of Guadalupe, Omaha (M)
St. Aloysius, Aloys (L)
St. Benedict the Moor, Omaha (L)
St. Bernard, Omaha (H)
St. Joan of Arc, Omaha (M)
St. Leo, Snyder (L)
St. Mary, Schuyler (L)
St. Mary's, David City (L)
St. Patrick, O'Neill (H)
St. Patrick's, Battle Creek (L)
St. Peter, Clarks (L)
St. Peter, Fullerton (M)
St. Peter, Omaha (H)

Orange (X)

Blessed Sacrament, Westminster (L)
Our Lady of Guadalupe, Santa Ana (L)
Our Lady of Lourdes, Santa Ana (H)
St. Bonaventure, Huntington Beach (H)

Orlando (X)

All Souls, Sanford (H)
Ascension, Melbourne (M)
Holy Name of Jesus, Indialantic (H)
Our Lady of Grace, Palm Bay (M)
Our Lady of Lourdes, Melbourne (M)
St. Charles Borromeo, Orlando (M)

St. Clare, Deltona (M)
St. Isaac Jogues, Orlando (M)
St. Mary's, Rockledge (M)
St. Michael, Wauchula (L)
St. Timothy, Lady Lake (M)

Owensboro (M)
St. Mark, Eddyville (L)
St. Martin, Rome (L)

Palm Beach (X)
Mary Immaculate, West Palm Beach (M)
Our Lady of Lourdes, Boca Raton (H)
St. Joan of Arc, Boca Raton (M)
St. Jude, Boca Raton (H)
St. Paul of the Cross, North Palm Beach (M)

Paterson (X)
St. George, Paterson (L)
St. Luke's, Hohokus (M)
St. Paul, Ramsey (M)
St. Thomas of Aquin, Ogdensburg (M)

Pensacola/Tallahasee (M)
Holy Name of Jesus, Niceville (L)
Little Flower, Pensacola (L)
Queen of Peace, Gainesville (L)
St. Ann, Gulf Breeze (H)
St. John the Evangelist, Chiefland (L)
St. Jude's, Ocala (M)
St. Madeleine, High Springs (M)
St. Thomas the Apostle, Homosassa (H)
St. Vincent de Paul, Madison (L)

Peoria (X)
Holy Family, Peoria (H)
Sacre Coeur, Creve Coeur (L)
St. Joseph's, Pekin (L)
St. Louis, Princeton (H)
St. Malachy's, Geneseo (L)
St. Mark's, Peoria (H)
St. Mary's, Pontiac (L)
St. Patrick's, Hennepin (L)

Philadelphia (M)
Mary, Mother of the Redeemer, North Wales (M)
Our Lady of Fatima, Secane (L)
Our Lady of Hope, Philadelphia (L)
SS. Cosmas and Damian, Conshohocken (M)
St. Casimir, Philadelphia (M)
St. Denis, Havertown (M)
St. Eleanor, Collegeville (L)
St. Gabriel of the Sorrowful Mother, New Garden Twp. (L)
St. John the Evangelist, Philadelphia (H)
St. Jude, Chalfont (M)
St. Mary Magdalen de Pazzi, Philadelphia (L)
St. Matthew, Conshohocken (H)
St. Peter, Pottstown (L)
St. Thomas of Villanova, Villanova (H)
St. Vincent de Paul, Richboro (L)

Phoenix (H)
Corpus Christi, Phoenix (L)
Most Holy Trinity, Phoenix (L)
Resurrection, Tempe (L)
St. Augustine, Phoenix (H)
St. Catherine of Sienna, Phoenix (M)
St. Germaine, Prescott Valley (L)
St. Gregory, Phoenix (L)
St. Henry, Buckeye (M)
St. Martin de Porres, Phoenix (M)

Pittsburgh (H)
Good Shepherd, West Middlesex (H)
Most Holy Name of Jesus, Pittsburgh (L)
Resurrection, Pittsburgh (M)
Sacred Heart, Pittsburgh (L)
SS. Peter and Paul, Beaver (L)
St. Albert the Great, Baldwin Boro (L)
St. Ann, Waynesburg (H)
St. Athanasius, West View (L)
St. Bonaventure, Glenshaw (M)
St. Christopher, Prospect (H)

St. Colman, Turtle Creek (L)
St. John the Evangelist, Uniontown (H)
St. John Vianney, Pittsburgh (L)
St. Joseph, Cabot (L)
St. Joseph, Sharon (H)
St. Joseph the Worker, New Castle (L)
St. Louise de Marillac, Pittsburgh (H)
St. Mary, Cecil (M)
St. Mary of Mercy, Pittsburgh (L)
St. Philomena, Beaver Falls (L)
St. Raphael, Pittsburgh (M)
St. Rita, Connellsville (L)
St. Stephen, Pittsburgh (L)
St. Teresa of Avila, Perrysville (M)
St. Winifred, Mt. Lebanon (M)
Transfiguration, Monongahela (M)
Transfiguration, Russellton (M)

Portland, Maine (H)
Holy Cross, Lewiston (L)
Holy Cross, South Portland (M)
Lakeway Ecumenical, Austin (M)
Our Lady of the Lakes, Oquossoc (L)
Our Lady of Wisdom, Orono (L)
St. Edmund, Westbrook (L)
St. James the Greater, Woodland (H)
St. Martin of Tours, Millinocket (L)
St. Mary's, Houlton (L)

Portland, Ore. (X)
Holy Trinity, Goldendale (L)
Resurrection, Tualatin (M)
St. Aloysius, Estacada (H)
St. Andrew, Portland (H)
St. Anne, Grants Pass (H)
St. Birgitta, Portland (M)
St. Clare, Portland (H)
St. John, Yamhill (M)
St. Mark, Eugene (M)
St. Mary, Star of the Sea, Astoria (M)
St. Patrick, Canby (M)
St. Philip Benizi, Redland (M)
St. Vincent de Paul, Portland (H)

Providence (X)
Holy Trinity, Central Falls (L)
SS. John and Paul, Coventry (L)
St. Anthony's, Pawtucket (L)
St. Anthony's, Providence (L)
St. Joseph's, Providence (H)
St. Lucy's, Middletown (H)
St. Mary's, Bristol (M)
St. Paul the Apostle, Foster (L)

Pueblo (H)
Immaculate Heart of Mary, Pagosa Springs (L)
St. Catherine's, Aledo (H)
St. Michael, Canon City (M)
St. Rose of Lima, Buena Vista (H)

Raleigh (M)
Good Shepherd, Hope Mills (L)
Immaculate Conception, Carolina Beach (H)
SS. Mary and Edward, Roxboro (H)
St. Anne, Edenton (M)
St. Catherine, Tarboro (L)
St. Elizabeth, Farmville (M)
St. Francis de Sales, Lumberton (L)
St. Mary, Goldsboro (M)
St. Mary, Garner (M)

Rapid City (X)
Blessed Sacrament, Bison (L)
Immaculate Conception, Winner (L)
Rosebud Reservation, St. Francis (L)
St. Anthony's, Hot Springs (L)
St. Michael, Herreid (L)
St. Paul, Belle Fourche (L)

Reno/Las Vegas (X)
St. Christopher, North Las Vegas (H)
St. Elizabeth Ann Seton, Las Vegas (L)

Richmond (H)
Christ the King, Norfolk (L)
Sacred Heart, Danville (M)
St. Edward the Confessor, Richmond (L)

St. George, Scottsville (M)
St. Gregory the Great, Virginia Beach
(H)
St. Jerome, Newport News (L)
St. Mark, Virginia Beach (L)
St. Mary of the Presentation, Suffolk
(M)
St. Mary's and Newman Community,
Blacksburg (L)
St. Olaf, Patron of Norway, Norge (L)
St. Patrick's, Chancellorsville (M)
St. Paul's, Richmond (M)
St. Rose of Lima, Hampton (M)
St. Therese, the Little Flower,
Gloucester (L)
St. Therese's, St. Paul (L)
St. Timothy, Tappahannock (M)

Rochester (H)
All Saints, Lansing (M)
Blessed Sacrament, Andover (L)
Bridget, East Bloomfield (L)
St. Charles Borromeo, Rochester (M)
St. Elizabeth Ann Seton, Hamlin (H)
St. John of the Cross, Whitesville (L)
St. John the Evangelist, Spencerport
(M)
St. Leo, Hilton (L)
St. Mary, Belmont (H)
St. Mary of the Assumption,
Scottsville (M)
St. Michael, Newark (H)
St. Michael, Penn Yan (H)
St. Patrick, Mt. Morris (L)
St. Thomas More, Rochester (H)

Rockford (H)
SS. Peter and Paul, Rockford (M)
St. Mary, Morrison (M)

Rockville Centre (H)
Our Lady of Lourdes, Malverne (M)
Our Lady of Mercy, Hicksville (M)
Our Lady of Peace, Lynbrook (M)
Sacred Heart, Cutchogue (M)
Sacred Heart, North Merrick (M)
St. Brigid, Westbury (H)

St. Francis de Sales, Patchogue (M)
St. Hugh of Lincoln, Huntington
Station (L)
St. Joseph's, Garden City (H)
St. Raymond's, East Rockaway (L)

Sacramento (H)
Holy Cross, West Sacramento (M)
Holy Rosary, Woodland (M)
Sacred Heart, Ione (L)
St. Anthony, Winters (M)
St. Boniface, San Francisco (H)
St. Thomas, Oroville (M)
St. Thomas More, Paradise (M)

Saginaw (L)
SS. Simon and Jude, Saginaw (L)
St. Helen, St. Helen (L)
St. Mary, Saginaw (M)
St. Mary, Mio (M)
St. Philip Neri, Coleman (M)

Salina (X)
St. John the Baptist's, Clyde (L)
St. Joseph's, Oakley (M)
St. Michael's, Chapman (L)

Salt Lake City (H)
St. Elizabeth's, Richfield (M)
St. Francis Xavier, Kearns (L)
St. Martin de Porres, Taylorsville (L)
St. Olaf, Bountiful (M)

San Angelo (M)
Holy Angels, San Angelo (L)
Our Lady of Guadalupe, Eldorado
(M)
Sacred Heart, Coleman (L)
St. Ann's, Sonora (L)
St. Joseph's, Fort Stockton (L)
St. Lawrence, St. Lawrence (L)

San Antonio (M)
Blessed Sacrament, Poth (H)
Divine Providence, San Antonio (H)
Our Lady of Guadalupe, Carrizo
Springs (L)

Our Lady of Mt. Carmel and St. Therese, San Antonio (M)
Our Lady of Perpetual Help, New Braunfels (H)
Sacred Heart, Eagle Pass (H)
San Francisco de la Espada, San Antonio (M)
St. Anthony of Padua, San Antonio (L)
St. Brigid, San Antonio (L)
St. Joseph, Beeville (L)
St. Joseph's, Nixon (L)
St. Jude, San Antonio (L)
St. Leonard's, San Antonio (M)
St. Martin de Porres, San Antonio (L)
St. Mary, Stockdale (L)
St. Matthew's, Jourdanton (L)
St. Peter's, Boerne (M)

San Bernardino (X)
Blessed Sacrament, Twentynine Palms (L)
Holy Spirit, Hemet (M)
Our Lady of Guadalupe, Riverside (L)
Our Lady of the Desert, Apple Valley (H)
Queen of Angels, Riverside (L)
St. Catherine of Alexandria, Riverside (M)
St. Frances of Rome, Lake Elsinore (L)
St. Martha's, Murietta (H)
St. Thomas the Apostle, Riverside (H)

San Diego (H)
Holy Family, San Diego (L)
Holy Trinity, El Cajon (M)
Mission San Luis Rey de Francia, San Luis Rey (H)
Our Lady of the Sacred Heart, San Diego (L)
St. Charles Borromeo, San Diego (H)
St. Richard, Borrego Springs (L)
St. Rose of Lima, Chula Vista (H)

San Francisco (L)
St. Andrew, Daly City (L)
St. Bruno, San Bruno (H)
St. Emydius, San Francisco (L)
St. Gabriel, San Francisco (L)
St. Joseph, Mountain View (L)
St. Nicholas, Los Altos (M)
St. Peter, San Francisco (H)
St. Simon, Los Altos (L)

San Jose (L)
Resurrection, Aptos (H)
St. Francis of Assisi/Evergreen Catholic, San Jose (M)

Santa Fe (X)
Cristo Rey, Santa Fe (M)
Immaculate Conception, Tome (L)
Our Lady of the Assumption, Jemez Springs (H)
San Antonio de Padua, Penasco (M)
San Isidro, Santa Fe (H)
St. Gertrude, Mora (L)
St. Therese of the Infant Jesus, Albuquerque (L)

Santa Rosa (X)
Blessed Kateri Tekakwitha, Hoopa (L)
St. Anthony of Padua, Novato (L)
St. John the Baptist, Healdsburg (L)
St. Mary of the Angels, Ukiah (H)
St. Patrick, Scotia (L)

Savannah (H)
Sacred Heart, Davenport (M)
Sacred Heart, Vidalia (L)
St. Anne, Richmond Hill (L)
St. Christopher, Claxton (L)
St. Frances Xavier Cabrini, Savannah (M)
St. Joseph's, Waycross (L)
St. William's, St. Simons Island (M)

Scranton (M)
Exaltation of the Holy Cross,
 Buttonwood (L)
Immaculate Conception, Lock Haven
 (L)
Our Lady of Mt. Carmel, Pittston (L)
St. Elizabeth, Smethport (L)
St. Patrick's, Nicholson (M)
St. Stanislaus, Nanticoke (L)

Seattle (M)
Holy Family, Kirkland (L)
Immaculate Conception,
 Mount Vernon (H)
San Antonio, Anaheim (L)
St. Brendan, Bothell (M)
St. Francis Xavier Mission, Toledo (L)
St. Gabriel's, Port Orchard (M)
St. John Mary Vianney, Kirkland (H)
St. Joseph, Seattle (H)
St. Luke, Seattle (H)
St. Madeleine Sophie, Bellevue (L)
St. Patrick, Seattle (H)
St. Vincent de Paul, Federal Way (M)

Shreveport (H)
Our Lady of the Holy Rosary,
 Shreveport (L)
St. John Berchmans, Shreveport (L)
St. Patrick, Lake Providence (L)

Sioux City (H)
Holy Name, Rock Rapids (L)
Immaculate Conception, Moville (L)
Nativity of Our Lord Jesus Christ,
 Sioux City (L)
Our Lady of Good Counsel, Fonda
 (M)
Our Lady of Good Counsel,
 Moorland (L)
Sacred Heart, Early (L)
Sacred Heart, Manilla (L)
Sacred Heart, Spencer (L)
SS. Peter and Paul, West Bend (M)
St. Francis of Assisi, Maple River (L)
St. Francis of Assisi, Rockwell City
 (M)

St. Joseph's, Milford (H)
St. Joseph's, Salix (L)
St. Mary's, Mallard (L)
St. Mary's, Spirit Lake (H)
St. Mary's, Storm Lake (M)
St. Patrick's, Estherville (H)
St. Patrick's, Sheldon (M)

Sioux Falls (X)
Holy Name, Watertown (H)
Sacred Heart, Aberdeen (L)
St. Anthony of Padua, Hoven (L)
St. Mary, Salem (L)
St. Michael, Mt. Pleasant (L)
St. Nicholas, Tea (M)
St. Paul the Apostle, Armour (L)
St. Rose of Lima, Garretson (M)

Spokane (H)
Holy Rosary, Pomeroy (H)
Immaculate Conception, Colville (L)
Immaculate Conception, Davenport
 (L)
St. Anthony, Spokane (H)
St. Charles, Spokane (M)
St. Thomas More, Spokane (H)

Springfield, Ill. (M)
Little Flower, Springfield (L)
Sacred Heart of Jesus, Oconee (L)
St. Agnes, Springfield (M)
St. Aloysius, Springfield (L)
St. James, Riverton (M)
St. Jude, Rochester (M)
St. Paul's, Danville (L)
St. Raymond, Raymond (L)
St. Thomas, Philo (L)

Springfield, Mass. (L)
Blessed Sacrament, Northampton (L)
Holy Cross, Springfield (H)
Holy Name of Jesus, Chicopee (L)
Holy Trinity, Hatfield (L)
Our Lady of Mt. Carmel, Pittsfield (L)
Sacred Heart, Holyoke (M)
St. John the Evangelist, Agawam (M)
St. Mary's, Thorndike (L)

Springfield, Mo. (L)
Holy Trinity, Springfield (L)
St. Agnes, Springfield (L)
St. Bernadette, Hermitage (M)
St. Marie du Lac, Ironton (L)
St. Vincent de Paul, Perryville (M)

St. Augustine (L)
Our Lady of Consolation, Callahan (L)
St. Catherine's, Orange Park (L)
St. Luke's, Middleburg (L)
St. Michael's, Fernandina Beach (L)

St. Cloud (H)
Christ, St. Cloud (M)
Holy Trinity, Royalton (H)
Seven Dolors, Albany (L)
St. Anthony of Padua, St. Cloud (H)
St. John the Baptist, Collegeville (L)
St. John's, Foley (H)
St. Joseph's, Waite Park (M)
St. Lawrence's, Duelm (L)
St. Louis, Paynesville (M)
St. Louis Bertrand, Foreston (H)
St. Mary, Little Falls (H)
St. Olaf, Elbow Lake (L)

St. Louis (H)
Christ, Prince of Peace, Manchester (M)
Immaculate Conception, Dardenne (M)
Immaculate Conception, Montgomery City (M)
Little Flower, St. Teresa, Richmond Heights (M)
Our Lady of Fatima, Florissant (M)
Sacred Heart, Troy (M)
St. Alphonsus, Millwood (H)
St. Alphonsus Liguori, St. Louis (H)
St. Catherine Laboure, Sappington (M)
St. Clement, Des Peres (L)
St. Elizabeth Ann Seton, St. Charles (M)
St. Francis Xavier, St. Louis (M)
St. Gerard Majella, Kirkwood (M)

St. John Bosco, Creve Coeur (M)
St. Joseph's, Neier (L)
St. Mary's, Moselle (L)
St. Monica, Creve Coeur (H)
St. Raphael the Archangel, St. Louis (M)
St. Rita, Vinita Park (M)
St. Simon of Cyrene, St. Louis (M)
St. Stephen's, Richwoods (M)
St. Vincent de Paul, Dutzow (M)
Visitation–St. Ann's, St. Louis (L)

St. Paul/Minneapolis (H)
All Saints, Minneapolis (M)
Annunciation, Minneapolis (M)
Annunciation of the B.V.M., Hazelwood (H)
Ascension, Minneapolis (L)
Corpus Christi, St. Paul (H)
Holy Trinity, Winsted (H)
Nativity of the B.V.M., Bloomington (H)
Our Lady of Peace, Minneapolis (M)
SS. Cyril and Methodius, Minneapolis (M)
St. Andrew, Elk River (M)
St. Anne, Hamel (M)
St. Casimir, St. Paul (L)
St. Charles, Bayport (M)
St. Edward, Bloomington (H)
St. Edward's, Princeton (M)
St. Francis of Assisi, Lakeland (L)
St. Genevieve, Centerville (L)
St. Helena, Minneapolis (M)
St. John the Evangelist, Little Canada (M)
St. Joseph, Rosemount (L)
St. Mark, Shakopee (H)
St. Odilia, Shoreview (H)
St. Olaf, Minneapolis (L)
St. Peter, Mendota (M)
St. Raphael, Crystal (M)
St. Victoria, Victoria (H)
St. Vincent de Paul, Osseo (H)
St. William of York, Stafford (H)
Transfiguration, Oakdale (M)
Visitation, Minneapolis (H)

St. Petersburg (X)
St. Rita, Dade City (L)
St. Theresa, Spring Hill (M)

Steubenville (H)
Assumption, Barnesville (M)
Christ the King, Athens (H)
St. Ann's, East Liverpool (H)
St. Henry, Harriettsville (M)
St. Mary, Lafferty (M)
St. Paul's, Athens (H)

Stockton (L)
Sacred Heart, Merced (L)
St. Anthony, Manteca (L)

Superior (L)
Holy Cross, Cornell (L)
Holy Rosary, Mellen (L)
Newman Community, Eau Claire (M)
St. Anne, Wausau (M)
St. Anthony, Tigerton (L)
St. Hyacinth, Antigo (M)
St. John the Baptist, Rib Lake (M)
St. John the Baptist, Webster (M)
St. Joseph, Stevens Point (M)
St. Lawrence, Wisconsin Rapids (H)
St. Mark, Rothschild (H)
St. Mary Help of Christians, Colby (H)
St. Patrick, Eau Claire (M)
St. Paul, Bloomer (M)
St. Pius X, Solon Springs (L)
St. Theresa, Westboro (L)

Syracuse (X)
St. Ann, Manlius (M)
St. Anthony of Padua, Chadwicks (L)
St. James, Syracuse (L)
St. John the Evangelist, Bainbridge (M)
St. John the Evangelist, New Hartford (M)
St. Joseph, Deposit (L)
St. Mark, Utica (M)
St. Mary, Auburn (L)
St. Mary, Minoa (M)

St. Mary of the Lake, Skaneateles (L)
St. Michael, Onondaga Hill (L)
St. Patrick, Owego (M)
St. Stanislaus Kostka, Binghamton (M)

Toledo (H)
Our Lady of Lourdes, Genoa (M)
Sacred Heart of Jesus, Toledo (H)
SS. Peter and Paul, Toledo (L)
St. Agnes, Toledo (L)
St. Aloysius, Bowling Green (L)
St. Anthony, Toledo (L)
St. Bernard, New Washington (L)
St. Francis de Sales, Toledo (M)
St. Mary of the Assumption, Toledo (L)
St. Michael, Kelley's Island (L)
St. Peter, Huron (M)
St. Rose, Perrysburg (H)
St. Wendelin, Fostoria (L)

Trenton (L)
Holy Angels, Trenton (L)
Holy Family, Union Beach (L)
Incarnation, Trenton (L)
Our Lady of Good Counsel, Trenton (M)
Our Lady of Peace, Normandy Beach (L)
Our Lady of Providence, Neptune (L)
Our Lady of the Lake, Sparta (M)
St. Anthony Claret, Lakewood (M)
St. Francis of Assisi, Trenton (L)
St. Gregory the Great, Trenton (M)
St. Michael, Long Branch (L)
St. Michael, Trenton (L)

Tucson (X)
Sacred Heart, Tombstone (L)
St. Andrew, Sierra Vista (M)
St. Cyril of Alexandria, Tucson (H)
St. Francis Apache Indian, Whiteriver (L)
St. John the Evangelist, Tucson (L)

Tulsa (X)
St. Bernard of Clairvaux, Tulsa (M)
St. Henry, Owasso (H)

Tyler (L)
Holy Cross, Pittsburg (H)
Immaculate Conception, Tyler (M)
St. Bernard, Fairfield (L)

Venice (H)
Epiphany, Venice (M)
Holy Cross, Palmetto (M)
SS. Peter and Paul the Apostles,
Bradenton (M)
St. Maximilian Kolbe, Murdock (M)

Victoria, Tex. (L)

Washington (X)
Holy Comforter–St. Cyprian,
Washington (L)
Our Lady of Victory, Washington (H)
Our Lady Queen of the Americas,
Washington (H)
Sacred Heart, Washington (L)
St. Anthony, Washington (M)

Wheeling/Charleston (H)
Good Shepherd, Glenville (L)
Holy Family, Richwood (L)
Mater Dolorosa, Paden City (L)
St. Andrew's, Union (L)
St. Anthony's, Follansbee (L)
St. Augustine, Grafton (L)
St. Charles, Jacksonville (L)
St. Elizabeth Ann Seton, Westover
(L)
St. Joseph the Worker, Weirton (H)
St. Joseph's, Wheeling (L)
St. Patrick, Hinton (L)
St. Peter's, Fairmont (L)
St. Sebastian's, Kingwood (L)
St. Stephen, Ona (H)
St. Theresa's, Morgantown (H)

Wichita (M)
Immaculate Conception, Wichita (H)
Our Lady of Lourdes, Pittsburg (M)
St. Francis, St. Paul (M)
St. Francis of Assisi, Wichita (H)
St. James, Augusta (L)
St. Joseph, Andale (H)
St. Joseph, Wichita (M)

Wilmington (H)
Christ Our King, Wilmington (L)
St. Mary Magdalen, Fairfax (M)

Winona (M)
All Saints, Madison Lake (L)
Holy Spirit, Rochester (L)
Nativity of the B.V.M., Cleveland (M)
Pax Christi, Rochester (H)
Sacred Heart, Winona (L)
St. Catherine's, Luverne (M)
St. Edward's, Austin (H)
St. John Vianney, Fairmont (L)
St. John-Assumption,
Faxon Township (H)
St. Joseph, Henderson (M)
St. Mary, Caledonia (M)
St. Mary, Le Center (H)
St. Mary's, Winona (L)
St. Michael, Kenyon (H)
St. Paul's, Minnesota City (M)
St. Raphael, Springfield (H)
St. Thomas, Jessenland (M)

Worcester (H)
Holy Cross, East Templeton (M)
Holy Spirit, Gardner (L)
Our Lady of the Rosary, Worcester
(L)
Sacred Heart of Jesus, Webster (H)
St. Cecilia, Ashland (M)
St. Columba's, Paxton (L)
St. Joseph's, Auburn (H)
St. Mary's, Southbridge (H)
St. Mary's, Uxbridge (L)
St. Michael, Hudson (M)

Yakima (L)
  Our Lady of Guadalupe, Granger (L)
  Our Lady of Lourdes, Selah (M)
  Our Lady of the Valley,
    Okanogan-Omak (M)
  St. Joseph's, Kennewick (L)

Youngstown (H)
  Blessed Sacrament, Warren (H)
  Christ Our King, Warren (M)
  Holy Spirit, Uniontown (H)
  Our Lady of Mt. Carmel, Niles (L)
  Our Lady of Mt. Carmel, Youngstown
    (H)

Our Lady of Peace, Canton (H)
St. Barbara's, Massillon (L)
St. James, Waynesburg (L)
St. Joseph, Warren (L)
St. Joseph, Youngstown (L)
St. Joseph's, Alliance (L)
St. Mary of the Immaculate
  Conception, Wooster (M)
St. Mary's, Warren (M)
St. Paul's, Salem (L)
St. Rose of Lima, Youngstown (L)

2. Catholic Colleges and Universities

Key:

H/High level of involvement = Adopt a parish or support for a special project
M/Medium level of involvement = Sponsorship or sending of personnel; support of a diocesan project
L/Low level of involvement = Fund raising

Note: From survey data as reported by the colleges and universities.

Austin	St. Edward's University (M)
Boston	Regis College (M)
	Weston Jesuit School of Theology (L)
Brooklyn	St. John's University (M)
Buffalo	Christ the King Seminary (H)
Burlington	St. Michael's College (M)
Chicago	Loyola University (H)
Cincinnati	University of Dayton (M)
Cleveland	Borromeo Seminary (M)
	St. Mary Seminary (H)
Davenport	St. Ambrose University (M)
Denver	Regis University (H)

Detroit	Madonna University (H)
	Sacred Heart Major Seminary (H)
Fargo	Cardinal Meunch Seminary (H)
Ft. Wayne/South Bend	University of Notre Dame (H)
Green Bay	Silver Lake College (M)
Hartford	Sacred Heart University (H)
Indianapolis	Marian College (M)
	St. Mary of the Woods College (M)
Kansas City-St. Joseph	Avila College (M)
	Conception Seminary College (M)
	Rockhurst College (H)
La Crosse	Viterbo College (M)
Lafayette, Ind.	St. Joseph's College (M)
Los Angeles	Mount St. Mary's College (M)
Manchester	St. Anselm College (M)
Mobile	Spring Hill College (H)
New Orleans	Loyola University (H)
	St. Joseph Seminary College (M)
New York	Fordham University (H)
	St. Thomas Aquinas College (L)
Newark	Seton Hall University (M)
Omaha	Creighton University (H)
Palm Beach	St. Vincent de Paul Regional Seminary (H)
Philadelphia	St. Joseph's University (H)
Pittsburgh	Carlow College (H)
	Duquesne University (H)
Portland, Ore.	University of Portland (H)
San Antonio	Incarnate Word College (H)
	Oblate School of Theology (H)
	Our Lady of the Lake University (L)
	St. Mary's University (H)
San Diego	University of San Diego (H)
San Jose	Santa Clara University (M)
Santa Fe	Immaculate Heart of Mary Seminary (L)
Scranton	College Misericordia (M)
Springfield, Mass.	College of Our Lady of the Elm (L)
St. Cloud	St. John's School of Theology (M)
St. Louis	Cardinal Glennon College (H)
	Fontbonne College (M)
St. Paul/Minneapolis	University of St. Thomas (H)
Wichita	Kansas Newman College (M)
Worcester	Assumption College (H)
	College of the Holy Cross (M)

3. Religious Communities

Key:

H/High level of involvement = Adopt a parish or regular commitment to a particulary country
M/Medium level of involvement = Sponsorship or sending of personnel; support of a diocesan project
L/Low level of involvement = Financial support (including support of health care institutions, social service organizations, or schools)

Note: From survey data as reported by the communities. Provinces are given when provided on the survey.

Adrian Dominican Sisters, Overseas Mission (H)
American Cassinese Benedictine, St. Benedict's Abbey (H)
American Cassinese Congregation, U.S.A. (L)
Apostles of the Sacred Heart, U.S.A. (H)
Assumption Abbey (H)
Assumptionists, North America (H)
Augustinians, Midwest (H)
Barnabite Fathers, North America (H)
Basilian Fathers, Southwest U.S.A. (H)
Benedictine (H)
Benedictine, St. Benedict's Abbey, Wisc. (M)
Benedictine, Swiss-American (H)
Benedictine Federation of St. Gertrude, U.S. and Canada (H)
Benedictine Sisters of Erie, St. Scholastica (H)
Benedictine Sisters of Mount St. Scholastica, Atchison, Kans. (H)
Benedictines, St. Vincent Archabbey (H)
Bernardine Franciscans, U.S. (H)
Brothers of the Christian Schools, Baltimore (H)
Brothers of the Christian Schools, Midwest (M)
Capuchin Franciscans, New York/New England (H)
Capuchin Franciscans of St. Joseph, Detroit (H)
Carmelite Sisters of St. Theresa (H)
Carmelites, Chicago/PCM (H)
Christian Brothers, New Orleans-Santa Fe (H)
Cistercians (Trappists), St. Joseph's Abbey (M)

Claretian Missionaries, U.S.A. Eastern (H)
Clerics of St. Viator, Chicago (H)
Comboni Missionaries, North American (M)
Congregation of Bon Secoure, U.S.A. (H)
Congregation of Christian Brothers, Western U.S. (H)
Congregation of Divine Providence (H)
Congregation of Our Lady of Mount Carmel (M)
Congregation of St. Catherine of Siena (M)
Congregation of the Holy Cross, Eastern (H)
Congregation of the Holy Cross, Southern (H)
Congregation of the Holy Cross, Southwest (H)
Congregation of the Holy Spirit, Mexican Apostolic Group (H)
Congregation of the Humility of Mary (H)
Congregation of the Sisters of St. Agnes (H)
Congregation of the Sisters of the Third Order of St. Francis of Perpetual Adoration,
    Central (M)
Consolata Missionaries, North America (H)
Conventual Franciscan Friars, Immaculate Conception (H)
Cordi-Marian Missionaries (L)
Daughters of Charity, Northeast (H)
Daughters of Charity, St. Vincent de Paul, Emmitsburg, Md. (H)
Daughters of Charity, St. Vincent de Paul, West Central (H)
Daughters of Jesus, North of Spain (H)
Daughters of St. Mary of Providence, U.S.A. (H)
Daughters of the Cross (L)
Daughters of the Cross, English (H)
De la Salle Brothers—Christian Schools, U.S.A-Toronto (M)
Discalced Carmelite Nuns (L)
Disciples of the Lord Jesus Christ, Amarillo (H)
Dominican (L)
Dominican, Western (M)
Dominican Fathers, St. Martin de Porres (H)
Dominican Men, St. Albert the Great (Central) (H)
Dominican Nuns, Springfield, Mass. Diocese (L)
Dominican Nuns of Perpetual Rosary, Southern (L)
Dominican Nuns of the Perpetual Rosary U.S.A./Sr. Joseph-Orele of Preache (L)
Dominican Sisters, Houston, Tex. (H)
Dominican Sisters, Springfield, Ill. (H)
Dominican Sisters, St. Mary of the Springs, Ohio (M)
Dominican Sisters Congregation (H)
Dominican Sisters of Oakford, U.S. (H)
Dominicans, Grand Rapids (M)
Felician-Franciscan Sisters, Assumption (H)
Franciscan Friars, Southwest/Our Lady of Guadalupe (H)
Franciscan Friars, Western U.S.A. (H)
Franciscan Friars of the Atonement (H)
Franciscan Friars of the Renewal (L)

Franciscan Sisters, Little Falls, Minn. (H)
Franciscan Sisters of Christian Charity (H)
Franciscan Sisters of Peace (H)
Franciscan Sisters of Perpetual Adoration (H)
Guadalupan Missionaries of the Holy Spirit (H)
Hermanas Catequistas, U.S.A. Region (H)
Holy Ghost Congregation, U.S.A.-East (H)
Holy Spirit Missionary Sisters, U.S. (H)
Holy Union Sisters, Groton, Mass. (L)
Incarnate Word and Blessed Sacrament, Corpus Christi (H)
Marian Fathers, St. Casimir (H)
Marianites of the Holy Cross, North America (H)
Marist Fathers and Brothers, Boston (H)
Marist Fathers and Brothers, San Francisco (M)
Marist Missionary Sisters, North American (M)
Marist Sisters, U.S.A. (H)
Marmion Abbey, Benedictines/Swiss-Americans (H)
Maryknoll Fathers and Brothers (H)
Maryknoll Sisters (H)
Medical Missions Sisters, North America (H)
Mercy, Vermont (M)
Minion Sisters of Mary Immaculate (H)
Missionaries of Africa (H)
Missionaries of the Precious Blood, Cincinnati (H)
Missionaries of the Sacred Heart (H)
Missionary Benedictine Sisters, U.S. (M)
Missionary Franciscans, American (H)
Missionary Fraternity of Mary, U.S. (H)
Missionary Servants of the Most Blessed Trinity (H)
Missionary Servants of the Most Holy Trinity (H)
Missionary Sisters of Jesus, Mary and Joseph, Texas-Mexico (H)
Missionary Sisters of St. Charles Borromeo-Scala, Our Lady of Fatima (H)
Missionary Sisters of the Sacred Heart of Jesus, Stella Maris (M)
Missionhurst, U.S. (H)
Monastery of the Blessed Sacrament (L)
Montfort Missionaries, U.S. (H)
Norbertines, St. Norbert Abbey (H)
Notre Dame Sisters, U.S.A. (H)
Oblate Sisters—Sacred Heart of Jesus (H)
Oblates of Mary Immaculate, Central U.S. (H)
Oblates of Mary Immaculate, Eastern U.S. (M)
Oblates of Mary Immaculate, Southern U.S. (M)
Oblates of St. Joseph, California (M)
Oratory of St. Philip Neri (PHARR) (H)
Order of Cistercians of the Strict Observance/Trappist (H)
Order of Preachers/Nuns, Monastery of the Infant Son (L)
Order of St. Augustine, U.S. and West Coast (H)

Sharing Faith Across the Hemisphere

Order of St. Augustine, Villanova (H)
Order of St. Clare (L)
Our Lady of Victory Missionary Sisters (H)
Pallottine Missionary Sisters, Queen of Apostles (H)
Poor Clare Nuns, St. John the Baptist (L)
Poor Handmaids of Jesus Christ (H)
Presentation of the Blessed Virgin Mary (H)
Presentation of the Blessed Virgin Mary, Costa Rica (H)
Redemptorists, Baltimore (H)
Redemptorists, St. Louis (H)
Religious of Mary Immaculate (H)
Religious of the Assumption, U.S.A. (M)
Religious of the Sacred Heart, Western America (H)
Religious Teachers Filippini, St. Lucy (H)
Salesians of Don Bosco, New Rochelle, NY (H)
School Sisters of Notre Dame, Baltimore (H)
School Sisters of Notre Dame, Dallas (H)
School Sisters of Notre Dame, Milwaukee (M)
School Sisters of Notre Dame, St. Louis, Miss. (H)
School Sisters of Notre Dame, Wilton (M)
School Sisters of St. Francis, Bethlehem (H)
School Sisters of St. Francis, U.S. (H)
Servants of Mary of Ladysmith (L)
Sister Servants of the Immaculate Heart of Mary (H)
Sister Servants of the Immaculate Heart of Mary, Immaculata, Penn. (H)
Sisters of Bethany, California (L)
Sisters of Charity, Blessed Virgin Mary (H)
Sisters of Charity, Cincinnati (M)
Sisters of Charity of Leavenworth (H)
Sisters of Charity of Nazareth, U.S. (H)
Sisters of Charity of New York (H)
Sisters of Charity of St. Augustine, Cleveland Diocese (M)
Sisters of Charity of the Incarnate Word (H)
Sisters of Christian Charity, Western (H)
Sisters of Loretto (M)
Sisters of Mercy, Cedar Rapids (M)
Sisters of Mercy, Merion (H)
Sisters of Mercy, New Hampshire (H)
Sisters of Mercy, New Jersey (L)
Sisters of Mercy, Omaha (L)
Sisters of Mercy, Pittsburgh (H)
Sisters of Mercy, Providence (H)
Sisters of Mercy of the Americas, Albany (H)
Sisters of Mercy of the Americas, Auburn, Calif. (M)
Sisters of Mercy of the Americas, Baltimore (H)
Sisters of Mercy of the Americas, Brooklyn (H)
Sisters of Mercy of the Americas, Burlingame, Calif. (H)

Sisters of Mercy of the Americas, Chicago (H)
Sisters of Mercy of the Americas, Connecticut (H)
Sisters of Mercy of the Americas, Detroit (M)
Sisters of Mercy of the Americas, Erie (H)
Sisters of Mercy of the Americas, Portland, Maine (M)
Sisters of Mercy of the Americas, Rochester (H)
Sisters of Notre Dame, Christ the King (H)
Sisters of Notre Dame, Covington, Ky. (L)
Sisters of Notre Dame, Toledo (L)
Sisters of Notre Dame de Namur, California (H)
Sisters of Notre Dame de Namur, Ohio (H)
Sisters of Our Lady of Christian Doctrine (H)
Sisters of Providence, Diocesan Congregation (H)
Sisters of Providence, Sacred Heart (H)
Sisters of Social Service of Los Angeles (H)
Sisters of St. Casimir (H)
Sisters of St. Dominic, Cleveland Diocese (M)
Sisters of St. Francis (H)
Sisters of St. Francis (H)
Sisters of St. Francis (M)
Sisters of St. Francis, Mount St. Clare, Clinton, Iowa (H)
Sisters of St. Francis, Oldenburg, Ind. (M)
Sisters of St. Francis of Assisi (H)
Sisters of St. Francis of Penance, Holy Name (H)
Sisters of St. Francis of Penance and Christian Charity, Sacred Heart (H)
Sisters of St. Francis of Penance and Christian Charity, West Coast (M)
Sisters of St. Francis of the Holy Cross (H)
Sisters of St. Francis of the Martyr St. George, St. Elizabeth (H)
Sisters of St. Francis Third Order Regular (H)
Sisters of St. John the Baptist, American (H)
Sisters of St. Joseph, Brentwood, N.Y. (H)
Sisters of St. Joseph, Chestnut Hill, Philadelphia (M)
Sisters of St. Joseph, Concordia, Kans. (H)
Sisters of St. Joseph, Rochester, N.Y. (H)
Sisters of St. Joseph, Vermont (L)
Sisters of St. Joseph, Watertown (L)
Sisters of St. Joseph of Carondelet (H)
Sisters of St. Joseph of Carondelet, Albany (H)
Sisters of St. Joseph of Carondelet, Hawaii (H)
Sisters of St. Joseph of Carondelet, Los Angeles (H)
Sisters of St. Joseph of Carondelet, St. Louis (H)
Sisters of St. Joseph of Carondelet, St. Paul (H)
Sisters of St. Joseph of Lyon, Maine (H)
Sisters of St. Joseph of Medialle (H)
Sisters of St. Joseph of Peace, West (M)
Sisters of St. Joseph of the Third Order of St. Francis (H)
Sisters of St. Joseph of Tipton, Ind. (H)

Sisters of St. Joseph of Wheeling (L)
Sisters of St. Mary, Buffalo/Eastern (M)
Sisters of the Holy Cross (H)
Sisters of the Holy Family (M)
Sisters of the Holy Spirit and Mary Immaculate (H)
Sisters of the Humility of Mary (M)
Sisters of the Most Precious Blood (H)
Sisters of the Order of St. Benedict, St. Joseph, Minn. (H)
Sisters of the Pious Schools, California-Mexico (H)
Sisters of the Precious Blood, Dayton, Ohio (H)
Sisters of the Presentation of the Virgin Mary (H)
Society of Helpers, United States (H)
Society of Jesus, California (H)
Society of Jesus, Detroit (H)
Society of Jesus, New England (H)
Society of Jesus, New Orleans (H)
Society of Jesus, Wisconsin (H)
Society of St. Edmund (H)
Society of St. Teresa of Jesus, St. Francis de Sales (H)
Society of the Divine Word, Southern (H)
Society of the Precious Blood, Kansas City (L)
Society of the Precious Blood, Pacific (M)
Society of the Sacred Heart, U.S. (M)
Sons of Mary—Health of the Sick, Boston (M)
St. Francis Mission Community (M)
Third Order Regular Franciscans, Immaculate Conception (H)
Ursuline (H)
Ursuline Nuns of Cleveland (H)
Ursuline Sisters, Paola (M)
Ursulines of the Roman Union, Central (H)
Vincentian Sisters of Charity, Diocese of Cleveland (M)
Visitation of Holy Mary, St. Louis (L)
Xaverian Missionaries, U.S.A. (H)

List of NCCB Bishops' Committee Chairmen and Secretariat Directors

Chairmen, Bishops' Committee for the Church in Latin America*

Cardinal Richard Cushing, 1962 to 1966
Most Rev. James McNulty, 1966 to 1968
Most Rev. Coleman Carroll, 1968 to 1970
Cardinal Humberto Medeiros, 1970 to 1973
Most Rev. John Fitzpatrick, 1973 to 1977
Most Rev. Nevin Hayes, 1977 to 1980

---

* From the early 1960s through 1970, an ad hoc committee of twelve bishops called the "Committee for Latin America" served the administrative board of the National Catholic Welfare Conference. The Committee was headed by Cardinal Richard Cushing until 1966. In 1970, the bishops established a standing committee.

Most Rev. Juan Arzube, 1980 to 1983
Most Rev. Patrick Flores, 1983 to 1986
Most Rev. Ricardo Ramírez, 1986 to 1989
Most Rev. Rene Valero, 1989 to 1991
Most Rev. Arturo Tafoya, 1991 to 1994
Most Rev. Raymundo Peña, 1994 to 1997

Directors, Secretariat for Latin America

Rev. John Considine, MM, 1960 to 1968
Rev. Louis Colonnese, 1968 to 1971
Rev. Frederick McGuire, CM, 1971 to 1975
Ms. Francis Neason, 1975 to 1983
Rev. David Gallivan, 1984 to 1989
Rev. George Emerson, 1989 to 1994
Rev. James Ronan, 1994 to present

Index

Betanzos, Domingo de, 11
Bishops, Latin American
  meeting in 1899, 66
  see also CELAM
Bishops, Mexican, 74, 75
Bishops, U.S.
  statement of solidarity on human
    rights, 181-183
  statements on social issues, 177
  see also National Conference of
    Catholic Bishops; United States
    Catholic Conference
Brazil
  Church's response to oppression in,
    169-171
  disappearances in, 174
  economic bonanza in, 168-169
  example of repression for other Latin
    American nations, 174
  military dictatorships in, 168, 169
  repression in, 171-173
  U.S. bishops' statement on, 182-183
Brummel, Dick, 217
Brummel, Jane, 216
Bureau for Latin America, 85, 107, 113
Burke, John
  and foundation of National Catholic
    War Council, 69, 70
  and Mexican crisis, 61-62, 78-80
  and National Catholic Welfare
    Council, 71
Burnier, Joao Bosco Penido, 172

Caccamo, Jim, 217, 219
Caccamo, Nancy, 215, 218
CAL (Pontifical Commission for Latin
    America), 84-85
Call for Forty Thousand, The, 82-83
Calles, Plutarco, 62, 74, 75, 78
Calvert, Cecil, 31-34
Camacho, Avila, 79-80
Cámara, Dom Helder, 84, 114-117, 120
Campesinos, 187
Capitalism, 135
Cárdenas, Lázaro, 79
Carmelites, 37
Carney, James, 193

Carroll, John, 34, 35, 36, 37, 38, 39, 51
Carter, Jimmy, 184
Casaldáglia, Dom Pedro, 172
Casaroli, Agostino, 93-94
Casas, Bartolome de las, 13-14
Castro, Fidel, 100-102
Catholic Action, methodology of,
    119-120
Catholic Church Extension Society,
    66-67
Catholic Church in Latin America
  challenged by Protestant missionaries,
    99
  diversity among nations, 66
  faith in, 146
  need for more clergy in, 65, 83
  new problems brought by
    independence of, 65-66
  in the 1960s, 96-99
  popular religiosity of, 98, 146-147
  state of, at Puebla meeting, 150-151
  see also missionaries; missions; *and*
    individual countries
Catholic Church in the United States
  Americanism in, 53-54
  call to conversion, 228-231
  education about Latin America, 113
  foundation of National Catholic War
    Council, 50
  future involvement with Latin
    America, 207
  immigration in, 39-44
  integrating national and religious
    aspects, 39
  missionary clergy in, 34
  national parishes in, 43
  nativism in, 44-46, 49-50
  in the 1960s, 99-100
  origins in Northeast, 31-37
  origins in Southwest, 46-48
  recognition as a mature Church, 55
  and separation of church and state,
    51-52
  trusteeism in, 38-39
  and Vietnam War, 178, 179-180
  see also missionaries; missions; survey,
    NCCB; *and individual dioceses*

Catholic Foreign Mission Society of
America, *see* Maryknoll
Catholic Inter-American Cooperation
Program, 113
Catholic Universe Bulletin, 186
Catholic World, The, 76
CELAM
critique of missions, 112
meeting at Medellín, 132-140
meeting at Puebla, 150-157
meeting at Santo Domingo, 224-228
organization of, 84
Censorship, 171
Center for Intercultural Formation, 107
Center of Intercultural Documentation,
126n. 40
Cerretti, Bonaventura, 71
Chile, 182
Chollet, Michele, 220
Christianizing
means of, in Peru, 1-2
see also evangelization; missionaries;
missions
Church and state, relationship of
new patterns in independent Latin
America, 64-66
Church and state, separation of
desired by liberals in Latin America, 65
in Mexico, 73-74
in United States, 51-53
Cisneros, Jimenez de, 24n. 5
Civil War, U.S., 50
Clarke, Maura, 189-190
Cleveland, Diocese of, 105
Cleveland, mission team of
murder of Donovan and Kazel,
189-190
work in the neediest areas, 142
Cofradias, 47
Collaboration
between episcopal conferences, 166
see also consultation; dialogue
Collections
for the Church in Latin America, 106,
205
for the Propagation of the Faith, 106

Colleges, Catholic in U.S.
see survey, NCCB, Catholic colleges
and universities
Colombia, *see* New Granada
Colonialism, 135
Colonnese, Michael, 292
Columbus, Christopher, 2-4, 6-7
Columbus, Diego, 12
Comblin, José, 152
Commonweal, 76
Communism
accusing church workers of, 188
combating dangers of, through
missions, 112
Communities, base ecclesial, 147-150,
155-156
Conference of Latin American Religious
(CLAR), 140-143
Conquest
divine right of, 6
evangelization by, 5-8
protest against, 13
Conquistador
mission mentality, 5-9, 16
Consalvi, Cardinal, 64
Considine, John, 81-83, 85, 95, 107, 292
Consultation
between bishops from North and
South, 185
see also collaboration; dialogue
Coolidge, Calvin, 90
Córdova, Pedro de, 13
Courtney, Maureen, 193
Criollos
defined, 25n. 25
and Latin American independence, 63
Cristeros, 75, 79, 89n. 27, 90n. 31
Cuba, 100-102
Culture
understanding of, in missions, 114-115
Curley, Archbishop, 77
Cushing, Richard, 85-86, 291
Cypher, Casimir, 186-188

D'Antonio, Nicholas, 187
Damboriena, Prudencio, 96
Dependence, 115, 139

Development
   discussion at Medellín, 134-135
   human, 228
   and liberation, 140
   in *Populorum Progressio,* 119
Dewart, Leslie, 102
Dialogue, 185, 209; *see also* collaboration
Diaz, Porfirio, 72, 78
Diego, Juan, 19-21
Dioceses, U.S.
   involvement with Latin America, *see*
      survey, NCCB, dioceses; *and*
      individual dioceses
Disappearances
   in Argentina, 174
   in Guatemala, 174
   in Latin American countries, 173-174
Dominicans
   and challenge of mission
      methodologies, 12-14
   and schools in New Spain, 11
   in Southwest United States, 46
Dongan, Thomas, 33
Donovan, Jean, 189-190
Dove, The, 31

Economic Justice for All, 185
Economics
   and evangelization, 230-231
   moral dimension of, 226
El Salvador
   murder of missionaries in, 189-190
   sister parish in, 215-220
   suspension of U.S. aid to, 192
Elizonda, Virgilio, 47-48
Emerson, George, 292
Encomiendas
   defined, 7
   effort to eliminate, 14
   and reductions, 9
England, John, 51
Esteban, 210
Evangelization
   in Andes, described by Poma, 16
   by conquest, 5-8
   mutuality of, 212

new stage of, announced by Paul VI,
   132
Evangelization, New, 227-231
Extension, 76
Fe y Alegría, 113
Ferdinand, 2
Ferdinand VII, 64
FERES (International Federation of
   Institutes for Socio-Religious
   Research), 96
Fitzpatrick, John, 291
Fitzpatrick, Joseph, 126n. 42
Flores, Patrick, 291
Food
   sent to Latin America, 115-116
Ford, Ita, 189-190
Franciscans
   in Peru, 104
   seminary at Tlaltiloco, 10
   in Southwest United States, 46
Freedom, religious, 34, 39
Fumasoni-Biondi, Pietro, 78

Gallivan, David, 292
Gaudium et Spes, 120
Gibbons, James
   Church envisioned, 51-52
   and Maryknoll, 67
   and Mexican Revolution, 73
   and National Catholic War Council,
      69, 70
   and separation of church and state, 53
Gines de Sepúlveda, Juan, 6
Goulat, Joao, 167, 168
Grail, the, 106
Grande, Rutilio, 190
Greaton, Joseph, 33
Greed, 4
Griffon, James, 230
Guadalupe, Virgin of, 19-22

Haig, Alexander, 191
Haiti
   independence of, 62
   power of the Church in, 65
Haiti Outreach Program, 214

Violence
  poverty as institutionalized, 136-138
  rejected by bishops, 89n. 27
  used by conquistadors and rebels, 9
  see also war
Voluntaryism, 44
Volunteers
  pros and cons of accepting, 116-117

Wall, Veronica, 143, 146
Walsh, James, 67-68, 127n. 52
War
  response to invaders, 8
  right to declare, against pagans, 5
  Spanish American, 57n. 8, 59n. 42
  Vietnam, 177-178, 179-180
  World War I, 50, 68-69, 74

Ward, Barbara, 97
Warris, Jerry, 215
Weakland, Rembert, 229-230
Weapons, interest of natives in, 3
Weigand, William, 185
Welsh, Lawrence, 194-195
White, Andrew, 35
Wilson, Woodrow, 73
Wolters, Alice, 144
Woods, William, 193
World War I, 50, 74
  and foundation of National Catholic
    War Council, 68-69

Zumárrago, Bishop, 19